NAFTA and the Campesinos

NAFTA and the Campesinos:

The Impact of NAFTA on Small-Scale Agricultural Producers in Mexico and the Prospects for Change

Editors: Juan M. Rivera, Scott Whiteford, and Manuel Chávez

UNIVERSITY OF SCRANTON PRESS
Scranton and London

Library of Congress Cataloging-in-Publication Data

NAFTA and the campesinos : the impact of NAFTA on small-scale agricultural producers in Mexico and the prospects for change / editors: Juan M. Rivera, Scott Whiteford, and Manuel Chavez.
p. cm.
Includes bibliographical references and index.
ISBN 978-1-58966-180-6 (pbk.)
1. Canada. Treaties, etc. 1992 Oct. 7. 2. Free trade--Mexico. 3. Family farms--Mexico. 4. Free trade--North America. 5. Mexico--Economic conditions. I. Rivera, Juan M., 1944- II. Whiteford, Scott, 1942- III. Chavez, Manuel, 1953-
HF1776.N33 2008
338.1'630972--dc22

2008038782

Distribution:
UNIVERSITY OF SCRANTON PRESS
Chicago Distribution Center
11030 S. Langley
Chicago, IL 60628

PRINTED IN THE UNITED STATES OF AMERICA

CONTENTS

Acknowledgments

DURING THE PREPARATION OF THIS VOLUME many people provided us with ideas, suggestions, guidance, and other contributions that helped to support and advance this project. Scholars William Glade and Lee Tavis encouraged us from the very beginning to focus our research on issues addressing development in the Mexican countryside. Business entrepreneurs John Nichols and John Caron kept reminding us to include the private sector as part of the solutions in our deliberations about Mexico's agricultural development. Alberto Nuñez and his Fundación Mexicana para el Desarrollo Rural offered actual examples of what could be accomplished when one reaches out to help rural families in the impoverished regions of Mexico. José Romero gave us his checkmarks and valuable observations on the original versions of the manuscript. Anne Golla, Michael Jaszkowiak, Kenny Miller, and Jennifer Molidor—all graduate students when this work was in progress—helped with field research and text editing for the various chapters. Finally, John Hunckler from University of Scranton Press was a critical and resourceful copyeditor who helped us with his useful suggestions and experienced editing advice. To all of these individuals we express our appreciation for helping make the publication of this book possible.

The Editors

Foreword

RURAL MEXICO IS AT A WATERSHED. The gradual opening of Mexican agricultural markets to efficient foreign competition, beginning with Mexico's joining the General Agreement on Tariffs and Trade (GATT) in 1986 and accelerating with their signing the North American Free Trade Agreement (NAFTA) in 1993, has dramatically increased competition within that country. Governmental attempts to enhance agricultural productivity have led to rescinding the land redistribution promised by the 1917 constitution, while the drive for agricultural productivity through mechanization and larger plots is forcing campesinos from the land without sufficient industrial expansion to absorb their labor. Small-scale farmers, accustomed to politically opportunistic governmental support, find themselves unable to cope with the new competition and governmental approach to subsidies. Rural living standards have actually declined. The portion of rural households at or below the poverty level in 1989 was 49 percent. By 1996, the proportion had increased to 53 percent. Rural Mexico is not thriving with open markets.

These deteriorating circumstances led the Program on Multinational Managers and Developing Country Concerns at the University of Notre Dame to convene a workshop on Mexican agriculture in April 1996. The purpose was to identify an appropriate role for agribusiness in this rapidly changing economic and political environment. Joining as partners in the venture were the University of Texas at Austin and Michigan State University. As with the Program's previous twelve workshops on poverty, debt, pharmaceuticals, and governmental regulation, with field work in the Philippines, Kenya, Mexico, Korea, Belize, and Honduras, a mixed group of participants was assembled. Included were agribusiness executives, academics, Mexican ejidatarios, and officials from nongovernmental organizations and governmental agencies. It was a tense time. At one session, a Mexican ejidatario looked the participating agribusiness executives in the eyes and shouted that big business was trying to steal his land, just as the Mexican government had been trying for decades. That statement captured the full challenge involved in working toward collaboration.

As we came to understand the depth of this issue and the antagonism among the actors, we realized the need to move our efforts from a campus in the United States to Mexico, and to get involved in the Mexican rural grassroots. The first step was to convene a workshop in Queretaro, Mexico in October 1997. California State University – Bakersfield, with an agricultural research history in the area, and the University of Queretaro joined the partnership. At this meeting, participants included Mexican and U.S. agribusiness executives (21), Mexican national and Queretaro state and municipal government officials (6), representatives of Mexican (9) and international (3) nongovernmental organizations (NGOs), and academics (12). The Queretaro conference participants observed that an open and frank discussion among such a diverse set of participants had not, to their collective knowledge, ever before taken place in Mexico.

The next step was field research. The University of Chapingo joined the partnership for this phase. The results of this decade-long effort are reported in this volume.

The NAFTA-related changes in the marketplace and the effectiveness and structures of governmental programs are analyzed in the initial essays. They document the failed governmental policies of the past and the challenge as addressed by the Fox regime and by the new administration in Mexico.

Following the initial macroanalysis and the discussion of the impact of NAFTA on the Mexican agricultural sector, the volume focuses on civil society—agribusinesses and NGOs—with specific case studies as these institutions work with small-scale producers to enhance their markets and development efforts. With global marketization, the power to direct development shifts from governments, who lose policy freedom, to the market—and the business institutions that comprise the market. As the determinants of agricultural development move from the government to business, the responsibility associated with that power also shifts. Given the deterioration of the living conditions in the countryside and the moral neutrality of the markets themselves, the entrepreneurial effort of some small-scale producers in this new environment and the efforts of agribusiness to draw them into the supply chain, as reported in these case studies, are noteworthy. Working with NGOs or seeking associations with corporate agribusiness can be central to this work—both for the small-scale producer attempting to gain access to the market systems and for the agribusinesses needing connections to the grassroots. However, these collaborative efforts, as indicated in the "goat milk" case (see Chapter 8), can demonstrate the difficulties of the partnering as well as that of the development task.

The most recent phase of the overall project (2005–2007) has been a joint venture between the University of Notre Dame's Mendoza College of Business, the Helen Kellogg Institute for International Studies, and the University of Guadalajara. The purpose of this partnership, funded by the USAID Teaching, Internship, Exchange, and Scholarship (TIES) Program, is to enhance economic development in Mexico by linking U.S. and Mexican universities and applying—in the field—lessons on management and entrepreneurship that are learned by faculty at their desks and students in the classroom. As part of this program, graduate business students from the University of Guadalajara and the University of Notre Dame worked with small-scale Mexican producers to improve productivity and help them gain access to global markets.

Juan Rivera has been the driving force of this Mexican project from the initial move to Mexico in 1997, through the field research reported here, to the

USAID TIES Program and the planning for a fourth phase concentrating on rural Mexican entrepreneurial skills and financing. The book that is presented here is but a stage in the quest for learning from the experiences of agriculture in Mexico under NAFTA, and for devising plans and actions to improve the well being of its small-scale and poor agricultural producers.

LEE A. TAVIS
Co-Director of the Program on Multinational Managers
and Developing Country Concerns
at the University of Notre Dame

Introduction

Mexican Agriculture and NAFTA—Prospects for Change

Juan M. Rivera and Scott Whiteford

The results achieved so far are only the beginning in a process to remedy the enormous income gap and the needs felt by thousands of rural families. Government and society need to redouble efforts to help the Mexican rural poor.

PRESIDENT VICENTE FOX, IV
State of the Nation Report
September 2004

AFTER MORE THAN A DECADE of the North American Free Trade Agreement (NAFTA) and twenty years of economic liberalization, the Mexican government and its people are searching for ways to improve economic and social conditions in their country. Debates among scholars and policy makers have centered on causes and effects, identifying winners and losers, and on learning from past experiences to rectify the path or change direction for the future. In principle, NAFTA was a deliberate and concerted mechanism adopted by three nations to dismantle barriers to trade and investments; judging by the changes experienced in those two areas, the results have been impressive. The United States, Canada, and Mexico assembled a market larger than the fifteen-member European Union, and their joint trade and investment almost tripled in the first ten years of NAFTA. The new trade treaty cemented an already strong trade relationship between the United States and Canada,[1] and transformed Mexico into the second largest U.S. trading partner, ahead of Japan —a position that Mexico is currently losing to China. NAFTA also made the United States more dependent on trade with its two neighbors, with trading flows that grew about twice as fast as those of the United States with the rest of the world.[2]

For Mexico, formalizing a trade partnership with the United States and Canada was a reconfirmation to the world that the government policies of free trade and open markets, introduced in the mid-1980s, would be permanently represented in future economic policies. In the process, Mexico's economy became more intertwined with the U.S. economy, and the flow of direct investment from the United States to Mexico became a significant factor for trade. Direct annual flows of U.S. investments to Mexico went from $1.3 billion in 1992 to $15 billion in 2001 (Pastor 2004, 27). The growth in total trade that Mexico experienced from the mid 1980s to 2001 ($289 billion) exceeded the total trade levels reported by all the rest of Latin America ($245 billion) for the same period (Luna Martinez 2002, 451).

Thanks to the presence of the United States, the North American market constitutes a potential engine for growth, since it represents a region that is larger in size and population than Europe, and also boasts a GDP that surpasses the combined GDP of the European Union (EU), even after the EU's expansion to 25 members in 2004. In all, after 15 years of operation, the North American market has produced neither the "giant sucking sound" of displaced labor to the South that Ross Perot predicted, nor the benefits of increased standards of living and economic integration—in particular, the weaker countries in the Agreement—which its ardent proponents estimated.

Part of the reason for these unfulfilled expectations is that NAFTA was not a trade agreement intended to mirror the policies and programs for development included in the EU accord. For one thing, the trade pact among the North American countries was not a pact of equals as much as was the case with the EU. More importantly, many in Mexico erroneously believed that simply opening trade with the rest of the world or its neighboring country would generate development; they found that their country needed to possess other elements in order to take full advantage of economic and trade integration. Now, as we reach the end of the fifteen-year phase-in for NAFTA's full and complete implementation, Mexico and its citizens face the unfulfilled dreams of economic opportunities that the proponents and signatories of NAFTA had originally envisioned.[3] While NAFTA helped Mexico to triple its exports and attract $153 billion in new foreign investments, it also made the Mexican economy more dependent on the ebb and flow of the U.S. economy.

It is difficult to isolate the net impact of NAFTA because of the concurrent influence of other economic events, such as the peso devaluation of 1995 and the deceleration of the U.S. economy after 2001. Nevertheless, real wages in Mexico are lower today than they were before NAFTA, and the flow of poor Mexicans illegally crossing the border to the United States in search of jobs is as intense as ever. The 1.3 million new jobs created in the Mexican manufacturing sector during the NAFTA years underestimated the wave of 500,000 new entrants added annually to the labor force in Mexico. Herein lie some of the challenges for the drafters of new economic and social policies in Mexico.

NAFTA and the Neo-Liberal Economic Policies in Mexico

Throughout most of the 1980s, the Mexican economy, like most of its counterparts in Latin America, was plagued by problems of high inflation, large budget deficits, slow or negative growth, increasing foreign debt, and periodic devaluations. The model of import substitution and market protectionism practiced since the 1950s was no longer able to produce an acceptable development path, and it could not deflect the changing winds of globalization that were sweeping the world at full force. As a response to a chronic economic malaise, the Latin American regimes embraced a new model for development that emphasized open trade and investment, fiscal and monetary discipline, large-scale privatization of state enterprises, deregulation of the economy, and in general, less government intervention. The set of economic policies known as "The Washington Consensus"[4] became very popular in the 1990s; most of the countries in Latin America subscribed to it. Mexico joined the trend and adopted many of these policies in the 1990s.

The new liberal economic policies and the benefits of trade liberalization contributed to a significant expansion of the foreign sector of the Mexican economy. Thus, the level of Mexican exports quadrupled from $40.7 billion in 1990 to $164.9 billion in 2003, as did its imports, which rose from $41.6 billion to $170.5 billion during those years. Partly due to free trade and open market policies, the Mexican economy achieved positive growth in GDP in all years after NAFTA (except in 1995, due mainly to the peso devaluation that produced the so-called Tequila crisis), with a growth in GDP estimated to reach 4% in 2004. While Mexico has reported a current account deficit in recent years, that deficit only represents a manageable 1.4% of its GNP.[5]

The trade boom for Mexico that NAFTA propelled has been heavily slanted toward the manufacturing sector, which in the early 1990s represented 85.6% of aggregate foreign trade, and has since grown at a 14.6% annual rate. By contrast, the share of primary products in total foreign trade is equivalent to only 4.9%, has grown at a rate of 7.5% annually since the implementation of NAFTA, and (other than in 1995) has consistently shown deficit trade balances (Luna Martinez 2002, 451). In absolute terms, the trade deficit in the primary sector averaged $1.4 billion per year during the years 1991 to 2001, and was caused mainly by agricultural food imports.

The "new" economic model imposed by the Mexican government was part of a Latin American trend introduced in the late 1980s, when the governments of the region acted on the realization that their policies of the past were no longer workable (David et al. 2000). Thus, the series of crises suffered by the Mexican economy in the early 1980s forced its government to look for alternatives to the traditional import-substitution model followed in the past and to concentrate on an industrialization-driven, export-oriented growth path. The country's policy makers thus embraced the new wave of global markets and open trade, an action that followed, and was consistent with, Mexico joining the General Agreement on Tariffs and Trade (GATT) in 1986. More significantly, during the Salinas regime from 1988 to 1994, Mexico's strategy for growth most emphasized open trade. It was during this period that pivotal measures on trade liberalization, privatization of government enterprises, reduction and control of government expenditures, re-privatization of commercial banks, and incentives to foreign investment were enacted or decreed. This process of economic neo-liberalism culminated with the implementation of the North American Free Trade Agreement (NAFTA) in the beginning of 1994.

As stated above, on a general macro level and for some sectors of the economy, the impact of NAFTA has been positive. The country recovered quickly from its devaluation-driven recession of 1995 and experienced an average annual growth of 5.2% in GDP during 1996–99, reaching a 6.9% growth rate in 2000 (U.S. Department of State 2002). Undoubtedly, the external sector—and particularly the effects of a stronger association with the trade partner to the north—helped fuel this thrust. Since the origin of NAFTA, annual foreign direct investment into Mexico tripled and reached $24 billion in 2001, 81% of which originated in the United States.[6] Likewise, Mexico's foreign trade (imports and exports) expanded exponentially, rising from $3.87 billion in 1970 to $340.8 billion in 2000; its share of GDP increased from 10.7% to 63.1% during this same period.[7] Notably, most of Mexico's foreign trade is with the United States, where Mexico exports 90% and imports 70% of its corresponding totals.[8]

The positive effects that NAFTA brought to Mexico during the expansionary cycle of the U.S. economy were mostly a benefit in terms of increased trade flows; however, this increase in trade did not, in most cases, trickle down to the rural poor.[9] The Mexican economy remains chronically afflicted with high poverty, unequal income distribution, disporportionate regional development, and an expanding productivity gap between agriculture and other sectors of the economy. The gap is even more pronounced when one looks at per capita income in Mexico, where the rural workers' average income is lower than the national average for any other economic sector. Data available for 1994 demonstrated the striking disparity between farming and non-farming income, when for that year urban households had nearly three times the monthly monetary income of rural households.[10] Furthermore, in 1996, 41.5% of Mexican farm workers earned less than the minimum wage.[11] Essentially, the new economic liberalism has worsened the losses of the Mexican rural poor[12] and left them unable to cope with the powerful forces of the open, global markets. Due to the impact on this group, this book is focused on evaluating the negative impacts—evidenced by the poverty levels and the ever-increasing trade deficits in agriculture—that NAFTA has had on the rural producers of Mexico.

The new economic liberalism is characterized by a strong emphasis on free-market mechanisms, by restraint and control of public finances, and by a government retreat from production-related tasks. For the agricultural sector in Mexico, the measures of the new economic model were characterized by significant changes in land property rights, deregulation of the labor markets, elimination of agricultural development banks, elimination of guaranteed prices for agricultural products, restrained investment in infrastructure, and elimination or reduction of government-supported agricultural extension programs.[13] Under these new circumstances, the Mexican policymakers at the time expected that the private sector would assume a more active role, guided by the invisible hand of the free market.

While reviewing the recent trends in agricultural employment and income in Latin America, Reardon et al. (2001) found that the structural adjustments and trade-liberalization schemes introduced in the 1980s and 1990s did not generate the flow of small-scale farming entrepreneurs that policy planners expected. Instead, some of the rural population switched to the services and contracted-labor farming sectors, which kept them at about the same level of subsistence income. The emphasis on trade-induced development contributed to the widening discrepancy in wealth—between the urban and relatively more industrialized north and central areas and the poor and predominantly rural south. The disparity in income levels and income inequality caused by the aggressive opening of the economy to the rest of the world has been identified before.[14] Labor income for people in states with high exposure to globalization shifted upwards relative to the distribution of income levels in states with less exposure to globalization. The new economic policies and the establishment of NAFTA favored the export-driven, large-scale corporate producers of fruits and vegetables, while the small-scale farmers, traditionally producing grains for the domestic market, became more and more disenfranchised.

Research on the impact of NAFTA on Mexican agriculture distinguishes two types of economic actors: those who are large producers with good access to capital and technology and those small and medium-size producers who have to do with persistent resource limitations and lack of attractive market outlets. The effects of NAFTA on the latter group, have been negative. As De Ita (2003, 2, 7) points out, the introduction of NAFTA brought an increase of basic grain imports and a change in crop patterns that favored big agricultural corporations that could adapt to and integrate the new market conditions. However, the small- and medium-sized producers of traditional staples—corn and beans—saw their crop prices plummet as a result of cheap and subsidized imports; they were unable to compensate for the drain by using economies of scale.

Audley et al. (2003, 7) add that Mexican rural farmers substituted income lost due to lower prices by cultivating marginal lands which resulted not only in lower production yields but also in deforestation in biologically rich areas of southern Mexico. Harris (2001) concurs with the general consensus that while a direct-payment program—such as the Pro Campo program introduced by Mexico at the start of NAFTA—has the potential to be more efficient than a system of subsidies and supports, it did not achieve the intended protection for the small producers who represent the great majority of agricultural households in Mexico. Because the system of direct payments is based on the extension of land owned, which makes no distinction between product crops, it again tended to favor the big agricultural landowners. On top of the small allowances that Pro Campo provided for small agricultural producers, the limited access to credit aggravated the feeble economic standing of the Mexican, small, rural producers. Puyana and Romero (2004, 25) have called attention to this by stating that since the beginning of economic reforms (and during NAFTA), rural credit was almost non-existent. This precluded the option of small agricultural producers adopting new production methods or switching to more profitable crops.

Coping with the Past, Challenges for the Future

In order to better understand the effects of NAFTA it is important to consider the programs already in existence when NAFTA was signed, and other programs that emerged around the same time.

Before the onset of economic liberalization, which occurred around 1985, the Mexican economy operated under a dysfunctional market system of government-regulated prices, import quotas, and nontariff barriers designed to protect the domestic manufacturing sector and to stem the pressures and fears of peso devaluations.[15] To reinforce the observance of government price controls on essential staples, the Mexican government created and operated CONASUPO (Compañia Nacional de Subsistencias Populares) as an official monopoly agency to supply and distribute basic goods—including agricultural products—at fixed prices. The free market and open border policies that were later instituted in Mexico prior to and in preparation for the move to NAFTA caused the demise of CONASUPO in 1991. In its place, but with a more limited role, a new government agency (ASERCA) was created to help in the transition to open markets. As part of this function, ASERCA can still provide subsidies to grain producers but only when the national price of those grains is below the proven production costs.

The liberalization of the domestic market and the borders opened to trade by globalization and NAFTA created a few new opportunities for the more sophisticated agricultural producers in Mexico, but left the small rural producers adrift in an ever more complex, uncertain, and competitive market environment. While some agricultural corporations—such as those in the northwestern state of Sonora, a state considered the main producer of wheat prior to NAFTA—became producers of nuts, peaches, asparagus, chickpeas, cucumbers, and watermelons for export, mainly to the United States,[16] the struggle of the rural Mexican poor for self-sufficiency continued with no apparent improvement in sight. The proportion of rural households at the poverty level increased from 49% in 1989 to 53% in 1996 (David et al. 2000, 1682).

The multiple factors that handicapped the rural sector in Mexico derived from two interdependent causes, namely, the inefficiency and inconsistencies of rural development policies applied by the government, and the lack of entrepreneurial skills and independence among agricultural producers. (The latter was a direct consequence of a traditional dependency by farmers on government handouts, which characterized the approach of the one-party-in-power system during the decades prior to the new liberal economic times.)

One of the social programs of the 1910 Mexican Revolution called for a redistribution of arable territory among the peasants who worked the land, giving the Mexican government the right to expropriate and distribute land among its rural population. Over time, 254 million acres, or more than half of the country, were allocated to poor Mexican peasants, creating farming communities (*ejidos*) of small communal plots which the peasants had the right to use and plant, but without rights of ownership. The land distribution reform that the Mexican constitution sanctioned soon became a political weapon of the official party and its federal government who, by distributing farming plots, gained (and for decades retained) the ballot preference of the rural masses. However, this system of land tenure handicapped the development of agriculture and made the communal farmers increasingly more dependent upon government subsidies. All this changed in 1992, when the Salinas regime amended Article 27 of the constitution, thus ending the program of land redistribution and giving the ejido peasants the right to own, sell, or lease their land.

The conditions that typically preclude the ability of the rural poor to advance with the rest of the economy were and still are present in the country. Thus, weak extension services; lack of affordable markets and suppliers for seeds, fertilizers, and financial services; inadequate infrastructure; and deficient market outlets for agricultural goods have been endemic in the Mexican agricultural sector. In essence, the Mexican agricultural producers, accustomed to heavily subsidized farm inputs and government-guaranteed grain prices in the past, were squeezed between the forces of NAFTA and Mexico's economic liberalization. On the one side, the prices of water supply, fertilizer, electricity, improved seeds, pesticides, and insurance rose to non-subsidized, market-driven levels. On the other side, opening the NAFTA gates brought in cheaper agricultural imports and subjected the Mexican farmers to international commodity prices and the seasoned competition from abroad.

To partially counterbalance the inequalities that the new liberalizing programs brought to the Mexican rural poor, the Mexican government tried new support mechanisms. One of these was the Pro Campo program, initiated in 1993, which consists of a direct cash support to each farmer who requests it at the beginning of the planting season. The payment is thus a direct decoupled subsidy per hectare owned by either private or communal (ejido) agricultural producers, and is independent of the type of crop planted or the region where the parcel is located. The Pro Campo payments were to remain constant for the first ten years of the NAFTA phase-in period and to be reduced over the following five years—after which time they would be eliminated.

Another government program to help the Mexican agricultural producers was the Alianza Para el Campo (Alliance for the Countryside),[17] launched in 1996, intended to improve agricultural productivity, and focusing on providing federal government support in infrastructure, process mechanization, and extension-type assistance. As a partial investment subsidy given to the farmer for the purchase of agricultural machinery or the improvement of cattle herds, it prescribes participation by the local state government to decentralize the federal apparatus and thus, try to reach the small agricultural communities.

In summary, inconsistent and ineffective government policies of the past have caused a deterioration of the economic and social fabric of the rural population, where nine out of every ten producers lack access to appropriate technology, and eight out of ten are not organized for productive work. There also have been serious imperfections in the market, specifically for grains and food staples, with unfavorable results for small producers. While there was an increase of 5% in the average productivity per hectare between 1993 and 1999, the relative price of agricultural products decreased by 25%. Considering this trend of low prices in basic grains and oilseeds, and in light of the high cost of production inputs and the retraction of government supports, the majority of the rural poor in Mexico live, and work, in precarious conditions. This situation is directly responsible for their migration from the countryside to Mexican urban centers or to the farming fields or barrios of the United States.

In recent years, the administration of President Vicente Fox, concerned with the structural problems afflicting the agricultural sector, began taking actions in line with a free-market approach to development. First, the Fox regime mapped rural development as part of the National Development Plan through a set of strategic objectives, projects, and programs for the agricultural sector—to be applied during 2001–2006 (SAGARPA 2001). Second, the enactment of a law on agriculture (at the end of 2001) formalized, for the first time, a comprehensive program for rural development and redefined the organizations and mechanisms to carry it through (Mexican Congress 2001, 45). Subsequently, in June of 2002, a presidential decree established a special concurrent program for rural development, which detailed the multiple programs and activities required to comply with the rural development law as part of a six-year, national plan (Mexico, June 17, 2002). Finally, in 2003, as a response to increasing public discontent and activism by peasant groups, the Fox regime issued emergency policies and channeled fresh funds to temporarily alleviate the unsolved crisis in the countryside.

On paper, the new legislation, programs, and plans for sustainable rural development introduced by the Fox government represented a comprehensive, multi-agency approach to improving the economic and social conditions of the rural poor. Thus, the 2001 Law for Sustainable Rural Development created an Inter-Ministerial Commission to be in charge of implementing its myriad of programs and projects. Furthermore, the law established a Mexican Board for Rural Development, a super-advisory unit charged with providing guidance about rural issues to the Mexican government. This board was integrated by the members of the Inter-Secretarial Commission and by representatives of producer associations and private organizations that had a direct interest in the agricultural sector.

The Rural Development Act aimed to increase the productivity and competitiveness of small agricultural producers, expand the market for agricultural goods, integrate the rural production units with the other links in the grain and staple-food supply chain, and create more rural enterprises. Such tasks were to be accomplished through multiple concerted actions managed by the Secretary of Agriculture and undertaken or overseen by the corresponding units of the Inter-Secretarial Commission for Rural Development, through a coordinated effort of units within the federal, state, and local governments. The multiple programs offered by this comprehensive approach to rural development included support for public and private investment; technology transfers; utilization of improved seeds; funds to improve crop insurance, warehousing, transportation, and working capital; training of rural producers in managerial, credit-use, and financing skills; and support for research and development applied to the characteristics of the Mexican environment.

The importance that the Fox regime placed on the agricultural sector was partially evident by the share of government funds earmarked for agricultural expenditures in the total budget: in the 2002 budget approved by the Mexican Congress, the Secretary of Agriculture was assigned the equivalent of $3.65 billion, representing 10.7% of the total government expenses, and an almost 20% increase over fiscal year 2001.[18] In the allocation of budget funds for 2002, the agricultural sector was second only to public education, which received $11.3

billion for its programs, or a 33% share of the total. However, even with this emphasis on funding programs for rural development, the spending gestures were too little, too late.

A closer review of specific items in the federal budget reveals that the Fox administration had assigned resources to improve the conditions of the rural population. For instance, in the 2002 budget, $582 million was allotted to support distribution and development of agricultural markets—almost three quarters of which was to help improve markets for basic grains and oilseeds.[19] Another entry in the budget, $82 million, was to help finance conversion of crops to better income-generating products. Lastly, the 2002 budget assigned $492.2 million for the Alliance for the Countryside (Alianza para el Campo), 60% of which was to benefit small producers in marginalized regions of the country.[20] In retrospect, when the new administration of Vicente Fox took office in 2000, the problems of the agricultural sector in Mexico continued to be an enormous challenge for any policymaker. It was already evident by then that the creation of new jobs in the export-oriented manufacturing sector was far from able to absorb the flow of new job seekers and displaced labor from the countryside.

The problems afflicting agriculture in Mexico have multiple roots in the past, and were magnified by the opening of the economy. There has never been a safety net to protect the small farmers in Mexico who were unfavorably affected by the new NAFTA-shaped environment. While export of fruits and vegetables by large-scale corporate farms benefited from increased trade, the other segment of Mexican agriculture—represented by small ejido farmers who concentrated on producing corn and beans—was left out of the market equation and the opportunities for progress. The series of support mechanisms introduced by the government to ameliorate the disadvantages that NAFTA brought were insufficient to move the small agricultural producers above and beyond the level of subsistence agriculture prevalent in the past. Given the economic realities, remaining options for survival for the poor peasants in small farming communities were reduced to part-time employment, remittances from relatives, and emigration to seek whatever opportunities could be found in the urban areas of Mexico or the United States.

In the more recent past, the government of Mexico has attempted to redirect more attention and resources to the agricultural sector, partly as a reaction to increasing demands raised by indigent farmers protesting in the streets of the Mexican capital. Thus, in 2003, the Fox government arranged to redistribute federal funds to provide emergency support measures for the poor agricultural producers. However, even with the best intentions and the most comprehensive approaches, too many variables and constraints limited the chances for any policymaker to stabilize Mexican agriculture.

Purpose and Structure of the Book

This book is not a magic wand for the Mexican policymakers to solve the uncertainties and limitations of the Mexican rural poor once and for all. It is, instead, an attempt to review the problems of the past in order to help identify action needed in the future. It is not a comprehensive approach to seeking improvements to the whole Mexican agricultural sector, nor to attending to the needs of all types of agricultural producers. The emphasis is on the small agricultural producer who owns a small plot of land and has to diversify his sources of income in order to survive.

This book comprises a series of cases documenting the good and bad experiences from the field—the favorable and unfavorable outcomes—of groups of Mexican agricultural producers who, in various segments of the sector, have tried to adjust to a new environment dominated by globalization and NAFTA. Some of these small, rural producers in Mexico represent economic units whose sources of income are diversified or complemented with non-agricultural wages such as income remittances from abroad or part-time employment by family members, all of which could cloud the true impact of NAFTA on their economic well-being. Thus, it is proper to state that the discussions of the cases in this book relate to rural households solely in their role as agricultural producers.

Chapter 1 presents an overview of the conditions of Mexican agriculture in recent years, which have been shaped by Mexico's joining NAFTA in 1994. Here, Manuel Gómez and Rita Schwentesius present arguments in support of the thesis that the NAFTA experiment, while opening export markets to integrated high-scale Mexican processors of fruits and vegetables, left the small agricultural producers of grains and oilseeds worse off and unable to compete under the new economic circumstances. The authors conclude that Mexico's trade balance in the agricultural sector has deteriorated as a result of NAFTA, and that the country has become more dependent on the United States for its supply of food staples.

In Chapter 2, which adds a sociological dimension to the economic discussion, Manuel Chavez analyzes the interaction between the forces of globalization and regionalism, and their influence on production, economic integration, government, and society. The formation of new regional trade blocs such as NAFTA and Mercosur reflects a response by governments and institutions to navigating the new waves of globalization and open competition. In this process of adaptation, several actors vie for more authority, control, and a larger portion of the economic pie. Thus, national governments, corporations, communities, and citizens in general face a complex competition where knowledge and information are essential, though expensive, weapons of choice. Chavez argues that in this game of global economic roulette, it is the poor rural sector in emerging societies that loses.

In Chapter 3, Mark Martinez and Gaspar Real Cabello provide an intriguing transition from the general context of globalization and NAFTA presented in the earlier chapters. Their study is a comprehensive and interesting analysis of how the domestic poultry industry—along with the multinational processing corporations and the individual poultry farmers—has adapted and flourished in Mexico within the context of NAFTA, or in spite of it. The authors' field research documents how many individuals and small poultry producer groups in central Mexico increased their production, improved their technology, and altogether grew and prospered after entering into supplier-producer associations with Pilgrim's Pride, a U.S. poultry company with processing plants in Mexico. This alliance between a U.S. multinational corporation and the small poultry producers was successful in part because of the market vision of the company and its willingness to create production opportunities for many small rural producers. The influence of Pilgrim's Pride in nourishing an expanding market and helping support individual chicken farmers spilled over in the industry and the region. Thus, small- and medium poultry producers joined in the push for better technology, better production, better competition, and better markets.

In Chapter 4, Gerardo Otero and Cornelia Butler Flora examine sugar as one of the most politically explosive topics in the three NAFTA countries. Sugarcane ranks as one of the most important crops in Mexico, measured in terms of growers, workers, and processing plants; farmers in 15 Mexican states grow sugarcane. World prices for sugar have been artificially manipulated by special trade agreements between countries as well as by internal price-support mechanisms in domestic markets. In their analysis, Otero and Butler Flora advance that the prevailing trade policies for the sugar industry in the NAFTA region are shaped by the relative power exercised by various competing groups—namely, cane and beet growers, industrial processors, workers, and consumers. In Mexico, the populist legacy of the Revolution influenced the state to cater to a wide variety of interests, including organized labor in sugar mills, organized peasant sugarcane producers, and sugar processors. The state-sponsored system under which the sugarcane industry operated in Mexico kept many constituents happy, but it was inefficient and costly to maintain. This chapter suggests ways for the NAFTA countries to coordinate NAFTA-region sugar policies to maximize employment while keeping the processing plants operating and increasing profits.

In Chapter 5, Juan Rivera presents another case study of alliances between Mexican small corn producers and two multinational agribusiness firms. As evidenced by the size of the surface planted and the 2.7 million corn producers out of a total four million farmers, corn is the most important crop in Mexico. Still, local production has not been sufficient to satisfy the local demand for many years, and the introduction of NAFTA brought more uncertainties to the domestic corn markets. That is, while the NAFTA signatory countries agreed to keep corn in Mexico outside of the duty-free trade path applicable to the rest of the products, the special duties and controls that the Mexican government was entitled to impose on corn imports were practically never applied. The result was a constant flow of cheap, subsidized corn from the United States into Mexico, with a consequent displacement of many domestic small corn producers. To partially ameliorate the conditions of the affected local farmers, two multinational agribusiness firms undertook programs to aid the small corn producers in Mexico. One of these corporations initiated a project to promote better technology that would improve production yields for those small corn farmers in targeted poor rural communities. The other corporation entered into contractual agreements with local producers to supply product for the corporation's corn-processing mill. The study of these cooperative arrangements suggests the potential benefit to forming such associations—between corporations and local agricultural producers—for a range of other products and in other regions of the country.

If there has been a segment of the agricultural sector in Mexico that has benefited from NAFTA, it is the frozen-vegetable industry in central Mexico. In Chapter 6, Elia Patlán and Juan de Dios Trujillo provide a comprehensive review of a thriving industry in the Bajio region that is heavily engaged in exporting vegetables to the United States. The field study by Patlán and Trujillo deals with contract agriculture between suppliers-producers of vegetables and large-scale frozen-vegetable processors. On the processor side, the field research includes the cases of a fully foreign-owned U.S. subsidiary, a partially foreign joint-venture firm, and a wholly domestic Mexican company. These corporations contract their supply of raw material from an array of Mexican agricultural producers represented mostly by small and medium-size farms. The contractual arrangements in the industry have worked well for all participating parties, with the firms providing technical support and financial security for the agricultural producers in the region. As a by-product, the expansion of the industry's operations through the years has helped somewhat to deter the flow of migration from the rural countryside.

One of the few other agricultural subsections in Mexico that can be considered successful and sustainable is that of organic agriculture. In Chapter 7, Laura Gómez and Manuel Gómez study the growing demand for organic products in the world, and then analyze how this type of production agriculture has started to develop in Mexico. While only a small portion (less than 1%) of total cultivated land is dedicated to organic farming, the positive impact on the economy of the peasants in those cultivated regions is noticeable, especially because the producers engaged in this market belong to groups representing the most marginalized and poorest peasants in Mexico. The market outlets for the Mexican organic products are in foreign lands. Thus, while the organic agriculture has developed as an independent and indigenous response against globalization, it is ironic that this subsection of Mexican agriculture is expanding sales and markets thanks in part to globalization.

Chapter 8 reports the results of an unsuccessful alliance among three agents in the highlands region of central Mexico. The case researched by Juan de Dios Trujillo, Elia Patlán, and Rita Schwentesius concentrates on the problems and constraints faced by a nongovernmental organization in bringing together goat-milk producers from the Matehuala region with a milk-processing plant that produces a goat-milk-based confectionary popular in Mexico. The processing plant came under the ownership of the Bimbo Group, a Mexican-based multinational conglomerate, that is the leader in baking products, snacks, and confectionary goods in Mexico and Latin America. The case study demonstrates how difficult it can be for an NGO—intent on aiding the small farm producers in Mexico—to negotiate the conflicting interests and priorities of the for-profit milk-processing plant on one side, and the small goat raisers on the other. The goatherd farmers in the study encountered bottlenecks and technical problems that precluded them from supplying the quantity and quality of goat milk required in the agreement with the milk processor. At the same time, the representatives from the NGO working on the project had to undertake so many diverse tasks on behalf of both the farmers and the plant (such as collecting and transporting milk, keeping track of quantities delivered, making payments to farmers, etc.) that soon they were unable to keep the administration of the project going. In addition to calling attention to the difficulties faced by the NGO, the case also brings into focus the need for more government participation in promoting and supporting the activities of the goat-keeping farmers in Mexico, some of the poorest peasants in the high desert areas of the country where alternative economic opportunities are hard to find.

The Conclusion explains how the lessons taken from the cases might provide guidelines and lead to recommendations for improving the conditions of the Mexico's rural poor.

Endnotes

1. Canada already had a free-trade pact with the United States, the Canada-U.S. Free Trade Agreement (CUSTA) that was implemented in 1989.
2. In 2000, U.S. trade with Mexico and Canada reflected 380% more in exports than Japan and China combined and 75% more than exports with the European Union. See Pastor, "North America's Second Decade," 124–35.
3. For a discussion of NAFTA accomplishments and shortcomings, see Alberto Aroyo, "NAFTA in Mexico's Promises, Myths and Realities," 5–22, and Audley et al. *NAFTA's Promise and Reality: Lessons from Mexico for the Hemisphere*, 1–88.
4. *The Washington Consensus* was a term used in 1990 by John Williamson from the Institute for International Economics to describe a set of economic prescriptions which had free trade and foreign investment as their cornerstone. See John Williamson, "After the Washington Consensus: Restarting Growth and Reforms in Latin America."
5. See "Tequila Slammer: The Peso Crisis, Ten Years On." *The Economist* (January 1-7, 2005): 55–58.
6. See INEGI—Mexico. *Banco de Información Económica*. Table on Foreign Direct Investment. http://dgensyp.inegi.gob.mx.
7. See Banco de Mexico (2000): 2–4.
8. While Mexico's close trade ties with the United States helped its progress up until 2000, it now hinders its growth. The contraction of the U.S. economy after September 11 translated into a 0.3% decrease in Mexico's GDP for 2001. This negative trend continued during the first quarter of 2002 when the Mexican economy contracted at an annual equivalent rate of 2%. See Banamex-Accival (2002): 255.
9. For a review of the performance of the Mexican economy in recent years, see Banco de Mexico (April 2000), and Grupo Financiero Banamex-Accival (2000). In addition, an excellent analysis of the changes in the Mexican economy from 1982 to 1998 can be found in Bensabat (1999): 71–87. As for the specific impact of these policy changes on the agricultural sector in Mexico, a good summary is found in J.L. Calva, et al., *El Campo Mexicano: Ajuste Neoliberal y Alternativas*, 230.
10. This income disparity continues, as evidenced from data for 1999. For that year, the per capita income in the Mexico City area was almost six times that in the state of Oaxaca, one of the poorest rural states in the country. See Linartas, "Desigualdad Regional in Mexico. El Efecto del TLCAN y Otras Reformas Estructurales," 25.
11. See Banamex-Accival, *Mexico Social 1998: Rural Mexico*, 29.
12. Included in this rural population are the indigenous people in Mexico, 65% of whom live in communities of fewer than 2,500 inhabitants where they are mainly engaged in primary-sector activities.
13. See David et al., "The Impact of the New Economic Model on Latin America's Agriculture," 1675.
14. See Hanson, "Globalization, Labor Income and Poverty in Mexico."

15. For a brief overview of economic conditions and support programs in existence prior to NAFTA, see Loria and Loria (2006).
16. See *The Economist*, October 28, 2000: 7; and Diaz-Bonilla and Reca, "Trade and Industrialization in Developing Countries. Trends and Policy Impacts," 220, 225. By supplying 13% of U.S. agricultural imports and buying 12% of U.S. agricultural exports, Mexico has become the third largest agricultural trading partner for the United States, after the European Union and Canada. On the other side, the United States is Mexico's main trading partner of agricultural products. Thus, for the year 1998, Mexico's agricultural trade with the United States represented $8.6 billion
17. In 1999, the Alianza Para el Campo (Alliance for the Countryside) paid 2.57 billion pesos in subsidies to Mexican farmers. This is even less than the 4.57 billion pesos ($480 million) of government subsidy on electricity for pumping water, which benefited mostly the northern region of the country. See *The Economist* (October 28, 2000): 1–16.
18. See Mexico. Secretary of the Treasury. *Decreto de Presupuesto 2002.* http://www.shcp.sse.gob.mx.
19. See ANEC. http://www.laneta.apc.org/anec.
20. ANEC, 19. http://www.laneta.apc.org/anec.

Bibliography

ANEC (Asociación Nacional de Empresas Comercializadoras de Productores del Campo). *Otro Presupuesto Rural 2002*. http://www.laneta.apc.org/anec.

Arroyo, Alberto. "NAFTA in Mexico's promises, myths and realities," in *Lessons From NAFTA: The High Cost of Free Trade*. Hemispheric Social Alliance Research Report (June 2003): 5–22.

Audley, John J., Demetrios Papademetriou, Sandra Polaski, and Scott Vaughan. *NAFTA's Promise and Reality: Lessons from Mexico for the Hemisphere*. Carnegie Endowment for International Peace (2004): 1–88.

Banamex-Accival. Division of Economic and Social Research. *Review of the Economic Situation of Mexico*. Banamex, vol. 78 (June 2002): 255.

———. *Mexico Social 1998. Rural Mexico*. "Wages and Income Section," 29.

———. Division of Economic and Social Research. *The Mexican Economy_Sectorial Report*. (2000).

Banco de Mexico. *The Mexican Economy: Performance, Strength and Recent Evolution. 1995–2000* Summary. Banco de Mexico Publication (2000): 2–4.

———. *Annual Report 1999*. Banco de Mexico Publication (April 2000).

Bensabat Kleinberg, Remonda. "Strategic Alliances: State-Business Relations in Mexico under Neo-Liberalism and Crisis." *Bulletin of Latin American Research* 18, no. 1 (1999): 71–87.

Calva, J. L., M. A. Gomez-Cruz, and Rita Schwentesius, eds. *El Campo Mexicano: Ajuste Neoliberal y Alternativas* (May 1997): 230.

David, Beatriz de A., M. Dirven, and F. Vogelgesang. "The Impact of the New Economic Model on Latin America's Agriculture," *World Development* 28, no. 9 (2000): 1673–88.

De Ita, A. "Los impactos socioeconomicos y ambientales de la liberación comercial de los granos básicos en el contexto del TLCAN: El caso de Sinaloa." Paper presented at the *Second North American Symposium on Assessing the Environmental Effects of Trade* (Mexico City, March 25–26, 2003).

De Janvry, A., M. Fafchamps, and E. Sadoulet. "Peasant Household Behavior with Missing Markets: Some Paradoxes Explained," *The Economic Journal* 101: 1400-1417.

Diaz-Bonilla, E., and L. Reca. "Trade and Industrialization in Developing Countries: Trends and Policy Impacts," *Agricultural Economics* 23 (2000): 219–29.

Garcia, Salazar, J. A. "Efectos de PROCAMPO sobre la Producción y Saldo de Comercio Exterior de Maiz," *Agrociencia* 35, no. 6 (2001): 671–83.

Hanson, Gordon H. "Globalization, Labor Income and Poverty in Mexico." *National Bureau of Economic Research*. Working Paper, no. 11027 (January 2005).

Harris, Lee R. "A Computable General Equilibrium Analysis of Mexico's Agricultural Policy Reforms." Discussion Paper, no. 65. International Food Policy Research Institute (IFPRI). Trade and Macroeconomics Division (2001).

INEGI—Mexico. *Banco de Información Económica*. Table on Foreign Direct Investment. http://dgensyp.inegi.gob.mx.

Levy, S., and S. van Wijnbergen. "Mexican Agriculture in the Free Trade Agreement: Transition Problems in Economic Reform." OECD Development Centre, Technical Papers, no. 63 (1992).

Linartas, Miguel Messmacher. "Desigualdad Regional in Mexico. El Efecto del TLCAN y Otras Reformas Estructurales." *Documento de Investigación No. 2000-4*. Dirección General de Investigación Económica. (Banco de Mexico, Diciembre 2000): 25.

Loría-Sagot, Miguel A. "El Sector Agricola Mexicano y NAFTA: Predicciones y Resultados. Lecciones Para Centroamerica." http://www.ruta.org/documentos_no_indexados/CAFTA_marzo06/ElSectorAgricMex_NaftaMLoria.pdf.

Luna Martinez, Sergio. "Agribusiness Foreign Trade." *Banamex: Review of the Economic Situation of Mexico* 923 Vol. 78 (November 2002): 451–55.

Mexican Congress. *Ley de Desarrollo Rural Sustentable* (Law of Sustainable Rural Development). Diario Oficial (Official Gazette), (December 7, 2001): 45.

Mexico. Secretaria de Agricultura, Ganadería, Desarrollo Rural, Pesca y Aliment ación. *Decreto* (Decree) which approves the special concurrent program for sustainable rural development. Government of Mexico. Diario Oficial (Official Gazette), (June 17, 2002): 128.

———. Secretaria de Hacienda y Crédito Publico (Secretary of the Treasury). *Decreto de Presupuesto 2002*. Presupuesto 2002 de Egresos de la Federación. http://www.shcp.sse.gob.mx

Pastor, Robert A. "North America's Second Decade," *Foreign Affairs* (January-February 2004): 124–35.

Puyana, A., and J. Romero. "Evaluación integral de los impactos e instrumentation del Capitulo agropecuario del TLCAN." In *Antecedentes y desempeño del sector agropecuario a partir del TLCAN: Preliminary Report* (February 2004).

Reardon, T., J. Berdegué, and G. Escobar. "Rural Non-Farm Employment and Incomes in Latin America: Overview and Policy Implications." *World Development* 29, no. 3 (2001): 395–409.

SAGARPA (Secretaria de Agricultura, Ganadería, Desarrollo Rural, Pesca y Alimentación). "Programa Sectorial de Agricultura, Ganadería, Desarrollo Rural, Pesca y Alimentación 2001–2006." In *Plan Nacional de Desarrollo* (2001).

The Economist. "Tequila Slammer: The Peso Crisis, Ten Years On," January 1–7, 2005: 55–58.

———. "Revolution Ends, Change Begins." Mexico Survey. October 28, 2000:1–7.

U.S. Department of Agriculture. Economic Research Service. Briefing Room. *World Trade. Mexico Trade*. Trade with the U.S.—Mexico. http://www.ers.usda.gov/briefing/mexico/trade/htm.

U.S. Department of State, Bureau of Economic and Business Affairs. *2001 Country Reports on Economic Policy and Trade Practices*, February 2002.

Williamson, John. "After the Washington Consensus: Restarting Growth and Reforms in Latin America." *Institute for International Economics*, 2003. http://www.iie.com/jwilliamson.htm.

Chapter 1

NAFTA's Impact on Mexican Agriculture: An Overview

Manuel Ángel Gómez Cruz and Rita Schwentesius Rindermann

THE NORTH AMERICAN FREE TRADE AGREEMENT (NAFTA) between Mexico, the United States, and Canada completed its tenth year on December 31, 2003, and since that date practically all agricultural products are free from tariff protection in the trade among the three countries. Only a partial defense mechanism for Mexico is left in place in the cases of corn, beans, sugar, poultry meat, and milk. The purpose of this chapter is to document and describe the economic and social impacts of the agricultural provisions (NAFTA, Chapter 7), both in the present and for the future, with the aim of justifying through objective data the urgent need to review that chapter of the trade agreement in order to establish protection mechanisms for some agricultural products.

This chapter presents a brief introduction to the panorama of Mexican agriculture just prior to and during the years of NAFTA, followed by a section on the asymmetries observed among the participating NAFTA nations. A third section offers an evaluation of NAFTA's effects on Mexican agriculture in general and on the small- and medium-size agricultural producers who represent the majority of Mexico's rural population. The fourth section is a discussion of the prospects of Mexican agriculture in the years ahead, and the chapter concludes with some proposals for change.

Background: Mexican Agriculture and NAFTA: 1981 to 2005

Research studies conducted by organizations of small, medium, and large producers, and by different academic groups in Mexico during the period since 1991, reached conclusions saying that, in general, Mexico has little to gain and much to lose from the trade agreement with the United States and Canada. Agricultural research groups such as CIESTAM recommended against negotiating from positions that jeopardize the domestic production of Mexico's most important foods (primarily grains, dairy products, and meat) in order to avoid severe damage to the national industry and to restrain a growing and unacceptable dependency in terms of food—and in economic, technological, and even political terms.[1] Given this scenario, some agents have insisted that a partial suspension of NAFTA's agricultural chapter is necessary.[2]

In the year 2002, the World Bank came to similar conclusions:

> It can be said that [the rural] sector has been the object of the most drastic structural reforms (trade liberalization as promoted by GATT and NAFTA, elimination of price controls, structural reform in relation to land ownership), however

> the results have been *disappointing* (emphasis added): stagnation of growth, lack of competitiveness in the international market, an increase in poverty in rural areas. . . . This sets forth a significant political problem, because effective in 2008, any last remaining import duty or trade barrier in the NAFTA region will be removed and the trade accord will be fully completed. The Mexican agricultural sector will then find itself in open and total competition with Canada and the United States.[3]

Since the end of 2002, Mexican farmers, who are organized in a wide variety of ways, have been clear about the situation they face and have been insisting that "the rural sector can't take any more *(El campo no aguanta más).*" A struggle began not only against the government and against transnational corporations, but also against Mexico's long-standing, corporate-style farmer organizations. On January 31, 2003, a protest march of more than 100,000 persons culminated at Mexico City's central plaza and was tolerated and accepted by the citizens of that huge city (although usually, marches of this type provoke a great deal of irritation), indicating the popular solidarity and sympathy felt for the farmers engaged in this struggle. It also demonstrates that the farmer movement has not died and has the capacity to renovate itself.

The struggle waged by Mexican farmers culminated on April 28, 2003, with the signing of the National Agreement for Agriculture *(Acuerdo Nacional para el Campo*—ANC).[4] This Agreement, signed by the federal government and some of the producer organizations, consists of a total of 282 points to be resolved in the short and medium term. Point 47 refers to an assessment of NAFTA, stating specifically: "The Federal Executive Branch will conduct a comprehensive assessment of the impacts and implementation of the NAFTA Agriculture Chapter. This assessment will be carried out with participation by farmer and producer organizations, and the productive chains, inviting the National Congress, local governments, universities and research centers, and should be completed by no later than December 31 of the current year."[5] Just as with many other points in the agreement, Point 47 has not been fulfilled at the time of this writing. This is because of the profound differences between the Mexican government and producer organizations with respect to the importance of agriculture in the national economy, and consequently, the difficulty in naming an entity to be responsible for carrying out such a study.

In Mexico, there are at least two positions that are completely opposite with regard to the agricultural sector's importance in the economy and NAFTA's impact on that sector. The first position measures the importance of this sector solely in monetary terms, based on its contribution to the GDP, and it evaluates NAFTA's impact exclusively through trade statistics.

The other position (presented here) considers the following: a) the multiplying effect of the agricultural sector, in both vertical and horizontal directions—in other words, it measures the impact on the manufacturing and inputs industries, and on the transportation, services, and trade sectors; b) the multifunctional nature of this sector, as the foundation for food and food sovereignty, and as a creator of jobs and foreign currency; and c) its impact on society, and its importance in maintaining peace in rural areas, for protecting the environment, biodiversity and the landscape, and as the basis for Mexican culture and national identity. This second position acknowledges the existence of a number of different rural sectors in Mexico, leading to the necessity for differentiated policies toward the types of producers and regions characterizing the country.

Nevertheless, the first position is the one that prevails in Mexico's current policies (realpolitik), and all the tendencies organized around the second perception are out of favor among policy makers. Measures are implemented to provide assistance[6] and protection[7] only for large agricultural producers and for groups associated with U.S. capital, while agricultural policy involving small producers is reduced to a type of charity that leads nowhere.

Asymmetries among NAFTA Partners

Trade relations between Mexico and its trade partners, the United States and Canada, are characterized by numerous asymmetries that explain, to a significant degree, NAFTA's negative impact on the agricultural sector as can be demonstrated by comparing Mexico's agriculture before and after the signing of NAFTA.

Before the signing of NAFTA, the following conditions prevailed:

1. The NAFTA countries brought to the table asymmetries in natural resources, technological level, producers' capitalization, assistance and subsidies received, etc. (See Table 1.)
2. Mexico carried a disadvantageous situation of noncompetitive production costs (due to higher prices for inputs such as diesel and electricity and steep financial costs) and higher costs in commercializing products (due to deficient, poor-quality infrastructure in highways and warehouse storage, lack of information, and similar factors). These are costs over which producers have no influence.
3. NAFTA was poorly negotiated for Mexico. The agreement was negotiated without considering the complete past experience of the Free Trade Agreement between the United States and Canada. Also, Chapters 19 and 20, referring to trade-related disagreements and controversies, are inadequate for genuinely resolving conflicts, and their procedures lead to a vicious cycle that holds no solutions. In addition to these disadvantages, the most sensitive products for Mexico were not excluded, as they were for Canada (poultry products, milk products); there are high import quotas for Mexico, with no tariffs accepted for a great diversity of products; there is no provision for the possibility of review, suspension, moratorium, or the use of other instruments for protecting domestic production.
4. There was an unequal legal standing. The United States negotiated a trade agreement, while, in Mexico, NAFTA is acknowledged as a treaty, bearing different legal implications, including limitations on reviewing it.
5. The United States has traditionally held and exercised greater negotiating capability and power. It uses lobbying, ongoing evaluation studies, and similar maneuvers to reinforce its negotiating strength.

Table 1
Asymmetries between Mexico, the United States, and Canada

	Mexico	United States	Canada
Population (1,000)[1]	100,368	285,926	31,015
Rural Population (1,000)[1]	25,555	64,539	6,535
Agricultural Population (1,000)[1]	23,064	6,162	766
Population density (people per sq. km)[2]	51	30	3
Surface area (1,000 hectare)[2]	195,820	962,909	997,061
Arable land (1,000 hectare)[2]	27,300	179,000	45,700
Irrigated land (1,000 hectare)[3]	6,500	22,400	720
GNP $ mill.million (1999)[4]	428.8 (place 12)	8,351.0 (place 1)	591.4 (place 9)
GNP per capita ($ 1999)[4]	4,400 (place 71)	30,600 (place 8)	19,320 (place 29)
GINI index[4]	53.7	40.8	31.5
Percentage share of income, highest 10%[4]	42.8	30.5	23.8
Competitiveness ranking, 2001[5]	51	2	11
Growth competitiveness ranking, 2001[5]	42	2	3
Public expenditure on agricultural research/ag. GNP (%)	0.52	2.60	
Public expenditure on education (% of GNP)[4]	4.9	5.4	6.9
Tractors per 1,000 agricultural workers[4]	20	1,484	1,642
Agricultural wages ($ per year), 1995/98[5]	908	n.d.	30,625
Agricultural productivity (1995 $ per agricultural worker)[4]	2,164	39,001	n.d.
Annual deforestation (annual % change)[4]	0.9	-0.3 *	-0.1*
Producer support estimates (% of value of production) 2001[6]	22	36	25
Food import, 1998/2000, value ($1,000)[7]	8,935,732	43,354,622	11,046,062
Food exports, 1998/2000, value ($1,000)[7]	7,157,371	55,508,420	15,253,898
Trade balance, value ($1,000)[7]	-1,778,361	12,153,798	4,207,837
Corn yields (tons/hectare)[8]	2.50	8.55	7.15

n.d. = not defined, * negative value means deforestation

Sources:

1. FAO, FAOSTAT, http://apps1.fao.org/servlet/XteServlet.jrun?Areas=33&Areas=231&Areas=138&Items=300 8& Elements=511&Elements=551&Elements=571&Years=2001&Format=Table&Xaxis=Years&Yaxis=countries&Aggregate=&Calculate=&Domain=SUA&ItemTypes=Population&Language=espanol&UserName=
2. FAO, FAOSTAT, http://apps1.fao.org/servlet/XteServlet.jrun?Areas=33&Areas=231&Areas=138&Items=1421&Elements=11&Elements=121&Elements=61&Years=2000&Format=Table&Xaxis=Years&Yaxis=Countries&Aggregate=&Calculate=&Domain=LUI&ItemTypes=LandUse&Language=espanol&UserName=
3. FAO, FAOSTAT, http://apps1.fao.org/servlet/XteServlet.jrun?Areas=33&Areas=231&Areas=138&Items=1423&Elements=51&Years=2000&Format=Table&Xaxis=Years&Yaxis=Countries&Aggregate=&Calculate=&Domain=LUI&ItemTypes=Irrigation&Language=espanol&UserName=
4. The World Bank, World Development Indicators 2002. Washington, DC, 2002,pp.64 y 65.
5. World Economic Forum. The Global Competitiveness Report 2001-2002, Table 1.Overall competitiveness ranking, p. 15, http://www.weforum.org/pdf/gcr/Overall_Competitiveness_Rankings.pdf.
6. OECD, Agricultural Compendium, Producer and Consumer Support Estimates 2002, base de datos, Beyond 20/20 Browser Files. París, Francia, 2002.
7. FAO, FAOSTAT, http://apps1.fao.org/servlet/XteServlet.jrun?Areas=33&Areas=231&Areas=138&Items=1882&Elements =62&Elements=92&Years=2000&Years=1999&Years=1998&Format=Table&Xaxis=Years&Yaxis=Countries&Aggregate=&Calculate=&Domain=SUA&ItemTypes=Trade.CropsLivestockProducts&Language=espanol&UserName=

8) FAO, FAOSTAT, http://apps1.fao.org/servlet/XteServlet.jrun?Areas=33&Areas=231&Areas=138&Items=56&Elements=41&Years=2001&Years=2000&Years=1999&Format=Table&Xaxis=Years&Yaxis=Countries&Aggregate=&Calculate=&Domain=SUA&ItemTypes=Production.Crops.Primary&Language=espanol&UserName=

After the signing of NAFTA, important conditions and events included the following:

1. With the new U.S. Farm Bill of 2002,[8] farmers there receive 70% more assistance. In Mexico, subsidies represented an average of 26% of the value of production in 1994–2001, while in the United States this percentage was 19%, and in Canada, 18% (Figure 1).[9] Thus, after NAFTA, the levels of assistance in the United States and Canada have been much greater than in Mexico.
2. Data—used by the OECD (Organization for Economic Cooperation and Development) for estimating government assistance to farmers—indicate a major inconsistency in agricultural assistance in Mexico vis-à-vis the other NAFTA partners. It is worth clarifying here that the OECD methodology illustrates the distortion caused by the exchange rate in the case of

Figure 1

Agricultural Producer Support Estimates for the United States, and Mexico, 1986–2004 (% of the Value of agricultural production, 1986–2004 market price support)

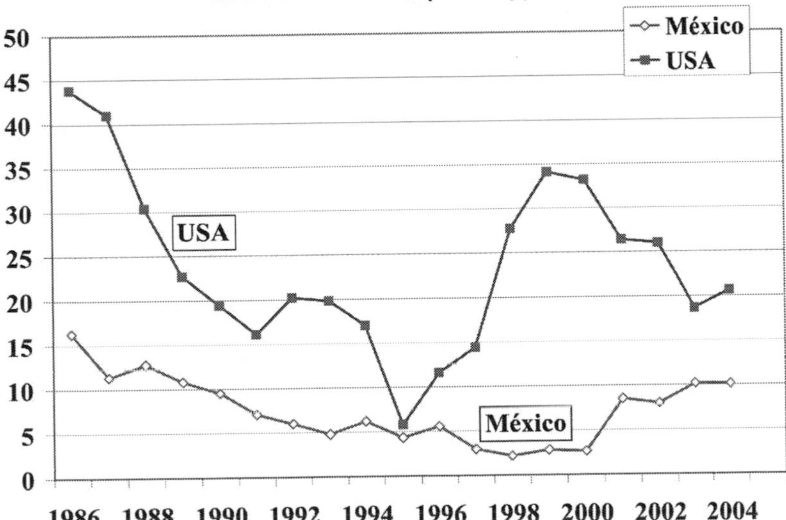

Source: Authors' calculations based on data from OECD, Producer and Consumer Support Estimates, OECD Database 1986–2004, http://www.oecd.org/dataoecd/33/50/32361372.ZIP, 2005.

Mexico. Since Mexico has had a notoriously over-valued exchange rate, agricultural assistance is over-estimated. If we use a balanced exchange rate, the subsidy decreases to 8% in 2003 in Mexico, or in other words, it represents 39% of the comparative government assistance provided to farmers in the United States.

3. As a basis for comparison, U.S. farmers receive assistance in the amount of $120.00 per hectare,[10] while in Mexico the assistance is equivalent to only $45.00 (OECD). U.S. producers farm an average of 29 hectares—

Mexican farmers, only 1.8 hectares (FAO, Statistical Database). Moreover, according to data from the World Bank, the productivity of a U.S. agricultural worker is 18 times greater ($39,000) when compared to a worker in Mexico ($2,164). (All dollar figures in this chapter are given in U.S. dollars.)

4. However, the asymmetries do not only exist in terms of the sizes of subsidies, but also in relation to their potential impact for the long term, and the capacity to generate technological innovations in a context of open competition. In this sense, Mexico's trade partners are promoting subsidies through services such as research and development, universities, infrastructure, commercialization, promotion, and stable reserves (see Figure 2). In 1994–2003, only an average of 8% of Mexico's subsidies were designated for services, while Canada and the United States reserved more than 25% of their resources for this area.
5. There are also asymmetries in the application of the limitations negotiated in NAFTA. In practice, Mexico has never charged tariffs on imports beyond the negotiated quotas for corn and dry beans, and consequently, the fiscal revenue lost during the NAFTA years represents more than $3.5 billion for corn, and $147 million for beans, in imports from the United States alone (see Tables 1 and 2.) Moreover, because of the limited capacity of Mexico's customs system, imported apples, beans, sugar, corn, pork, beef, and poultry products escaped the payment of

Figure 2

General Services Support Estimate in relation to Total Support Estimate in the United States, Canada, and Mexico, 1986–2003 (% of total support)

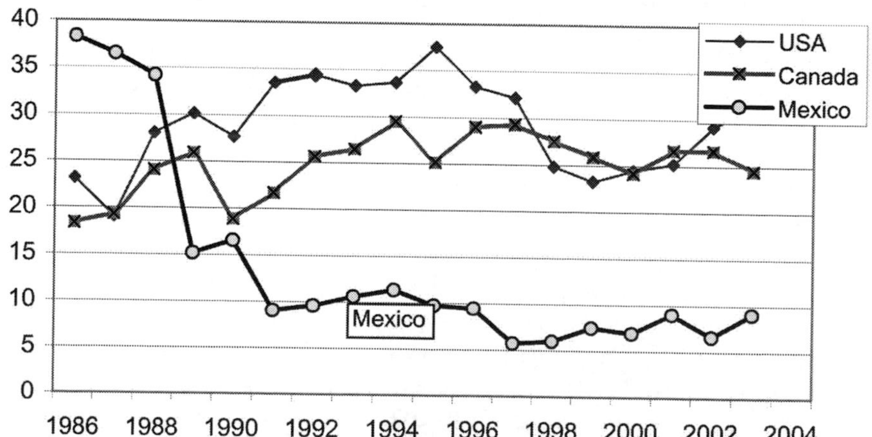

Source: Authors' calculations based on data from OECD, Producer and Consumer Support Estimates, OECD Database 1986–2004. http://www.oecd.org/dataoecd/33/50/32361372.ZIP, 2005.

safeguards, compensatory quotas, and general import taxes equivalent in value to approximately 50% of traded volumes.[11]

6. Exports to Mexico reported by the U.S. Department of Agriculture (USDA) contrast with the designation of import quotas by Mexico's Secretary of Economy. In the case of corn,[12] the designation as of December 31, 2003, was a total of 3.8 million tons, or 2.3 million tons less than the amount registered by the United States.[13] Another source of statistical information on imports reports the introduction of over 5.76 million tons, or 200,000 more tons than was registered by the United States. In the case

Table 2

Mexico's theoretical loss of fiscal revenue from US corn imports exceeding NAFTA quotas, 1989/93-2008

Year	*Import* (tons)	*Quota* (tons)	*Over-quota* (tons)	*NAFTA Tariff* ($/ ton)	*Fiscal loss (US $)*
1989/93	2,148,215				
1994	3,058,148	2,500,000	558,148	197	109,955,156
1995+	5,945,500	2,575,000	3,370,500	189	637,024,500
1996	6,314,387	2,652,250	3,662,137	181	662,846,797
1997	2,566,264	2,731,817		173	0
1998	5,247,763	2,813,771	2,433,992	164	399,174,688
1999	5,068,619	2,898,184	2,170,435	156	338,587,860
2000	5,146,666	2,985,129	2,161,537	139	300,453,643
2001	5,592,398	3,074,682	2,517,716	121	304,643,636
2002	5,326,755	3,166,922	2,159,833	104	224,622,632
2003	5,589,645	3.261,930	2,327,715	87	202,511,205
2004	5,613,794	3,359,788	2,254,006	69	155,526,414
2005	5,799,044	3,460,581	2,338,463	52	121,600,076
2006		3,564,399		34	
2007		3,671,331		17	
2008		Free		0	
Total (94-03)	49,843,911		25,954,482		3,456,946,607

The United States changed the data of volume exported to Mexico in the year 2000 to 2,871,567 tons, while the FAO database continued to use 5,945,500 tons. (http://apps.fao.org, consulted Feb. 7, 2004).

Source: Authors' calculations based on information from USDA, ERS, Foreign Agricultural Trade of the United States (http://www.fas.usda.gov/ustrdscripts/USReport.exe, consulted June. 14, 2006) and SECOFI, 1994, Tratado de Libre Comercio de América del Norte, Fracciones arancelarias y plazos de desgravación, Mexico, Miguel Ángel Porrúa, 78–80.

of beans, there is a difference of 11,602 tons between the statistics of the two countries.

7. As mentioned before in point 5, Mexico always imported more corn and dry beans than they had negotiated in the NAFTA agreement, and the Government never collected the over-quota tariff. This failure to apply

the tariffs theoretically[14] caused significant fiscal losses for corn and beans, (See Tables 2 and 3.)

8. Mexico has not achieved the necessary progress in defining and applying quality standards and has not established enough adequate facilities for enforcing sanitation controls, all of which limits the application of special duties or fines on imported goods, such as meat products.

A Ten-Year Evaluation of NAFTA

After ten years, NAFTA's impact is more dramatic than predicted:

1. Mexico's overall agro-food sector is not competitive in the NAFTA region. (See Figure 3.) Although it was competitive in the 1960s, Mexico has gradually lost ground. In the period since NAFTA, went into effect, it has not created the expected conditions for improving the situation and reversing the tendency toward less competitiveness. Thus, Mexico has not been able to narrow the gap with respect to the United States.

Table 3

Mexico's theoretical loss of fiscal revenue from US and Canadian bean imports exceeding NAFTA quotas, 1989/93–2008

Year	*NAFTA quota+*		*Import*		*Import Above tariff-free quota*	*Tariff Above quota*	*Fiscal loss*
	US (tons)	*Canada (tons)*	*US (tons)*	*Canada (tons)*	*(tons)*	*($ / ton)*	*(US$)*
	A	B	C	D	(C+D)–(A+B)		
1994	50,000	1,500	54,964	1,262	4,964	460	2,283,440
1995	51,500	1,545	24,048	696	--	441	-
1996	53,045	1,591	119,972	4,877	70,213	422	29,629,886
1997	54,636	1,639	86.628	1,685	32,038	403	12,911,314
1998	56,275	1,688	189,973	6,336	138,346	384	53,124,864
1999	57,964	1,739	121,617	1,736	63,653	364	23,169,692
2000	59,703	1,791	84,708	1,791	25,005	324	8,101,620
2001	61,494	1,845	115,557	8,600	60,818	283	17,211,494
2002	63,339	1,900	73,404	4,189	2,289	243	556,227
2003	65,239	1,957	23,298	9,000	--	202	
2004	67,196	2,016	29,415		--	162	
2005	69,212	2,076				121	
2006	71,288	2,139				81	
2007	73,427	2,203				40	
2008	free	free				free	
Total			1,022,600 tons				$146,988,537

+ Negotiated tariff-free quota.

Source: Authors' calculations based on BANCOMEXT, World Trade Atlas. Foreign Trade Statistics. Information on CD-Rom, various years; and SECOFI, 1994, Tratado de Libre Comercio de América del Norte. Fracciones arancelarias y plazos de desgravación, Mexico, Miguel Ángel Porrúa Book Publisher, p. 66.

Figure 3

Competitiveness of Mexican and U.S. agro-food sectors in the NAFTA region (1961-2003)

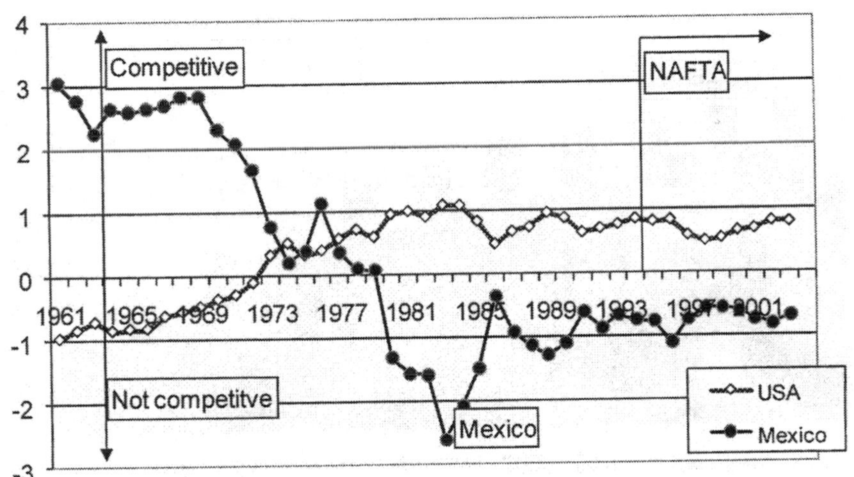

Source: Authors' calculations based on Index of Vollrath,[1] and data from FAO, FAOSTAT, http://faostat.fao.org/faostat/form?collection=Trade.CropsLivestockProducts&Domain=Trade&servl et=1&hasbulk=0&version=ext&language=ES, May, 2005.

[1] Vollrath, Thomas L., and Paul V. Johnston. "The Changing Structure of Agricultural Trade in North America, Pre-and Post-CUSTA/NAFTA: What Does It Mean?" AAEA/CAEA poster paper, (annual meetings), Chicago, August 5–8, 2001. http://www.ers.usda.gov/briefing/nafta/PDFFiles/ Vollrath2001AAEAPoster.pdf.

Figure 4

Mexico's food imports and agro-food trade balance, 1989–2004 (Millions of dollars)

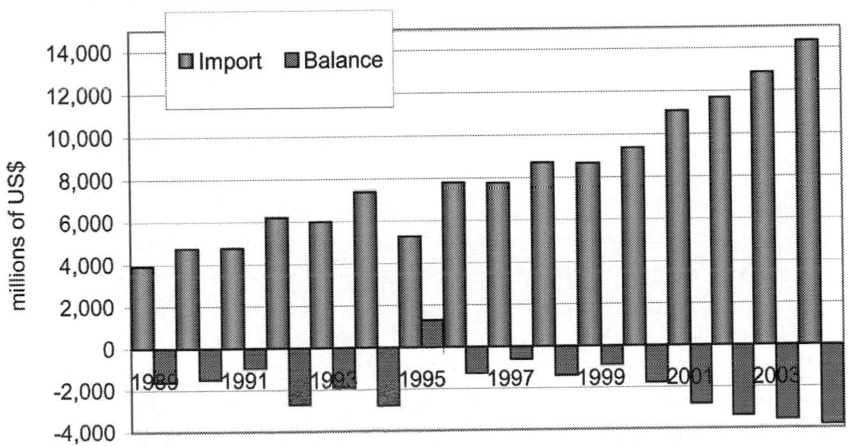

Source: Authors' calculations and elaboration based on INEGI, http://www.inegi.gob.mx, May 20005.

2. Due to its lack of competitiveness, Mexico has a chronic trade deficit in agriculture, with an increasingly worsening trend. Ten years after NAFTA went into effect, this deficit reached $17.1 billion, equivalent to 4.3 times the budget for Mexican agriculture for the year 2003 (see Figure 4). This deficit is in addition to the foreign debt that has been hanging over the country since the oil crisis of the early 1980s. Since NAFTA went into effect, Mexico has spent the exorbitant amount of $90 billion on purchasing food, an amount greater than the country's public debt ($87.7 billion).[15] As we begin the 21st century, Mexico's food imports are as high as the value of revenue obtained by its oil exports, and represent a third of the total food imports in all of Latin America.[16]
3. In 2004, Mexico's agro-food deficit reached a new historical record, nearly

Figure 5
Mexico's tendency toward losing self-sufficiency in grains 1961–2003 (% of consumption)

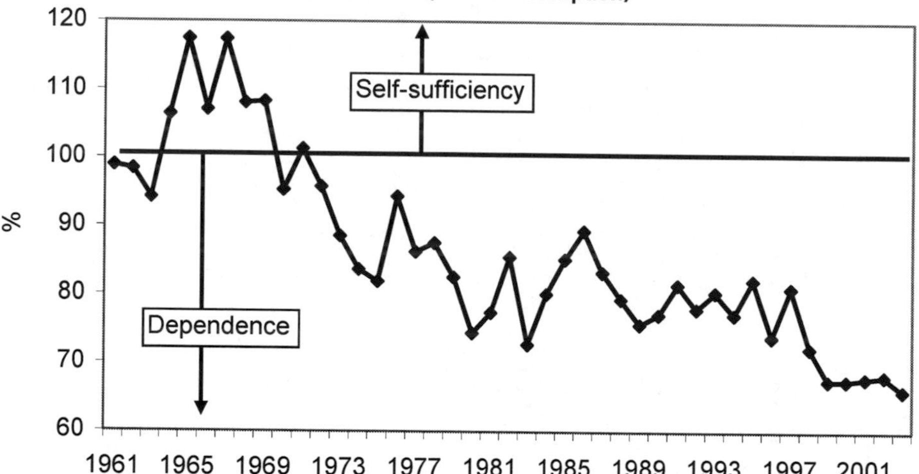

Source: Authors' calculations, based on FAO, FAOSTAT, 2005 http://faostat.fao.org/faostat/form?collection=Trade.CropsLivestockProducts&Domain=Trade&servl et=1&hasbulk=0&version=ext&language=ES, May, 2005.

$4 billon, (see Figure 4.)

4. Mexico is a major exporter of agricultural and processed food products. However, its export structure points to two problems: first of all, exports are concentrated (22%) in the alcoholic beverage industry, which is transnational in nature, signifying that not all the benefits from this trade remain in Mexico; and second, the multiplying factor from agriculture exports is relatively low due to the high component of imported inputs for production and manufacturing.
5. In 1993, before NAFTA, Mexico imported 8.8 million metric tons of grain and oil seed. However, it is estimated that in 2003 Mexico imported more than 20 million metric tons, or 2.3 times more. Since NAFTA, 148

million metric tons have been imported. In grain and oilseed alone, Mexico imported the equivalent of $32 billion between 1994 and December 2003,[17] and every year, the amount of imports increased. Despite a decreasing tendency in international grain prices, Mexico has, during NAFTA's ten years, registered a 7% annual average growth rate in the

Table 4

Mexico. Population employed in agricultural and food industry activities, 1993–2003

13. **Year**	**1993**	**1995**	**1997**	**2000**	**2003**	**Difference 1993-2003**
14. **Total population***	86,613,285	90,163,107	93,378,680	97,378,680	103,636,353	
15. **Employed population****	32,832,680	33,881,068	37,359,758	38,983,855	40,633,197	7,800,517
16. **Employed in agricultural agricultural activities**	8,842,774	8,378,344	9,020,277	7,060,706	6,813,644	-2,029,130
17. **Agricultural as percent of Total**	29.93	24.73	24.14	18.110	16.77	-37.73
18. **Employed in the food industry**	1,180,654	1,106,388	1,532,994	1,561,033	1,707,939	527,285

Sources:
* Consejo Nacional de Población, Población de México en Cifras, http://www.conapo.gob.mx/m_en_cifras/principal.html.
** Department of Labor and Social Security (Secretaría del Trabajo y Previsión Social—STPS). Encuesta Nacional de Empleo. Población ocupada por sexo y rama de actividad económica. 1993–2000; http://www.stps.gob.mx/01_Ofic.-na/ 05_cg peet/302_0055a.htm, 9.11.2002. 2003; http://www.stps.gob.mx/01_oficina/05_ cgpeet/302_0156.htm, 14.02.2004.

value of imports.[18] The situation for meats, tropical fruits, etc. is similar.

6. Statistics indicate that Mexico is losing its food sovereignty, and instead has a greater dependency on imports (see Figure 5.) Because of NAFTA, food imports are coming more and more from the United States—replacing other countries (such as Uruguay in the case of rice, and Brazil in the case of soybeans) that have traditionally supplied the Mexican market.
7. Mexico's high agricultural imports have displaced national producers—increasing unemployment in rural areas, and destroying part of the country's infrastructure. Unemployment in rural Mexico has increased at an alarming rate (see Table 4.) According to data from Mexico's Department of Labor and Social Security, more than two million jobs have been lost, and of that amount, nearly 600,000 are related to basic grain production. It is estimated that 40% of pork producers have stopped producing, and 24% of potato producers have done the same, with similar experiences in the cases of rice and corn producers.
8. Indirectly, imports also have a negative effect on natural resources and the environment, since farmers are left without sustainable, profitable alternatives. The increasingly reduced options for crops in the country's different regions force farmers to limit their production to single-crop production, to the detriment of soil fertility. For example, cotton and soybeans are no longer options in the state of Sonora, and rice, sugarcane, and cotton have disappeared from the fields of Sinaloa.
9. Despite the claim that NAFTA would attract more foreign investment in agriculture, as well as create more jobs and increase workers' renuner-

Figure 6

Mexico's basic food-basket prices and prices paid to agricultural producers, 1994–2004 (1994=100)

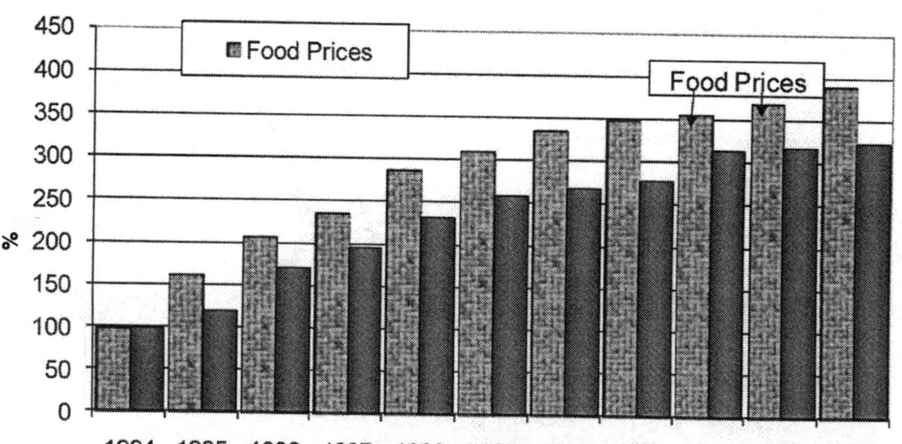

12. Source: Authors' calculations based on data from the President's Office, 4o Informe de Gobierno, September 1, 2004. Annex, 239–40.

ations, poverty in Mexico's rural areas has increased. According to official statistics, 69.3% of the total rural population is poor.[19] Since NAFTA went into effect, foreign investment in the agricultural sector has dropped to only a tenth of what it was in pre-NAFTA years. From 1990 to 1993, an average annual amount of $45 million in foreign investment was introduced into Mexico's primary production sector; however this amount dropped to less than $4 million in the 2001–2003 period.[20]

10. The alleged advantages for consumers based on greater access to less expensive imported food products never developed. From 1994 to 2004, the prices in the basic food basket increased by 292%, while prices paid to agricultural producers rose only 224%, according to statistics from the Mexican government. In other words, mass importing has placed more pressure on prices for primary agricultural products than on consumer

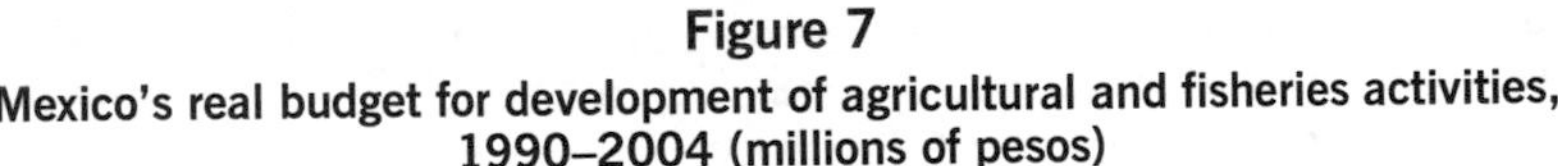

Figure 7

Mexico's real budget for development of agricultural and fisheries activities, 1990–2004 (millions of pesos)

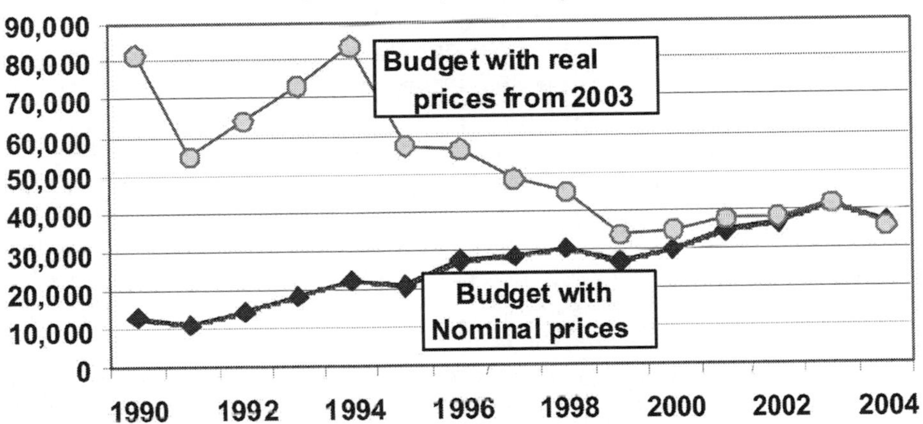

Sources: 1990–2002; Mexico, President's Office, 3er Informe de Gobierno. September 1, 2003, p. 250. 2003 and 2004; Comisión Intersecretarial para el Desarrollo Rural Sustentable. Deflated with INPC.

prices, and the latter continue to increase (see Figure 6). There are two different interpretations for the differential in the price increases—food received more transformation and/or the imports and middlemen gained more profit.

11. When the Mexican government signed NAFTA at the end of 1992, it was fully aware of the asymmetries between Mexico and its future trade partners. Consequently, it should have seen the need to implement policies for narrowing the existing gaps through an increased budget and new programs, in accordance with the reality of NAFTA. Instead, the budget for the agricultural and fisheries sectors decreased steadily (in real numbers) during the period from 1990 to 2004 (see Figure 7). This budget dropped from 83.5 billion pesos in 1994, when NAFTA went into effect,

to less than 42% of that amount by 2004. To make matters worse, in 2001, the Mexican government did not conduct the Agricultural Census which had been compiled every ten years since 1930 to provide the necessary information for appropriately focusing government actions within the agricultural sector. Consequently, agricultural policy is increasingly carried out blindly, and is disconnected from reality.

Prospects for the Year 2008

NAFTA has triggered the most drastic and profound transformation in the history of agriculture in Mexico. The present and future for this sector have been totally changed, and the option of continuing to live in the country's rural areas has been placed into question for the great majority of producers. Organizations of small, medium, and business-level producers of corn, soybeans, wheat, beans, rice, potatoes, cotton, apples, pork, cattle, etc.—representing most of Mexico's agricultural and livestock producers—are calling for NAFTA's suspension, or at least, its renegotiation, since no more than a thousand individuals have benefited from NAFTA,[21] while millions are on the losing end.

As of January 1, 2003, nine years after NAFTA's implementation, the minimal tariff protection was annulled for all imported agricultural products, with the exception of corn, beans, powdered milk, and sugar, and the protection for these latter products is only on paper.

Among the products affected the most, now and in the coming years, are poultry, pork, potatoes, animal fats, barley, apples, and fresh cheeses. These products had tariff protection ranging from 25% to 50% and/or import quotas, but that changed effective January 1, 2004, with no restraints in the form of import duties or special restrictions remaining. As expected, importers took advantage of the new circumstances.

Since January 2003, poultry and pork production is no longer protected through import quotas. According to well-informed sources at Apoyos y Servicios a la Comercialización Agropecuaria (ASERCA),[22] there are reports that during recent years, importers of poultry and pork requested up to ten times more than the negotiated, tariff-free quota allowed. A dramatic increase in the importing of these products is expected, and will not only negatively impact Mexico's poultry and pork sectors, but also the beef-producing sector. In the fall of 2002, many cattle ranchers in the states of Tabasco and Veracruz were liquidating their herds and no longer investing in this activity. The importing of meat also negatively impacts the production of animal feed, for which the national demand is constantly decreasing.

Protection will also disappear for barley and malt production, which could turn Mexico into a country "outsourcing" its beer.

Already free from tariffs is an incredible list of primary and processed products including the following: rice, tropical fruits, wheat, edible by-products, even coffee (roasted and processed), dairy products (except powdered milk), milled products, fresh-grape wines, canned and other processed goods, tobacco, vegetable oil and fats, copra, and sheep (meat and live animals).

In addition, it will be more and more difficult for Mexican agricultural products to be exported to the United States as this country increases its controls for importation. Cases of alleged dumping by Mexican tomato exporters and a prohibition on Mexican cantaloupes entering the United States—supposedly due to sanitation problems (all not fully proven)—are but two examples of the still "invisible" barriers to a free flow of trade to the North in the NAFTA region.

The year 2004 brought a slight respite for the difficult situation confronting Mexico's agricultural sector. The scarcity of grains at the international level has impacted prices, and imports are not increasing as projected. Also, the cases of "mad cow disease" in Canada and Mexico have forced the Mexican government to close the border, temporarily promoting domestic production.

But the United States will make it increasingly more difficult for Mexican products to enter its market. Regulations in the area of food sanitation represent a 10% increase in production costs for vegetable exporters in Mexico, without any increase in price. There are also new provisions in the Biosecurity Act in the United States. In short, the reduction in tariffs obtained through NAFTA has been replaced by new non-tariff barriers.

After ten years of NAFTA, the agreement has not fulfilled the expectations created by the governments that signed it, and the dismal results predicted by diverse researchers and analysts have become reality.

Proposal for Consideration

Before advancing a proposal regarding NAFTA, it is important to ponder a key precedent in trade relations between Mexico and the United States: the role of the U.S. Congress in the area of transportation. Despite the fact that NAFTA established the unrestricted movement of vehicles between Mexican and U.S. territories beginning in 1995, the United States used a moratorium to prohibit Mexican vehicles from entering the United States. After many years of controversy, on February 6, 2001, the WTO issued a decision in favor of Mexico. On June 5, 2001, President George W. Bush finally gave authorization (on paper) for Mexican trucks to enter the United States and ordered the lifting of the 1995 moratorium. However, the U.S. Congress approved U.S. access for Mexican cargo trucks to begin in the year 2002, with the condition that sufficient inspectors could be contracted. On August 1, 2001, however, the U.S. Congress backtracked, calling for a blockade, using as justification, questions about the safety of Mexican trucks on U.S. highways.[23] Thus, the U.S. Congress has set an example that could be followed by their Mexican counterparts. Despite NAFTA's free–trade policies, the United States forcefully protects their transportation sector, their sources of employment, and their national interests.

Similarly, the importance of agriculture in Mexico as a source of employment, producer of food, and protector of the environment—with all the social and cultural implications—cannot be denied. Given that there are no compensation funds to lessen the effects of NAFTA, and that whatever budget is designated will never be enough to allow Mexico's agricultural sector to be competitive with the agricultural sector in the world's most powerful country; and in consideration of Article 21 of the WTO (on the consequences of a Treaty) and Article 89 of the Mexican Constitution, Section 10 (unequal legal status, see Appendix); and given the faculties granted by the nation to the legislative branch, the NAFTA agriculture chapter should be reviewed. Mexico should not give up its national sovereignty and should take advantage of all the provisions stipulated in its Constitution.

This proposal is not only justified by the unfavorable consequences that NAFTA has already brought to the Mexican rural sector but also by the potential harm that it could cause to the sector in the future.

A review and the partial suspension of NAFTA to alleviate the open-economy pressures on Mexico's most sensitive products will affect some individual interests, especially those of importers and intermediaries for agricultural products. This would aid in the installation of additional support programs that could help to balance the pressures from eager low-price importers. However, as we have demonstrated, the benefits for consumers as argued in official circles have not proven to be true. And, Mexican exporters will not feel any negative effects as long as they make use of the "latitudes for maneuvering" permitted to developing countries by the WTO.

It is also important to take into consideration the direct and indirect monetary costs for the entire Mexican society that have already been generated by trade liberalization—as well as those still to come. The liquidation of the National Bank for Rural Credit (Banrural) alone will cost the overall Mexican society 42 billion pesos (an amount that surpasses the agricultural budget for the entire year of 2002). Banrural's failure cannot be explained solely due to administrative errors, but rather due to the lack of profitability in agriculture as a result of the State policy of abandoning its responsibilities.

Finally, the Mexican Government implemented the policy of economic liberation and signed NAFTA. Notwithstanding any potential revision or renegotiation of the treaty that might occur in the future, the role of the Mexican Government should still be the adjustment and adapting of its policies to seek economic and social well-being of its whole population.

Endnotes

1. CIESTAAM (1992), 10.
2. Agriculture Committee of the House of Representatives (2000).
3. World Bank (April 23, 2002), 12–13. http://bancomundial.org.mx/ pdf/EAP_Documento_Principal.pdf.
4. The complete text of this document is available at http://www.sagarpa.gob.mx/cgcs/acuerdo.
5. ANC, p. 17. In-depth information regarding ANC can be found in Schwentesius, et al. (2003).
6. In early 2003, the Mexican government reduced, for example, the prices of electricity and diesel fuel used in agriculture, although numerous bureaucratic hurdles are involved.
7. The Mexican government established measures for safeguarding the nation's poultry industry, which is the most technologically advanced, and furthermore, the industry that is most integrated with the United States, due to the capital originating from that country.
8. USDA, Farm Bill 2002, Information Homepage, http://www.usda.gov/farmbill/index.html.
9. OECD, *Producer and Consumer Support Estimates,* OECD Database 1986–2003, http://www.oece.org/dataoecd/33/50/32361272.ZIP.
10. Authors' calculation based on information from OECD, 2002.
11. José Guzman "El TLCAN tomó por sorpresa a las aduanas," El Financiero, April 26, 2004.
12. Canada is not exporting corn to Mexico. See (February 7, 2004) http://www.economia.gob.mx/pics/p/p1294/MMAI_AE5.XLS.
13. Zahniser, St. and William Coyle, "U.S.-Mexico Corn Trade During the NAFTA Era: New Twists to an Old Story," in USDA/ERS: *Electronic Outlook Report from the Economic Research Service,* FDS-04D-01, May 2004, http://www.ers.usda.gov/publications/FDS/may04/fds04D01/fds- 04-D01.pdf.
14. It isn't possible to estimate real fiscal losses, because if Mexico would have collected the negotiated duties, the imports would have been lower.
15. Mexico. President's Office, 2002, *Segundo Informe de Gobierno,* September 1, Appendix, 237.
16. Authors' calculation based on information from FAO.
17. INEGI, *Banco de Información Económica* (BIE), Foreign Sector, Import of merchandise by product and economic activity of origin (April 12, 2003), http://www.inegi.gob.mx/difusion/espanol/fbie.
18. Authors' calculations based on INEGI, http://www.inegi.gob.mx.
19. Cortés Cáceres, et al. (2002), 19.
20. Mexico. President's Office. *3er Informe de Gobierno.* (3rd State of the Union Report) September 1, 2003. Appendix, 332.
21. Those benefiting are agro-industrialists producing beer and tequila; producers and packers of export vegetables and tropical fruits; importers of meat, grains, fruit, and agricultural inputs.
22. http://www.infoaserca.gob.mx.
23. Information from Efrén Marín López (2002), 90–102.

Bibliography

Agriculture Committee of the House of Representatives, 2000, *¿Cuánta Liberalización aguanta la Agricultura? Impacto del TLCAN en el sector agroalimentario.* Mexico City: House of Representatives, UACh, CIESTAAM, CECCAM, 2000, 348 pp.

Agro business, October 2002, No. 119.

CIESTAAM, 1992, *La agricultura mexicana frente al Tratado Trilateral de Libre Comercio,* Mexico City: Juan Pablos.

Cortés Cáceres, Fernando, et al., 2002, *Evolución y características de la pobreza en México en la última década del siglo XXI, SEDESOL,* August, p. 19.

Department of Labor and Social Security *(Secretaría del Trabajo y Previsión Social—* STPS) National Employment Survey. Employed population, by sex and by branch of economic activity. http://www.stps.gob.mx/01_oficina/05_cgpeet/302_0055a.htm, 9.11.2002.

El Financiero (newspaper), November 4, 2002, 26.

FAO, Statistical data base, http://apps.fao.org.

Guzman, Jose, "El TLCAN tomó por sorpresa a las aduanas," *El Financiero,* April 26, 2004.

INEGI, *Banco de Información Económica* (BIE), External Sector, Importing of commodities by product and by economic activity of origin, http://www.inegi.gob.mx/difu sion/espanol/fbie.html. 4.12.2002.

Mexican President's Office, 2002, *Segundo Informe de Gobierno,* September 1, Appendix.

Marín López, Efrén. 2002, "La solución política: ¿Opción a la insuficiencia de los capítulos 19 y 20 del TLCAN?" doctoral dissertation, UAM, Xochimilco, Mexico City, December.

OECD, 2002, *Agricultural Compendium,* Producer and Consumer Support Estimates 2002, data base, Beyond 20/20 Browser Files. Paris, France.

SECOFI, 1994. *Tratado de Libre Comercio de América del Norte. Fracciones arancelarias y plazos de desgravación,* México: Miguel Ángel Porrúa Publishers.

USDA, *Farm Bill 2002,* Information Homepage, http://www.usda.gov/farmbill/index.html.

USDA, Foreign Agricultural Trade of the United States, http://www.fas.usda.gov/ustrd scripts/USReport.exe.

Vollrath, Thomas L. and Paul V. Johnston. "The Changing Structure of Agricultural Trade in North America, Pre and Post CUSTA/NAFTA: What Does It Mean?" AAEA/CAEA poster paper, (annual meetings), Chicago, August 5-8, 2001 http://www.ers.usda.gov/briefing/nafta/PDFFiles/Vollrath-2001AAEAPoster.pdf.

World Bank. Memorandum from the President of the *Banco Internacional de Reconstrucción y Fomento and the Corporación Financiera Internacional* to the Executive Directorate, on "Estrategia de Asistencia para el País del Grupo del Banco Mundial para los Estados Unidos Mexicanos. Unidad para Colombia–México–Venezuela." Report No. 23849-ME, April 23, 2002, http://bancomundial.org.mx/pdf/EAP_Documento_Principal.pdf.

———. World Development Report 2000/2001. "Attacking Poverty". Washington, DC, 2001

———. World Development Indicators 2002. Washington, DC, 2002.

World Economic Forum. *The Global Competitiveness Report* 2001–2002, Table 1. Overall competitiveness ranking, http://www.weforum.org/pdf/gcr/Overall_Competitiveness_Rankings.pdf.

Chapter 2

Asymmetry of Resources, Access to Information, and Transparency as Structural Challenges Facing Rural Areas

Manuel Chávez

Globalization and regionalization in the last 20 years have imposed new mechanisms on many social and economic systems all over the world. To survive global economic restructuring, rural communities in developing countries face challenges that are new to them. Most of these challenges are structural, with external and domestic forces affecting the traditional systems of producing, transporting, and marketing products. Producers in rural areas confront these new demands with inefficient and insufficient resources. The remote location of these communities also poses additional challenges to their ability to receive timely information and access to governmental services. The changes in communication technology for disseminating information as well as the reduction or elimination of governmental extension services further compound these barriers. Having information about markets, incentives, subsidies, access to capital, regulations, and competition is imperative for producers and companies to adapt to—and survive—rapidly changing conditions.

The basic elements of production, such as capital, technology, upgraded inputs, and information about markets and regulations, are not available to these communities. Institutional systems to aid rural producers in organizing and competing in a new environment are critical, but often lacking. Now more than ever, the very survival of these small producers is connected to internal support systems.[1]

Mexico's process of economic reform in the 1980s caused major transformations to traditional social forms of operation and production. Few small producers have been able to adapt and survive; most suffered major impacts in their household incomes, resulting in massive internal and international migrations (Schwentesius and Gomez Cruz 2000). Family members were forced to enter the labor market at early ages in order to contribute to household finances. As a result, these contributions by school-age family members affected their future educational training and, ultimately, graduation. As young adults, members of

1 For the purpose of this chapter, small producers are agricultural producers who sell more than 40% of their annual production and who own no more than five hectares per producer. These represent more than half of the total agricultural producers in Mexico (CEPAL-SAGARPA 2004).

the family dropped out of school, limiting their chances for upward social and economic mobility.

In North America, regionalization has affected small producers in the United States and Canada, but the new forms of production and marketing have been more demanding on Mexican producers (Yunez-Naude 2002). Regional forces have layers of interaction which tend to benefit those who have the best access to processes of production and, ultimately to information. Government, corporations, producers, associations, and small producers have different capacities, resources, and access to official and "privileged" information that, in turn, affects participation and survival.

Communication scholars in rural studies argue that populations living in poor, under-serviced communities are the least likely beneficiaries of the resources, alternatives, and opportunities that derive from greater access to information. This communication analysis studied access and uses of information and its availability to disenfranchised rural communities throughout most of the 1980s and 1990s (Rogers 2003). This was true when the policies and regulations of NAFTA (North American Free Trade Agreement) were formulated in Mexico. Clearly, not everyone had the same access to the process and the information that would directly affect communities, families, and individuals. Before the approval of the agreement, different private and public actors had access, resources, and information about the planned restructuring policies.

A variety of actors—such as legislators, federal and state officials, agricultural lobbyists, and representatives of the working agrarian sector—participated in the NAFTA negotiation process with differing degrees of influence. Their participation represented the interests and objectives of their constituencies and stakeholders, thereby reflecting the politically strong State-led objectives and corporate interests very well, yet very few of these participants represented small communities (Arroyo 2000). While local agro-industries prepared themselves for the competition to come, agrarian leaders did not create mechanisms to prepare small producers for the changes. Moreover, the State did not provide two important elements present in other countries engaged in regionalization: the creation of safety nets to buffer the economic impacts of the reforms, and the creation of special extension outreach services to provide the necessary means to adapt and compete effectively.

The asymmetry of information created many small producers who were not prepared or knowledgeable of how to succeed in the new open-market competition. Adding to structural vulnerability, the lack of timely, accurate, and usable information negatively affected producers, their families and communities. Ultimately, they were unable to prepare, adapt, and protect themselves from the coming events resulting from NAFTA's implementation. As illustrated in this chapter, the Mexican state failed small producers, not only on specific structural negotiations and sectors and products to be protected or subsidized, but also in failing to disseminate the basic information that commonly empowers citizens. This chapter analyzes the major structural forces at play at the global and regional level, the regional trade conditions under NAFTA, the information and communication models; and the role of the State. This chapter uses official data for macro-level analysis, and data from focus groups and interviews conducted by the author for micro-level analysis.

The Forces of Globalization

While small producers are affected more negatively by the structural conditions of their location, the forces of globalization and regionalization affect everyone to a certain degree. Nations and their national companies, communities, and citizens, face a complex competition where information, knowledge, and rapid decisions are critical to survival. This section provides a historical overview of the development of globalization and how some countries have responded.

According to some scholars, the process of (and adjustments to) globalization started before World War II, when corporations from the United States were actively extracting natural resources from underdeveloped nations, particularly from Latin America and the Caribbean. Companies that most often benefited from this model of direct extraction have operated in agriculture, energy, and mining (Williamson 1997). In many cases, the operation of American corporations was linked to an intrusive foreign policy formulated in Washington. The benefit from decades of operation fell to corporations, the local elites that protected them in Latin America, and a managerial class that served as direct intermediaries. Little or no documentation of positive benefits exists for the local populations or workers who participated in these operations (Cardoso 1967; Quijano 1967).

After World War II, the direct extractive model added a manufacturing-assembling element in which a corporation would invest in manufacturing in a country where fundamentals were favorable. These included cheap labor, reduced tax burden, and little governmental intervention, which provided both a docile labor force and a package of fiscal incentives to reduce the burden on the corporation. The principal assumption for the hosting countries was that the creation of jobs would induce benefits for the entire country. The transnational corporations originally operating under this concept included automobile, textile, and appliance/electronics manufacturers. Later, the list of industries expanded to include the pharmaceutical and agro-industrial sectors (Chomsky 1999).

Globalization is a historical process that has existed for centuries. Examples from the past include the Phoenician trade in most of the Mediterranean; the Roman Empire's domination of most of Europe, North Africa, and most of the Middle East; and Spain's arrival in and domination of the New World. Subsequently, globalization increased by communication, innovation, and rapid technological progress, particularly in the second half of the twentieth century. Globalization refers to the increasing integration and interdependence of national economies around the world, particularly through trade and financial transactions. It also refers to the movement of labor and information-knowledge across national borders and to the mobility of portions of the manufacture of a product trademarked by a transnational corporation. These forces are not new, but recently the intensity and speed of these forces have grown remarkably more demanding (Gilpin 2000).

The ideological thrust behind globalization is the presumption that markets promote efficiency through competition and international division of labor—in other words, that specialization allows each nation and its people to concentrate on what they do best. Global markets allow for greater segments of customers around the world. This ideology also assumes that access to capital investments, technology, less costly imports, and larger export markets are available when a nation engages in the world market. However, the realities are not nearly this simple. National leaders have developed policies to enhance each their own competitive advantage, but that often required structural adjustments that caused negative internal impacts (Heredia 1997). A socially accountable government needs to consider economic strategies that include programs to prepare their citizenry to compete and benefit from globalization, while at the same time offering social initiatives to re-train, reeducate, and protect negatively-impacted populations.

International organizations such as the International Monetary Fund (IMF) and the World Bank (WB) have also stimulated the process by advising debtor nations to open their economies to foreign investment as a strategy for development. Likewise, these institutions have asked debtor countries to increase and accelerate their processes of privatization and deregulation, under the assumption that this will bring more rapid benefits. These measures first took place during the 1980s and accelerated particularly among countries with little political capital to negotiate. The recommendations to open economies, deregulate, and privatize were touted as formulations that, in time, would bring positive results—in other words, that the market would take care of structural dislocations. These policies were known in Latin America and the Caribbean as "neo-liberal" reforms or "the Washington Consensus." The so-called economic structural adjustment was the introduction of neo-liberal reform to developing countries (Buckley 2005). The reforms imposed on people of the Americas included: strong reductions in public expenditures (including social and health areas); increases in fiscal control; monetary liberalization of domestic currencies; reduction of subsidies for food; and wage controls.

As new rules emerged from the changing economic environment, governments responded differently. Some nations formed blocs to compete effectively under the new rules, others emphasized protectionist measures, and still others chose to open their economies more rapidly to foreign players. These, too, are examples of globalization that call for significant adaptations, structural changes and critical maneuvering from various actors such as governments, industries, producers, and ultimately, consumers (Stiglitz 2002).

Vulnerable areas were the domestic sector, highly mobile foreign investments, and the populations in rural areas that had little information about the impending changes. For the agricultural sector, the opening of national economies and rapid deregulation of official mechanisms facilitated the process of production expansion by a few, which is evident in almost all sectors of a domestic economy. Small- and medium-size producers were exposed to the full throttle of reform with few defenses to protect themselves. Indeed, no sector of the economy was shielded during the negotiation process (Gómez Cruz et al. 2003).

Regionalization and Global Institutions

After World War II, the need for general rules on products, tariffs, and trade norms led to the creation of the General Agreement on Tariffs and Trade (GATT). Regional trading blocs evolved as extensions of this—equalizing standards, norms, and the treatment of countries participating in world trade. A major assumption was that countries participating in global trade under a subscribed agreement increase their chances of growth. Excluded was the assumption that resources and the capacity to trade vary from country to country given the importance of historical processes, institutional development, and political maturity (Hockman and Kostecki 2001).

The case of Mexico entering the North American regional trading bloc illustrates this point. Mexico faced structural challenges to becoming an equal partner in NAFTA. Negotiations were difficult and the opportunities elusive (Chambers and Smith 2002); failure was particularly evident in the formulation of social policies to protect the populations most vulnerable to the affects of the changes. While the United States and Canada had safety nets to protect industries, sectors, and workers, Mexico lacked such provisions. The expectation of Mexican policy makers, was that the market would take care of the adjustments and that people would, by necessity, change rapidly and willingly. Ten years later, the disappointment of this expectation underlines the importance of social safety nets and the provision of basic information.

Current, major, regional trading blocs include the EU (European Union), NAFTA, ASEAN (Association of Southeast Asian Nations), and MERCOSUR (Common Market of South America). Figure 1 illustrates the interactions be-

Figure 1

Major Regional Trade Blocs

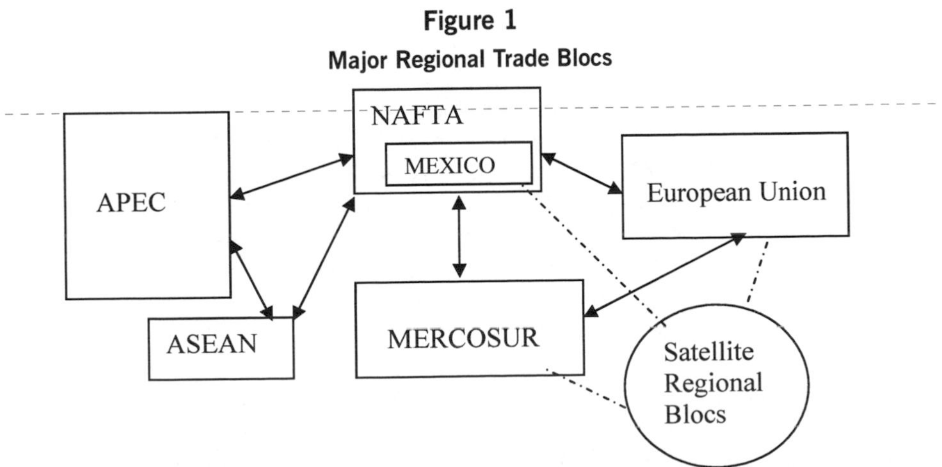

tween major blocs within the context of current east-west, north-south assumptions. Solid lines indicate that trade, economic exchanges, and investments are active between countries within the blocs, and dotted lines show less active interactions. The circle titled "Satellite Regional Blocs" includes either small or dormant blocs that have no significant volumes of trade. These include the Andean Pact, the Central American Common Market (CACM), the Caribbean Community and Common Market (CARICOM), the Common Market for Eastern and Southern Africa (COMESA), the Southern African Development Community (SADC), and the Economic Community of West African States (ECOWAS). The square labeled MEX and its connections with satellite blocs, the European Union, and MERCOSUR relates to Mexico's tendency to sign free-trade agreements with other nations and blocs on an individual basis rather than as a NAFTA bloc. Mexico's tendency is due in part to the difficult and complex political environment within the United States in regard to approving free-trade agreements with other nations and trading blocs.

The World Trade Organization (WTO), as a result of the 1994 GATT agreement, is a permanent institution overseeing trade agreements, enforcing trade rules, and settling trade disputes. Since the United States proposed the creation of the WTO during the GATT meetings, it was expected that they would lead the organization. The American Congress approved it in 1995, with an immediate affiliation of 110 nations. By 1997, there were 129 members and by 2006, WTO had 150 members that represented almost 97% of world trade. Recently, the WTO has been attacked politically for its tendency to favor certain nations, which is unacceptable under the spirit of the agreement. In addition, the organization has received criticism for its insistence on accelerating reforms and gaining open access to markets, particularly those of developing countries. These nations, seeking to conform to the WTO requirements, often implement reforms without the proper social and economic safety nets, provoking internal inequalities and regional imbalances (Hockman and Kostecki 2001).

The International Monetary Fund and the World Bank provide assistance to nations under two different sets of rules. The IMF offers loans to countries that face serious challenges in their internal fiscal conditions or in meeting their international obligations. Loans are negotiated and offered on condition of policy changes requiring strict controls on public expenditures. The World Bank, on the other hand, offers loans for long-term development projects—mainly to developing nations. The World Bank is known for imposing loan requirements that favor policies of market openness, privatization, and deregulation. In some cases, the loans are based on specific programs offered by the Bank with little space for a nation to maneuver out of them. In the last decade, both institutions have been openly criticized for being responsible for most of the economic decline of developing nations in the last twenty years (Wade 2001; Stiglitz 2003). By the early 2000s, both institutions shifted their loan policies to less demanding requirements and with a new approach to investing in social sectors.

Some economists have argued that regional trade blocs—which account for 60% of world trade—have opened markets, but they cannot substitute for worldwide reciprocity (Bergsten 1996; Hockman and Kostecki 2001; and Stiglitz 2002). The negotiation of low tariffs for greater market access should be reciprocal even when most trade is concentrated in the northern part of the world. In the end, industrialized rich nations benefit not only by being able to offer products to poor nations, but also by allowing the entry of products of those countries at a preferential rate, thus helping production that, in the end, should be seen as mutually beneficial.

The formation of blocs among unequal partners brings economic, social, and political asymmetries. It is inevitable that if one country is stronger within

Table 1
REGIONAL TRADE BLOCS
(2005 data)

Name	Initiation	Member Countries	Population in Millions	Economic Output (GDP) in $ Trillions
EU	1957	25	459	14,760
NAFTA	1994	3	425	17,120
APEC*	1989	21	2,185	7,478
MERCOSUR	1991 (a)	4	231	2,005
ASEAN	1967 (b)	10	567	1,072

* The APEC includes the United States, Mexico, Canada, Peru, and Chile, all of which are included in other regional blocs. (Population and economic outputs are adjusted.)
(a) The agreement was signed on 1991, but the formal initiation took place until 1995,
(b) The initial agreement started in 1967, but the consolidation of the trade block took place in 2002.

Sources: IMF, World Economic Outlook Database, 2006; WTO, Statistics Database 2007; EU Statistics 2007.

the bloc, that it would tend to dominate most of the negotiations and conditions. This dominance tends to be economic and, therefore, has significant consequences for the contents of bi-national or multilateral negotiations. The weaker partners try to persuade the stronger as to the benefits of complementation and supplementation—but, very often, unsuccessfully. As seen in Table 1, world regional blocs have significant variations in population and economic outputs. Clearly, in terms of economic output, NAFTA and the EU dominate world trade, with $17 and $14 trillion dollars of GDP respectively. (Note: All dollar figures in this chapter are given in U.S. dollars.)

By the beginning of 2000, the Latin American and Caribbean region had five regional blocs with different degrees of trade and economic interaction.

These are: NAFTA, MERCOSUR, CACM, CARICOM and the Andean Pact. Of these, NAFTA and MERCOSUR are the most active and significant in terms of volume, and (as seen in Table 1) the former has an aggregated output of more than $17,120 trillion, while the latter has close to $2,005 trillion. Other sub-blocs, such as the Caribbean and Central American blocs, have fallen short due to their low industrial output. However, trade in the Latin American region among countries and sub-blocs almost tripled from $23 billion in 1990 to $58.5 billion in 2002 (ECLAC 2005). This shows a tendency toward high volumes of trade within the region, which has been able to maintain relatively small but positive increasing levels.

In 2005, the Free Trade Area of the Americas (FTAA) was expected to be formalized as an alliance of American nations united on trade, as well as political, environmental, and social issues. The trade proposal was previously endorsed and supported by every nation in the Americas (with the exception of Cuba, which did not participate in the Summit of the Americas in Miami in 1994). Yet, the readiness of most countries is still unclear. Commissions organized by the Organization of American States have held meetings to set the requirements that countries need to comply with in order to achieve affiliation with the continental bloc (OAS 1998). Implementation requirements, deadlines, and specific contents of the prerequisites are still being negotiated. As seen in Table 2, countries in the Americas have different degrees of participation that relate to their corresponding per-capita incomes and their GDPs.

The FTAA is expected to help countries in the Western Hemisphere compete globally and to improve their structural conditions (see Table 2). The agreement not only relates to trade and economic fundamentals, but also to public policies related to democracy, human rights, judicial reform, environmental regulation, and social investments. Institutional capacity of every nation is being required to be up to the standards of others. Yet, trade-divergent perspectives

Table 2
Latin American and Caribbean Region
Socio-economic Characteristics by Sub-regional Groups—2004

Level as location in PCI/GDP	*Region in LA and the Caribbean*	*Bloc in LA and the Caribbean*	*Member Countries*	*PCI/GDP in U.S. dollars*	*FTAA participation*
Upper Income	North and South	NAFTA MERCOSUR	Brazil, Argentina, Chile, Uruguay, and Mexico	$ 7,100 – 13,000	Very active
Middle Income	South Central and Caribbean	Andean Pact CACM CARICOM	Venezuela, Colombia, Perú, Ecuador, Costa Rica, Panamá, D.R., Paraguay	$3,100-7,000	Active
Low Income	Central and Caribbean	Andean Pact CACM CARICOM	Guatemala, Belize, Haití, Nicaragua, El Salvador, Bolivia	$ 800-3,000	Low-moderate

Source: Table prepared with data from ECLAC-UN, Overview of the Economies of Latin American and the Caribbean, 2005.

and the lack of support from the U.S. Congress have derailed the possibility of having the completed agreement any time soon.

MERCOSUR (*Mercado Común del Sur*) is the regional bloc of South America. The original objective was to create a customs union and a free trade area between Brazil, Paraguay, Uruguay, and Argentina. After additional negotiations, MERCOSUR accepted Chile as an associate member. The group formalized negotiations in 1991 and the agreement was implemented despite the several macroeconomic problems of its members. The main purpose of the group is to create a free-trade area that could expand throughout the entire South American continent. Membership does not stipulate any other regulatory frameworks, or clauses of political cooperation (MERCOSUR 1994). The strongest member of this bloc is Brazil, which from 1999 to 2003 faced economic problems that provoked a more than 25% devaluation of the *real*, which resulted in negative impacts on its trading partners. Argentina and Uruguay had faced serious reductions in their exports to Brazil, directly impacting their export-import balances. Despite this apparently short adjustment, Brazil has recovered internally and was still favored by investors as evidenced by direct investments, which in 2004 were almost $17 billion (World Bank, 2005).

NAFTA and Agricultural Trade

NAFTA is the regional bloc of North America—Canada, the United States, and Mexico—that officially started on January 1,1994. Negotiations began in 1991, and although Canada and the United States signed an agreement of free trade in 1988, Mexico and the United States began formal talks to expand their bilateral trade to a trade area of North America as early as 1989. The original proposal considered the reduction of tariffs and elimination of barriers, but a wide political movement of labor and environmental groups forced the parties to include comprehensive parallel agreements in those areas. Although technically the agreement is not a treaty, the tri-national obligations and commitments have been implemented by the enactment of domestic laws. The agreement was a product of a highly contested political process played out from 1988 to 1992, and then approved by their respective legislative bodies in 1993 (Chavez and Whiteford 1996). Although the agreement did not include wide cooperation, additional accords signed years later have added cultural and educational cooperation/coordination components. Recently, in March of 2005, the three members of NAFTA signed the Security and Prosperity Partnership of North America (SPP) to widen their collaboration in areas of security, trade, manufacturing, energy, and health (Chavez 2006). The stronger member of this bloc is the United States, which, as evidenced in Table 3, shows a larger share of the regional GDP—almost 88% of the total. More than half of the population lives in the United States, and its per-capita income is the highest in the region.

Trade, as predicted in the agreement, has increased significantly in North America. Mexico has become the largest supplier in North America of appliances, electronics, computer and auto parts, and a variety of agricultural products. Energy resources, especially oil and gas exports, have placed Mexico as a major supplier of these resources to the U.S. market, closely behind Canada. Services, from financial data-entry to hospital equipment repair and servicing, have increased as well in the entire region. It is still unclear how much of this growth is sustainable and whether the economic growth generated in northern Mexico is transferable or replicable in other parts of the country.

Taken together, trade has increased significantly since 1994. As seen in Table 4, the total trade in North America increased by almost 120% in the last ten years. The increase is notable even in the trade relationship that was already well established—as between Canada and the United States, which increased by 100% from 1995 to 2005. In the case of Mexico-U.S. trade, the increase was more than 125%. This interaction is growing as the sectors of energy—including oil, gas, and electricity—grow faster than other sectors. As of today, NAFTA trade generates more than $2 billion dollars of trade daily, and with the elimination of the remaining tariffs in agricultural products and the facilitations of rules of origin, trade is expected to grow even more.

Total trade between Mexico and the United States has increased almost four times in the last five years, as noted in Table 5. In fact, Mexico's trade with the United States places it as the second-largest trading partner following Canada. However, in a closer study of sector indicators, not all have registered positive results. At first, exports to Mexico grew as much as its exports to the United States, but in the last five years the latter grew at a slower rate. Competition from other labor-intensive industries in Central America and the Caribbean has created flat employment growth in this unskilled sector.

Table 3
North America and European Union
Selected Indicators 2005

COUNTRY OR REGION	POPULATION thousands	GDP $ Trillions	LABOR FORCE thousands	GDP per capita $	MANUFACTURING WAGE $/hour average
CANADA	32,369	1,850	17,431	35,200	16.55
MEXICO	105,100	1,320	39,107	10,250	6.17
UNITED STATES	288,200	13,950	151,673	43,500	18.24
NORTH AMERICA	425,669	17,120	208,211	SKW	SKW
EUROPEAN UNION	459,100	13,010	222,700	29,900	19.8

Sources: Statistics Canada 2006; Mexico, INEGI, STPS, 2006; U.S. Census Bureau, 2006; and EU Economic and Social Statistics selected reports, 2006.

In terms of agricultural trade, the scenario for Mexico is not as favorable as in the industrial sector there. Mexico is now importing more from the United States, and traditional agro-industries in Mexico have been forced to close their operations. As seen in Table 6, regardless of the increase in trade in the sector (this increase is in raw value of trade, as manufacturing as a percent of GDP has only increased slightly since NAFTA came into effect, and the share of total

Table 4

Total Trade—North America, 1993–2005

(In Millions of Dollars)

	1993	*1995*	*1993–1995 %change*	*2000*	*1995–2000 %change*	*2005*	*2000–2005 %change*
U.S.-MEX	88,145	120,102	36.3	255,260	112.5	292,810	14.7
CAN-MEX	2,744	3,362	22.5	14,120	320.0	18,203	28.9
U.S.-CAN	210,660	217,084	3.0	405,603	86.8	499,200	23.1
TOTAL	301,549	340,548	12.9	674,983	98.2	810,213	20.0

Sources: U.S. Dept. of Commerce, International Trade Administration, National Trade Data, 2006.

employment in manufacturing has decreased slightly), the tendency shows that more is being imported. Product specialization and productivity rates are factors playing on both sides of the border. However, this makes the commodities requiring less capital investment more vulnerable. Competition for market share and the horizontal and vertical consolidation of groups in the agricultural sector have contributed to the loss of markets for Mexican agricultural producers. In conclusion, the Mexican agricultural sector, particularly when it relates to the segment represented by its small and medium agricultural producers, is one of the losers under NAFTA (see the chapters written for this volume by Gomez Cruz and Schwentesius). Even when the total agricultural trade is $17 billion dollars, it only represents a mere 6% of the total value of trade between Mexico and the United States.

Table 5

Total Trade—United States and Mexico, 1993–2005

(In Millions of Dollars)

	1993	**1995**	***1993-1995 %change***	***2000***	***1995-2000 %change***	***2005***	***2000-2005 %change***
Exports to Mexico	45,295	53,828	18.8	109,610	103.6	121,710	11.04
Imports from Mexico	42,850	66,273	54.7	145,640	119.8	171,125	17.50
TOTAL TRADE	88,145	120,10 1	36.3	255,250	112.5	292,835	14.72

Sources: U.S. Dept. of Agriculture, Economic Research Services, 2006 and U.S. Dept. of Commerce, International Trade Administration, National Trade Data, 2006.

Strategic policy questions remain as Mexico, Canada, and the United States position themselves for economic growth in North America. Leading up to 2000, under the assumption of all things being equal among the partners, the market was supposed to act as the arbitrator for production and pricing. However, Canada and the United States had mechanisms that served as social-welfare safety nets for those workers or companies that had been negatively affected by NAFTA, as either direct aid or subsidies. In the United States, the year following the signing of the agreement, the Clinton administration passed the NAFTA-Transitional Adjustment Assistance Program to aid workers who were affected directly by the agreement. The remedies included job training, career counseling, and various financial allowances to the workers and their families. Canada did not have an assistance program, but had federal mechanisms to aid those who lost their income. The Mexican policy completely lacked such remedies.

Agro-industries, particularly from the United States, were very active in the Mexican market before NAFTA passed. In 1993, the total amount of foreign direct investment was four billion dollars—invested primarily in the manufacturing sector. Nevertheless, in 1994 and 1995, the first two years of NAFTA, the levels invested increased by 50% to six and seven billion dollars, respectively. The difference in amounts of investment is related to the sectors that receive the infusion of investment; in this case, it was the agricultural sector. Agro-industries moved rapidly to invest in Mexico and to advance their control in the local market. Others saw the opportunities for investment in the production of items that would be shipped to the United States. Those industries that invested in this period focused on frozen vegetables, poultry, baby food, milk products, and fruits. Grains producers and food conglomerates such as ADM (Archer Daniels Midland Company) and Monsanto positioned themselves strategically to buy out local producers and dominate the market.

Table 6
Agricultural Trade – United States and Mexico, 1990-2005
(In Millions of Dollars)

	1990	1995	1990-1995 % change	2000	1995-2000 % change	2005	2000-2005 % change
Exports to Mexico	2,830	3,540	25.1%	6,410	81.1%	9,362	46.1%
Imports from Mexico	2,828	3,835	35.6%	5,077	32.4%	8,340	64.3%
TOTAL	5,658	7,375	30.3%	11,487	55.8%	17,702	54.1%

Source: U.S. Department of Agriculture, Economic Research Services, 2006

Like the producing companies, food retailers saw an opportunity to dominate the local distribution market. Companies such as Costco, Wal-Mart, Carrefur, and H-E-B moved rapidly with plenty of capital to acquire local supermarkets and retailers. By 2001, transnational retailers controlled three-quarters of food retailing in Mexico. While many retailers were transnational in their capital composition, the dominant companies were American firms such as Wal-Mart, which bought CIFRA (one of the top companies in Mexico during the 1970s and 1980s). Alliances were also common and PriceMart, Vons, and other U.S. companies forged joint ventures (Chávez 2002) by approaching companies like Comercial Mexicana and Gigante. Therefore, in the end, the challenges faced by the Mexican agricultural sector were more than production; they actually went to marketing, distribution, and finally, all the retailing process.

Unprepared Markets Facing Regionalization

Globalization has brought both opportunities and challenges to nations all over the world, but regional blocs feel its forces more rapidly. In the face of globalization, some governments have responded by plunging into the process, while others have sought to build upon existing relationships of economic interdependence. Induced by the forces of the international and financial sectors of highly developed countries, and coupled with the rapid development of new information technologies, the pace of economic restructuring and its consequences accelerated greatly in the last twenty years. The social and economic consequences of globalization processes have been diverse and often contradictory. The loss of jobs, markets, and the plundering of national resources have forced governments to develop new policies to regulate some aspects of globalization.

The experience of structural adjustment and neo-liberalism in Latin America over the last 20 years has been bitter, particularly for workers and the agrarian poor. The impacts have varied depending on the country and the nature of its economy. Countries which opened their economies and enacted privatization left their long-protected sectors—such as agriculture and mid- to small-size — to foreign competition. The competition between countries to attract direct foreign investment has been intense. Latin American nations have competed with each other and with Asian nations by exploiting their proximity to the U.S. market, the quality and productivity of their labor force, and the limited power of their unions. At the same time, Latin American countries have also opened up their previously protected sectors. Major foreign companies with capital and technology have entered these countries by purchasing smaller and previously protected enterprises. In all of these cases, the policies were intended to stimulate economic growth, but in fact, these policies were responding to global forces, as well.

In contrast, some Caribbean countries, which are dependent upon tourism, have felt much less impact than the large countries of Latin America where inflation has been controlled at a high social and economic cost. In the Caribbean, economic strategy has emphasized investment tax havens and tourism, which has maintained an economic growth also linked to globalization. Their competition has been regional, from countries in the same area, and their competitive advantage has been based on their fiscal incentives to protect investments and in their intrinsic natural resources offered as attraction to international travelers (Brohman 1996).

In regional blocs, issues of proximity and interdependence have special importance for communities living close to each other. National economies were integrated and synchronized into trade blocs intended to build on economic interdependence already informally in place. NAFTA, for example, evolved in this manner when the tri-national agreements expanded to link a range of activities including cooperation concerning labor, education, and the environment. While the economic gains, unfortunately, have been uneven and unequal, for both regions and sectors, the evolution of *transnationalism* from this context has generated changes on top of the forces of globalization and regionalization (Portes et al. 1999).

Economic interdependence and spatial proximity in the context of globalization generate another set of processes and linkages known as *transnationalism*. As globalization increased and penetrated societies, transnationalism subtly permeated the members of those societies through culture, ideology, and customs. Most of the countries in Latin America and the Caribbean have experienced the influence of global consumption induced by developed countries. Mexico, in particular, has experienced a rapid transformation in consumption and production that has impacted all regions by imposing tastes and preferences characteristic of the United States. Yet, the increasing presence of communication technology and modernization of infrastructure has induced some changes in information access, accountability, and empowerment. Unintentionally, access to information has provoked changes in the social and political participation of citizens in their respective communities and, therefore, more widely in their countries.

Massive Mexican migration to the United States, some of which has been generated by the economic changes resulting from globalization and NAFTA, has created new non-territorial communities which transcend national boundaries economically, socially, and politically. Linked through the Internet and community radio, people are renegotiating their identities, sense of community, economic activities, and power relationships, and are challenging traditional ways of defining national boundaries (Fox 2005). These new relationships, while not restricted to the NAFTA countries, constitute an important new socio-economic underpinning to the regional political alliance. Since these communities will become more politically active, mobilization may include the seeds of resistance and coordinated opposition to new economic changes. One example is the bi-national support to the Mexican agricultural movement *El Campo no Aguanta Mas* (*THE COUNTRYSIDE CANNOT TAKE IT ANY MORE*) that created, in 2002, a massive political problem for the Fox administration.

The Role of the State, Access to Information, and Transparency

At the core of rural problems in Mexico is the State. One of the major contradictions of governance in Latin America, especially in Mexico, is the negative relationship between democratically elected government and the mandate to serve the people who elected that government. Accountability, transparency, and access to information are traits that governments must guarantee and which, in Mexico, are absent. The democratic value of the public good must be a constant in governance, regardless of the political ideology of the government. It is essential to maintain stability, development, and the infusion of democratic values in all members of the society.

Governments may generate policies that do not always reflect the vast and varied interests of members of the electorate. Good governance and policy formulation are key elements of the responsiveness and accountability of governments in democratic societies. When these elements are lacking, the electorate may choose to remove the government in a subsequent election (Ferejohn 1999).

In Mexico this notion has been unattainable, first because of an unresponsive government, and then because of a disconnected political system. Until the year 2000, the political party in control, the PRI, was a dominant force for so long that it was not surprising that the politics of the country did not reflect the interests of the electorate. This is particularly true in rural Mexico, where the dominance of the PRI was strong, whether through co-optive tactics or by means of fossilized organizations, such as the CNC (*Confederación Nacional Campesina*). In 2002, after a switch to another political party—the PAN or the National Action Party—public officials responsible for the agricultural policy were as arrogant and unresponsive as their counterparts in the previous PRI administrations. A case in point is the lack of recognition by the Secretary of Agriculture (SAGARPA) officials of the need for an agricultural extension service that helps rural producers become competitive. Their insistence on creating *empresarios del campo* (peasant entrepreneurs) is a demonstration of the oversimplification of the complexities of rural Mexico. The assumption that any rural producer can become an entrepreneur with key products is flawed because of the lack of basic infrastructure and information about markets, prices, and government support. The notion that small entrepreneurs can function by market forces is unrealistic. Producers need information, knowledge, skills, and orientation about what to produce, how to produce better, and how to distribute more efficiently. This is a governmental function of disseminating information, and providing transparency. Citizens need to know about policies, their impacts, and the alternatives in order to successfully face those policies. Even the creation of a best-practices model is unrealistic in a country where the small producers in their *ejidos* and communities have little or no access to information. Having a best-practices model may be a realistic option in a country where producers, communities, and their families are informed about them.

The lack of accountability, transparency, and access characterizes many governments in Latin America and the Caribbean. This is particularly true during the 1980s and half of the 1990s in which Mexico's incorporation into GATT, and later into NAFTA, had significant repercussions for the rural population. An example of the failure of accountability occurred during the process of trade negotiations where little, if any, information was shared with small producers.

Press accounts published in Mexico indicated that leaders of the agrarian sector were informed of the coming reforms and did little or nothing to modify it (Ortega 1993). The peasant leadership caused additional problems as a result of its symbiotic relationship with the federal government and ultimately with the

PRI, as the information did not trickle down to the constituency. When the three governments approved NAFTA, it was too late for the producers to be prepared.

Another failure involved transparency. In different states of Mexico, the process of assisting small producers with loans has been handled politically, through the traditional channels of political co-option. Further, at the time when agro-industries were calculating and planning strategies to penetrate all areas of production and marketing, small producers were kept in the dark. Small producers had no access to knowledge and information concerning the process, the type of problems which were expected to be generated, the formulas in place to face the challenges, and the expectations for them. Transparency was not a factor in the formulation of economic reforms, and more importantly, it was not a factor during the process of implementation.

It is clear that by the beginning of the 1990s, it was too late to stop the NAFTA negotiations, but it was not too late to protect the producers. If only the producers had been informed about the possible effects that they would be exposed to, they could have had the opportunity to prepare and adjust. This failure to protect was a reflection of the political incapacity of the PRI (Salinas) administration to be accountable and responsive to the entire citizenry (Alcocer 1993). Transparency cannot be achieved in any country where the political system practices secrecy, exclusion and privilege. In Mexico, traditionally, transparency meant losing control, and the government was not interested in openness and accountability.

Access to information is one of the most basic components of democratic countries, even in those with a bias for the market. The assumption is that people and citizens in general have a right to know the businesses of the government and how its actions can harm an individual, community, region, or particular group. Access to information is not new; laws that allow citizens to access government information were passed in the Netherlands in the eighteenth century. In the United States, laws were passed thirty years ago—the Freedom of Information Act approved in 1976—to expand the rights of American citizens, the media, and any organization to closely examine the functioning of the government.

In Mexico, the Law of Access to Information and Transparency was passed in 2002 and implemented at the beginning of 2003. The passage of the law by the Mexican Congress took place ten years after NAFTA was approved and signed. Mexico is now wrestling with the implementation of the law, and while it may be helpful in the future, it was not there 15 years ago to help the producers, or any citizen, to learn more about an agreement that their government was negotiating. The proper provision of information was critical as the impacts derived from the agreement had an immediate effect as well as long-term consequences for many in the agricultural sector.

The disadvantage experienced by rural communities and small producers was structural—given the level of knowledge and the conditions of governance and public administration in Mexico. First, information was not available, regardless of how and by whom requested; and second, the flow of information passed through different and selective stages, making the information obsolete.

Clearly, those communities, associations, and small producers who had little access to timely, adequate, and accurate information were not and will not be able to compete in the open market. In a society where access to information is asymmetrical, it is unrealistic to expect that all members of that society will be able to benefit from said information (Schmid 2004).

In the case of groups and communities with significant access to information, they are able to place their products at the best price and to use new forms of conservation and preservation for their products—in other words, they have greater possibilities to survive. Information allows for the modification of traditional strategies used to participate in the market. Such was the case for producers of kiwi fruit in the Mexican state of Colima who were able to place their products in the American market by 1999. With state aid, the producers were able to modify their production to U.S. requirements and to design an efficient logistical model to place their products across the border (Chávez 2001). Unfortunately, in most cases the opposite was true, not many producers knew about market opportunities for their products

One producer of mangos in Nayarit noted, "No one told us that the new regulations would cause major damage to our company. Otherwise me and my family would have been better prepared" (Chávez 2001). In many cases, the regulations imposed on their products would not allow them to compete on fair terms. If they had been informed, small producers could have prepared or at least not have been surprised by the changes. Prices, subsidies, and costs of production were factors that modified the opportunities for producers; by not having access to that information, the vast majority of small producers were affected negatively.

When the agro-industries participated in the lobbying for policies, they had information about how the markets and the producers would be related. They knew what logistics, incentives, subsidies, and access to capital would be. They were able to anticipate impacts from policies more rapidly. However, the process was not equal, and not all companies had access to accurate information. Therefore, small producers were at a distinct disadvantage. They did not have access to the policy-formulation process and the resources to inform were scarce, inefficient, or controlled by some members of their political organizations. This is a process known as asymmetry of information by which, in most economic conditions, one party will have insufficient or deficient information (Schmid 2004).
In sum, the Mexican state failed to compensate for the weakness of the market and the asymmetry of information. The agricultural sector, in this "open" market, does not work on the basis of fairness since information was not equally available to all. In fact, the inequality of the process created serious challenges to rural areas in Mexico. Actors did not have the same access to information, and therefore their reactions reflected the poor timing, quality, and amount of information they had available.

Small Producers in Rural Areas as a Vulnerable Social Group

In addition to the disadvantage of not being included in the policy process, other barriers confront these small producers in rural communities. The challenges that communities face in the information age are formidable. If structural limitations play a role, knowing about subtle elements—such as timing and amount of information—are as critical as having the resources to face reforms. If this is true in rural communities in such developed countries as the United States, the challenges for rural populations in developing societies are more demanding (Allen and Dillman 1994). Additionally, the lack of consistency in fulfilling promises and the lack of government anticipation of and responsiveness to challenges facing the small producers hinder adjustment to economic changes and their possible effects.

The second part of the problem of accountability is related to the lack of alternatives to protect people from the unintended consequences of policies. In the case of Mexico, it was clear that the neo-liberal reform and its efforts to activate the Mexican economy would cause negative externalities. Such is the paradox of subsidies and free trade. The negotiators were offering the opening of the economy and the reduction of subsidies in exchange for a percentage reduction of tariffs that in turn would cause more damages than benefits. Other questions affecting rural areas that remained unanswered were these: For whom were the official negotiators working? Were the official negotiators representing the national interests and therefore an electorate that in theory elected them democratically? Or were they representing the interests of a reduced number of elites who would profit from trade and not from production?

To mitigate social, economic, and potentially political crises among the rural and small-producer communities, the state had an obligation to prepare its citizens for what would come. In areas where producers lost costumers, market share, and income, their claim could not have been more basic: "We heard from other producers that NAFTA would kill us, but nobody told us what to do it about it. In fact, I resent that no one from the government came to tell us what other alternatives we had. I would have changed my products, used different seeds, or even got together with others, but nobody here knew about that" (Chávez 2001).

The lack of responsive policies from the government was evident in the comments of small producers: "The government in the state of Nayarit offered nothing. When NAFTA was passed, no agency came to advise us about what to do." State and federal governments failed to be accountable on this front. "In one of the meetings of the producers association, we asked if the government was preparing ways to help us; no one knew. Our own leader did not know much and promised to talk to the office in Tepic, but nothing happened. One thing was clear, *los federales* didn't show up to help us" (Chávez 2001).

Without the government's visible assistance, the presence of the transnational companies offered little comfort. Producers' intrinsic distrust of the transnational corporations yielded denial that did not facilitate the adjustments: "The executives of Gerber mentioned that changes would be coming soon. But, you know, they are working for a company that profits from us; we knew that. We thought that they simply were trying to scare us" (Chávez 2001).

Even if companies intended to mitigate the effects, their policies of implementation did not generate a group of producers supporting or cheering for the American corporations. In sum, small producers and their communities felt abandoned by both the government agencies and the companies; for them, the State and the market failed.

Public Policy with Positive Impacts for Rural Areas

Under globalization, the transnational corporations, nongovernmental organizations, and multilateral trade organizations have joined the cast of economic actors affecting policies within states. Economic globalization has intensified at the beginning of the new millennium. As the chapters in this volume suggest, globalization within NAFTA, and in Mexico in particular, has favored urban growth over rural growth, the northern states over the southern states, and the sectors of the population that have economic resources, education, and access to new technologies over those that do not. In order to mitigate the social and economic crisis among poor and rural populations, the policy formulation process needs to be comprehensive. It needs to include representatives from all stakeholders in order to identify issues, and to address concerns and dislocations. In the case of the small agricultural producers in Mexico during the NAFTA implementation, providing information and resources in a timely fashion may have eased the transition. Additionally, education and retraining opportunities, as well as financial assistance, would have helped those who chose to leave the agricultural market because they could not compete. Implementing these changes could have potentially affected migration rates—as well as the educational attainment and future earning power of young people.

As the trend of globalization continues and evolves, especially with the possible FTAA (Free Trade Area of the Americas), the Mexican government will need to modify its policy process if it seeks to learn lessons from the NAFTA experience and better prepare all stakeholders affected. Recommendations for possible implementation include, but are not limited to: a) macroeconomic stability to create the adequate conditions for investment and savings; b) outward oriented policies to promote efficiency through increased trade and direct foreign investment; c) social policy programs to provide safety nets for dislocated workers, companies, states, or municipalities affected by globalization; d) a permanent program to offer accountability, transparency, and access to information; e) programs to ensure strong institutions, effective governments, fiscal responsibility, and transparency in public affairs; f) education, training, and research and development to promote productivity; and g) promotion and provision of incentives for models that foster sustainable development.

The critical areas for policy-makers in dealing with globalization are multiple and challenging. In particular, Mexico needs better policies not only on a national scale, but also on state and local levels, as well. To reduce inequalities, the consolidation of regions under national, state, and local developments needs to be considered.

Globalization and its consequences in Latin America, especially in Mexico, are not taken passively, but have generated social movements, cultural resistance, and new forms for mobilizing identity and resources. An inclusive, accountable, and transparent policy-development process will better ensure comprehensive policies to meet the interests of the nation.

Bibliography

Alcocer, Jorge. "El Mito del Mercado y el TLC," *Proceso*. Mexico, D.F. Feb 20, 1993.

Allen, John C., and Don A. Dillman. *Against All Odds: Rural Community in the Information Age*. Boulder, CO: Westview, 1994.

Arroyo Picard, Alberto. *El TLCAN: Objetivos y Resultados, 7 Años Después*. Universidad Autónoma Metropolitana, Centro de Estudios para el Cambio en el Campo Mexicano. Mexico, D.F.: Versión impresa, 2000.

Audly, John J., Demetrious Papademetriou, Sandra Polaski, and Scout Vaughn. *NAFTA's Promise and Reality: Lessons from Mexico for the Hemisphere*. Carnegie Endowment for International Peace. Carnegie Endowment Report, Washington, DC, 2003.

Baños Ramirez, Othon. *Neoliberalismo, Reorganización y Subsistencia Rural: El caso de la zona henequenera de Yucatán, 1980-1992*. Mérida: Universidad Autónoma de Yucatán, 1996.

Belous, Richard S., and Kelly L. McClenahan. *Global Corporations and Nation-States*. Washington, DC: National Planning Association, 1991.

Bergsten, Fred. "Globalizing Free Trade," *Foreign Affairs* 75, no. 3 (May–June 1996).

Bergstrand, Jeffrey. "Going Global: 25 Keys to International Operations," *The New York Times*, Pocket MBA Series, 2000.

Brohman J. "New directions in tourism for third world development," *Annals of Tourism Research* 23, no. 1 (London: Elsevier Science, 1996), 48–70.

Buckley, Richard. *Winds of Change in Latin America: Populism versus US Imperialism*. Cheltenham, England: Chapman Partnership, 2005.

Calva, José Luis. *El Neoliberalismo Mexicano*. México, D.F.: Editorial Trillas, 2000.

Cardoso, Fernando H. "The Industrial Elite." In *Elites in Latin America*. Edited by Seymour Martin Lipset and Aldo Solari. Oxford: Oxford University Press, 1967.

Casas, Rosalba, ed. *La Formacion de Redes de Conocimiento: Una Perspectiva Regional desde México*. UNAM, Insituto de Investigaciones Sociales. Barcelona, España (and Mexico, D.F.): Anthopos Editorial, 2001.

———. "La Transferencia de Conocimientos en Biotecnología: Formación de Redes a Nivel Local." En *La Formacion de Redes de Conocimiento*, edited by Rosalba Casas.

CEPAL-SAGARPA. "Tipologia de Productores Agricolas de los Ejidos y Comunidades en Mexico." Comisión Economica para América Latina y el Caribe. United Nations. Santiago, Chile and Secretaría de Agricultura, Ganadería, Desarrollo Rural, Pesca y Alimentación, Mexico, D.F., 2004.

CEPAL. "Social Panorama of Latin America." Comisión Economica para Latin America y el Caribe. United Nations. Santiago, Chile: 1996.

Chambers, Edward, and Peter Smith. "NAFTA in the New Millennium: Questions and Contexts." In *NAFTA in the New Millennium* edited by Edward Chambers and Peter Smith. University of Alberta Press and Center for U.S._Mexican Studies, University of California-San Diego. San Diego: 2002.

Chávez, Manuel, and Scott Whiteford. "Beyond the Market: The Political and Socio-economic Dimensions of NAFTA." In *Policy Choices, NAFTA, Free Trade Among Nations*, edited by Karen Roberts and Mark Wilson. East Lansing: Michigan State University Press, 1996.

Chávez, Manuel. Author interviews with members of a fruit producers group in the Pacific Coast of Mexico, the Garcia Family Group in La Peñita, Nayarit, 2001.

———. "NAFTA and the Transformation of Commercial Networks in Mexico: The Policy Perspective." *Development Policy Review* 20, no. 4 (September 2002).

Chomsky, Noam. *Latin America: From Colonization to Globalization*. Melbourne: Ocean Press, 1999.

Dervin, Brenda. "Information and Democracy: An Examination of Underlying Assumptions," *Journal of the American Society for Information Science* 45, no.6 (July 1994): 369–85.

ECLAC (Economic Commission for Latin America and the Caribbean). Economic Survey of Latin America and the Caribbean, 2004–2005. United Nations. Santiago, Chile: August 2005.

Featherstone, M., and S. Lash. "Globalization, Modernity and the Spatialization of Social Theory: An Introduction." In *Global Modernities,* edited by Mike Featherstone, Scott Lash, and Roland Robertson. London: Sage Publications, 1995.

———, et al., eds. *Global Modernities*. London: Sage Publications Ltd., 1995.

Ferejohn, John. "Accountability and Authority: Toward a Theory of Political Accountability." In *Democracy, Accountability, and Representation,* edited by Adam Przeworski, Susan Stokes, and Bernard Manin. Cambridge: Cambridge University Press, 1999.

Fox, Jonathan. "Mexican Rural Communities in the Transformation of Transnational Networks." Keynote Presentation to the Annual Meeting of the Mexican Association of Rural Studies, Oaxaca, Mexico, 2005.

Frankel, Jeffrey A. *Regional Trading Blocs in the World Economic System*. Washington, DC: Institute for International Economics, 1997.

Germain, G. C., and D. Bray. "*Global Change and Embeddedness: A Critical Analysis of Shifting Points of Reference*," University of Alberta, Department of Sociology, 1994.

Gilpin, Robert. *The Challenge of Global Capitalism: The World Economy in the 21st Century*. Princeton, NJ: Princeton University Press, 2000.

Gómez Cruz, Manuel, Rita Schwentesius, Fernando Cervantes, Scott Whiteford and Manuel Chávez. **"Social Capital and Small-scale Milk Producers in México". In** *Social Capital and Poverty Reduction in Latin America and the Caribbean: towards a New Paradigm,* compiled by Raul Atria and Marcelo Siles. Santiago, Chile (and New York): United Nations, ECLAC, 2004.

Heredia, Blanca. "Prosper or Perish? Development in the Age of Global Capital," *Current History* (November 1997): 383–88.

Hockman, Bernard M., and Michael M. Kostecki. *The Political Economy of the World Trade System: The WTO and Beyond*. Oxford: Oxford University Press, 2001.

Kapstein, Ethan B. "Workers and the World Economy," *Foreign Affairs* 75, no.3 (May-June 1986).

MERCOSUR (Mercado Común del Sur). *Protocolo de Ouro Preto,* Secretaria del MERCOSUR. **Montevideo, Uruguay: Sector de Normativa y Documentacion, 1994.**

OAS (Organization of American States). *Second Summit of the Americas, Plan of Action, Santiago, Chile*. Washington, DC: Summit of the Americas Secretariat. 1998.

Ortega Pizarro, Fernando. "Los Empresarios Mexicanos Pidieron y no les Dieron." *Proceso*. Mexico D.F., Nov. 20, 1993.

Plan Nacional de Desarrollo: Programa Nacional de Agricultura, Ganaderia, Desarrollo Rural, Pesca y Alimentacion 2001–2006. Mexico, D.F.: Presidencia de la República, 2001.

Pineyro, J. L. "Geopolitics and National Security in Latin America: A View from History and Political Theory; Geopolitica y seguridad nacional en America Latina: vision historica y teorico-politica," *Sociologica* 9, no. 25 (1994): 75–94.

Portes, Alejandro, Luis E. Guarnizo, and Patricia Landolt. "The Study of Transnationalism: Pitfalls and Promise of an Emergent Research Field," *Ethnic and Racial Studies* 22, no. 2 (1999) London: Routledge, 217–37.

Chapter 3

Globalization, the State, and the Role of Agro-Industry in Mexico's Development

Mark A. Martinez and Gaspar Real Cabello

This chapter analyzes the evolving relationship between the State, globalization, and the role of agro-industry in rural Mexico. In particular, by focusing on the role of transnational capital in rural Mexico, this chapter provides a better understanding of the impact of globalization on Mexican agriculture and rural communities. To date, characterizations of how globalization (as embodied by transnational capital and multilateral arrangements like NAFTA) has impacted Mexico fall into two distinct categories: negative and positive. From the negative position, it is argued that globalization has contributed to a bi-modal process of production, in which technology-oriented production increasingly dominates those who continue to produce along traditional lines. The primary argument here is that transnational capital does little more than undermine or displace local producers and communities, while consolidating the role of producers who can afford to embrace technology. On the positive side, globalization is seen as beneficial in that competition pushes Mexico's agricultural sector to become more sophisticated and efficient. The end result is competitive industries that are better prepared and capable of competing internationally. In the process, local and rural communities are remade by local entrepreneurs who are increasingly capable of working with large transnational interests, which contributes to the larger goals of the State. To gain insight into these dynamics, we look at the evolution of Mexico's poultry industry in general and the role of the Pilgrim's Pride Corporation in Mexico more specifically. We argue that Mexico's experience with globalization is still open to debate, but its relationship with transnational agribusiness in the poultry sector has been more positive than negative.

Globalization in Mexico's Poultry Industry

In historical terms, globalization can refer to dynamics like the transfer of language and religious beliefs to new geographic centers, as has been the case throughout most of human history. More recently, globalization is broadly identified with the opening of markets, the movement of capital, and regional economic integration, which have created new investment and political patterns the world over. Because of Mexico's previous inward-looking and protectionist policies, and its delayed embrace of free-market competition, economic globalization came rather late (at least compared to the Asian experience). It nonetheless has had the anticipated impact of altering larger production processes. For example, in Mexico's poultry industry, small and technologically unsophisticated local producers found that they would have to adopt modern feed and care techniques if they were to compete and grow in the 1970s and 1980s. While many small producers did not adapt, others began to embrace market-oriented practices as early as the 1960s. This helped plant the seed of market competition, which successive Mexican presidents later championed in the 1980s and 1990s. To help institutionalize, deepen, and spread market-oriented production processes, Mexico signed a regional trade pact, the North American Free Trade Agreement (NAFTA), with Canada and the United States.[1]

While changes from globalization and regional economic integration (private enterprise, competition, etc.) were expected and even welcomed, persistent patterns of subsistence in rural Mexico provoked new questions about the benefits of globalization and private enterprise. For example, market-oriented policies have created a series of challenges as past modes of survival have increasingly been replaced by new subsistence activities. Survival strategies are consistently being abandoned or remade in rural Mexico—from migration to Mexico's major cities (or to the United States) to the increased reliance on expensive technology to produce competitive goods. This, in turn, has created new pressures that neither the State nor Mexico's internal markets are prepared to meet. To facilitate the process of producing competitive goods in the countryside, large-scale agro-industry has increasingly combined forces with small producers.[2] It is our goal to demonstrate, by focusing on Mexico's poultry industry, how these relationships have impacted small producers in rural Mexico. This is an important task because a primary concern in Mexico is to determine whether globalization and competition will have a long term-positive impact on the country's economic and political future.

In this process, we address the argument made by several observers that globalization has contributed to a "new international division of labor" (Sanderson 1990), where low-wage and raw-material-producing nations are seen as little more than potential profit areas to be exploited. Contending that the presence of agro-industry has fundamentally altered local social and economic patterns throughout rural Mexico (Sanderson 1990, 57), one perspective suggests that dislocation and manipulation are the primary results of globalization and competition. While many might be inclined to view globalization negatively, especially as it applies to developing countries like Mexico,[3] there is another perspective that views transnational capital as a vital component necessary for the development of rural sectors throughout the world (Feder 1976; 1984). This has especially been the case since the early 1990s when the Washington Consensus helped to establish the parameters for broader neo-liberal policy prescriptions that promote increased investment, advocate market efficiency, and push competition throughout the developing world. Mirroring earlier modernization vs. dependency debates, it is helpful to understand that the underlying tensions of both approaches (modernization-dependency creating positive-negative effects) are largely a product of differences of opinion that come from seeing the development issue from two distinct levels of analysis. Proponents of the market-oriented approach tend to focus on producers, and the capacity to adapt to innovation. Critics of globalization, however, point to a country's position in the "international division of labor" and the conditions that create financial and market dependency (Valenzuela and Valenzuela, 1986). Wherever one falls on the modernization-dependency divide, there is little doubt that the globalization (and the more specific NAFTA) debate cannot be understood without looking at the history of transnational capital in specific industries and regions.

In this chapter, we look at the evolution of the poultry industry in Mexico and analyze how poultry producers at various levels (small, medium, and large) have fared or come to adapt in an increasingly technologically oriented and competitive industry. As well, we look at how a large-scale transnational firm, Texas-based Pilgrim's Pride, has affected Mexico's poultry market while, at the same time, becoming an important social actor by transforming social and economic relations on many levels in the central region of Mexico. In the process, we will show that the presence of Pilgrim's Pride has helped to alter and diversify Mexico's poultry market by transforming the ways agricultural goods are produced, marketed, and consumed.

Our primary objective, however, is to explain how globalization affects local production processes in rural Mexico. To do this, we focus on the role of technology and illustrate how access to and control of technology in the poultry industry has significantly altered the structure of options available to poultry producers. To understand these dynamics, we begin by looking at the poultry market in the central state of Querétaro, the Mexican headquarters of Pilgrim's Pride.

Phase I: Transforming "Backyard Farms" in Querétaro, Mexico

The history of Querétaro's—and to a large degree, Mexico's—poultry industry can be divided into two phases after the 1950s. In phase one, the focus was primarily on increasing production from a small number of poultry producers. During the late 1950s, poultry production in the state of Querétaro was dominated by a small-scale production process that, according to one source, "required little more than a backyard." On these "farms" the number of chickens produced varied from 100 to more than 500 birds per cycle (at that time, four cycles per year). Poultry was generally marketed locally while still alive, although many birds were slaughtered before being brought to market. Because consumption patterns and lifestyles in the city of Querétaro were tied to the ebb and flow of rural Querétaro, what the city consumed was very much influenced by rural production patterns in the state. Illustrating how urban demand helped define the broader limits of market potential in the late 1950s, one observer wrote, "In what is now part of Ezequiel Montes Avenue, the bus terminal was located, where different rural communities arrived from throughout the states of Querétaro and Guanajuato. . . . Buses arrived loaded with diverse goods from the countryside, like turkeys, grown chickens, little chicks, eggs, etc., all of which came from family farms and were sold live."[4]

It was during this period that today's modern poultry industry began to emerge. In fact, many producers who began during this period continue to operate on a larger scale today, which has meant that producers who raised and sold poultry in the city of Querétaro were the early pioneers of modern poultry production techniques in Querétaro.[5] Apart from understanding the early complexities of modern production processes, they also continued in a difficult industry rife with high risks and relatively low profit margins. As production techniques became more sophisticated (medicines, special feed, etc.), these producers helped to modernize and expand production techniques in the region by the late 1950s. Querétaro's poultry industry, however, still did not include specialized installations for raising and processing poultry. Nor were there specialized slaughter houses for birds sold locally. As well, because reproduction and incubation were done traditionally (i.e., manually), incubation was a marginal part of the production process. This meant that an industrialized poultry sector did not exist in central Mexico during the 1950s and into the early 1960s.

Once small incubators started to appear and became more widely available, ambitious producers began to think in terms of modernizing production techniques in order to manage the increasing amount of birds produced. This in turn led to the building of larger and specialized hatcheries (*casetas*) that would help produce the conditions necessary for the mass production of poultry on large poultry farms (*granjas*). It was at this time that various groups within the poultry industry realized the importance of technology, and began looking for ways to incorporate modern techniques and equipment into production facilities (Castro 2001). As production techniques became increasingly technical, the arrival of Ralston Purina helped push Mexico toward new levels of poultry production and innovation (Castro 2001).

Phase II: PURINA and Querétaro's Poultry Industry

The second development which set the stage for the evolution of Querétaro's poultry industry began in the 1950s with the arrival of Ralston Purina from the United States. Headquartered in St. Louis, Missouri, Purina emerged by the 1950s as the principal U.S. producer of mixed-grain feed for cattle and other animals.[6] In Mexico, Purina first established distributorships and, later, built feed-production facilities in central Mexico, which served the needs of farm and other animals. At the same time, local producers in Querétaro began to develop more dynamic and complex techniques for producing poultry, and Purina's arrival helped spur the mass-production process (Purina inaugurated its first facility in 1957). While it is difficult to ascertain whether Purina was the *key* variable necessary to push Mexico's poultry industry on the road to modernization, there is little doubt that Purina's presence (which coincided with the early phases of agro-industry's globalization in Mexico) had a significant impact on central Mexico's poultry industry.

Indeed, as Purina expanded beyond Querétaro in the 1970s, and established processing plants in different states, its growing client network became increasingly interested in moving beyond the small-scale, cottage-industry production levels that had characterized much of the region's poultry production through the 1960s. Purina's strategy for encouraging small producers to grow was to promote the raising of chicks in Mexico's rural communities by providing "poultry packages" to rural communities and small ranches. Among the package items were chicks, literature explaining how to take care of poultry, and even five kilograms of feed for the chicks. As well, information regarding improved birds, vaccinations, and different feed (produced by Purina) was distributed (Zúñiga 1999). Interested producers who wanted in on these packages were later required to buy both chicks and feed from Purina. While these processes helped to enhance competition and local knowledge of basic production processes, one thing was missing from Purina's initial attempts to improve and enhance poultry production—there was little effort to provide for specialized facilities, or *casetas*, which would become necessary for raising chicks on a large scale. Many budding poultry farmers used facilities originally designed for other purposes (including housing). In this manner, new businesses (including *Bachoco*, Pilgrim's Pride's primary competitor in Mexico today) emerged and prospered by providing additional services and technical assistance that Purina did not provide.

It was at this point that Mexico's poultry industry began to split along traditional and modern lines across the country. Many smaller, nonintegrated poultry producers continued to function like backyard, artisan-style producers of the past, where most of the work continued to be done manually, and products were sold in local open-air markets. In contrast, a growing number of technologically oriented producers (both *non-ejido,* private entrepreneurs and, later, ejido farmers) began to invest in new methods, buy specialized hatcheries, and seek out new forms of production. This helped create a small but increasingly important technological divide that appeared across regions throughout Mexico. For example, manual labor dominated in Baja California, while states like Sonora were filled with producers (such as the Mezquital del Oro Company, the modern prototype in Northwest Mexico) who were more and more technically sophisticated. In sum, technological contrasts emerged throughout Mexico by the late 1960s and early 1970s.

Another Poultry-Industry "Model" in Mexico?

Today one of the more popular and widely accepted beliefs in Mexico regarding its poultry industry is that Mexico had the option of following two distinct industry paths early on. It is argued that the first path that Mexico could have followed was the "farmer model" that many poultry producers utilized in the United States (including Pilgrim's Pride founder, Bo Pilgrim: www.pilgrimspride.com/company/story.asp). According to this model, Mexico's rural producers would start with a small number of birds and grow as their markets expanded. The second option was the emerging model of large-scale farming that Purina helped advance during the 1960s and 1970s. The argument here is that Mexican agro-industrialists could have encouraged large producer networks to help push an increasingly complex and technologically dynamic poultry sector. Highly technical and organizationally complex, this model proved to be difficult for a variety of reasons—a lack of resources (tied to the government's urban-industrial focus), government corruption (once it began to promote poultry farms in the countryside), incomplete national market networks, and undeveloped economies of scale in the industry. Mexico had small pockets of technically evolving producers, but was dominated by small-poultry farmers, who were limited by a lack of technological sophistication and financial resources. Several state-sponsored attempts to increase poultry production in the 1970s and early 1980s failed largely because they required a level of technical assistance and commercial experience that local and small farmers in Mexico lacked—and the national government failed to provide.[7]

Another factor that helped to maintain the small backyard "farmer model" was the government's recognition that a structure dependent upon small farmers afforded many rural Mexicans a reasonable level of subsistence, as was the case earlier in the United States.[8] In a country like Mexico, where resources were few and largely dedicated to urban and industrial development, this was an important consideration. Because the farmer model contributed to building economies of scale in the poultry industry in the United States and was viewed as a success, it was seen as a legitimate plan to follow in Mexico. The goal then was to find an approach that could help pave the way for larger poultry production initiatives which could then become national in scale. This approach meant encouraging small producer groups to move beyond subsistence. Thus the state encouraged and subsidized the creation of consortiums in the 1970s, which would include 10 to 20 families. These consortiums were then supplied an average of 50 chickens, and were promised assistance until the group could become independent commercial producers in local markets (Maya 2000). While these projects never had the immediate commercial impact State planners hoped for (i.e., creating wide-scale commercial farming classes), a practical effect was that families still had access to basic foodstuffs and household goods because, as was the case earlier in the United States, families were able to exchange eggs for sugar, cooking oil, and other items.

The overall goal of these consortium projects was undermined, however, by spotty technical assistance and a lack of financial resources to help care for what were supposed to become commercial birds. Apart from the fact that small farmers did not have a dependable network of technical assistance and credit, the project was damaged by what one observer sarcastically called the project's "only real achievement"—the spreading of diseases. Although some economies of scale had been reached, limited access to (or even knowledge of) cures and medicines meant that outbreaks of diseases spread quickly. This was due in part to the fact that sporadic or incomplete "eradication efforts only served to allow [diseases] to return much stronger in mutated viral forms, like New Castle, which was much more difficult to control" (Maya 2000).[9] As viruses began to spread to other areas in the countryside, the program was seen as an unmitigated failure (Maya 2000).

Pilgrim's Pride and the Making of Mexico's Modern Poultry Industry

During the 1980s the Mexican government began altering the economic landscape of Mexico to give private capital a freer hand. Mexico's decision to join the General Agreement on Tariffs and Trade (GATT) in 1986 helped push Mexico's new policy approach along and began the process of opening up the Mexican economy. These nascent "neo-liberal" policies, which were initiated by the Miguel de la Madrid administration (1982–88) and implemented with a passion by the Carlos Salinas de Gortari administration (1988–94), soon dominated the thinking of policy-makers at the national level and were institutionalized when NAFTA came into force in 1994.[10] While the logic for joining international trade agreements varies from country to country and region to region, two of the primary goals for Mexico were to improve its development prospects and to enhance the competitive position of its agro-industry. While Pilgrim's Pride had made the decision to invest in Mexico before its 1986 GATT decision (discussed below), the arrival of the Texas-based company helped Mexico in both of these areas.

Ranked as the third-largest producer of poultry products in the United States, and currently the second-largest producer in Mexico, Pilgrim's Pride stands distinct, and its presence has altered Mexico's agro-industrial landscape. Indeed, the Pilgrim's Pride Corporation has encouraged market-oriented producers to employ new techniques and processes—ventilating systems, genetics, feed, heating systems, insulation, and medicines, among other improvements the Pilgrim's Pride Corporation has helped pioneer—that reduce the amount of time necessary to grow a four-pound chicken from nine-and-one-half weeks (1970) to just six weeks today.[11] What this means is that four production cycles per year (1960s) have been increased to 5.7 cycles per year because of improvements in technology and management.

In addition, the Pilgrim's Pride Corporation has been part of a process that has reduced the number of man-hours necessary to raise a three-pound bird—from two hours and thirty-seven minutes to just fourteen minutes—and lowered the real labor costs necessary for production.[12] In fact, by the late 1990s, roughly 25% of the poultry industry's profits depended on human labor, meaning that 75% of the industry's profits depended on technology (Teissier 1997). In more practical terms, because of technological advancements, where it once required two people to manage a single hatchery (early 1980s), one individual can now take care of ten automated hatcheries. The benefits derived from reducing the number of man-hours are numerous, and some justify displacing man-hour labor. For example, while some might complain about the need to create jobs for Mexico's rural communities (discussed below), automation reduces the amount of human contact, and thus the potential for carrying pathogens from hatchery to hatchery. The result is that the chances of disease outbreaks are reduced, which benefits small and local owners because production cycles are not exposed to as many viral outbreaks.

In the process, producers who want to keep pace, and who hope to ally with companies like Pilgrim's Pride, have found it profitable to invest in technology and new machinery. What this means is that changes made by large local producers (60,000 or more birds per cycle) within the poultry industry are now being copied at the small-producer level (15,000 or fewer per cycle). These changes are part of a market-driven process that has become an integral part of globalization at many levels around the world. In addition to technological changes, new approaches in the poultry industry, such as packaging and commercialization (refrigerated instead of open air-markets, store modifications, color, presentation, etc.) have played as significant a role in reshaping Mexico's poultry industry as have higher quality and lower prices. All of this has pushed the poultry market to become more competitive and helped restructure production relationships throughout Mexico.[13] For example, many observers might be quick to argue that large companies "displace" or "undermine" local producers. But for many, Pilgrim's Pride has helped create secure markets for small producers (as buyers), provided much needed resource support (medicines, feed, etc.), and even served as a business-saving source of financing for small producers who are ignored by Mexico's private banking system. The experience of Querétaro's small and medium-sized producers offers an interesting perspective on this.

Producer Alliances, Small Producers, and Shared Risk

Because critics of globalization and NAFTA often start from the premise that large corporations benefit at the expense of smaller producers, any discussion of producer alliances requires that we look at production responsibilities and risks at the small- and medium-size producer level. By doing so, we are better able to determine not only the burdens and responsibilities of production, but also the attitudes toward such partnerships. Understanding these attitudes is necessary because of the inclination to view responsibility and risk as simply participating in, and sharing, good and bad results. Here, casual observers may be inclined to focus primarily on economic (quality and quantity) and legal (formal obligation) responsibilities. We have found, however, that understanding shared responsibilities and risks encompasses more than economic and legal obligations. Rather, we have found that local-level attitudes toward production and risk are very much determined by a producer's sense of commitment to Pilgrim's Pride. To determine how Pilgrim's Pride is viewed by small- and medium-size partners, we conducted a series of interviews in the late 1990s which indicate that a producer's *production history* and *economic status* contribute significantly to how producers view Pilgrim's Pride. In particular, the closer a producer was to a negative experience in the market, and the fewer resources he had to deal with these challenges, the more he found the new relationship with Pilgrim's Pride to be a positive one. In the process of reaching these conclusions, we found three different *aparcero* (producer group) tiers which provide a good deal of insight into producer commitment and shared risk.

These producer tiers include those who see Pilgrim's Pride: a) as their economic salvation, b) as part of their economic base, or c) as a matter of economic convenience and/or legal obligation. The first two groups are small-scale producers with many *ejidatarios* involved as *aparceros*, while the last group encompasses both medium- and large-scale producers who view themselves as potentially self-sufficient.[14]

Producer Relations as Economic Salvation

Those who hold the view that Pilgrim's Pride is crucial to their economic salvation are very much affected by their production history. In every case we reviewed among the small-scale producers (two hatcheries, or 30,000 birds per cycle), there was a long and storied history of what local producers considered to be outright abuse and exploitation by the National Bank for Rural Credit (*Banrural*).[15] In particular, the business relationship between many small producers and Banrural deteriorated to such an extent that there was no confidence, no initiative, no commitment, and no profits to speak of as far as the small producer was concerned. Indeed, every small-scale producer we spoke to recounted numerous stories of what they considered to be deception, denial, and debt on the part of Banrural. For example, one producer pointed out how Banrural managers would arrive and take home a few chickens or, on special occasions, up to two hundred chickens for agency or personal parties. In one case we were told how, after the 1985 earthquake in Mexico City, trucks arrived

Table 1

Farms (Numbers of Hatcheries)	**Production** (Birds per Cycle)	**History with Past Producers**	**Economic Status Before 1988**	**Relationship with Pilgrim's Pride**
≤2	30,000	Exploited	Weak	Personal/Loyal
2–4	30,000–60,000	Mixed	Varied/Surviving	Loyal/Market
≥5	60,000 +	Growth-oriented	Surviving/Stable/	Market/Distant

to take away 30,000 chickens "for disaster relief." In none of these cases were producers compensated for their work or expenses.

Every group we spoke to was emphatic that, with the arrival of Pilgrim's Pride, regular grain shipments, professional oversight, proper medicine, clear price structures, etc. solved the problems they experienced with *Banrural*. For these producers, the arrival of Pilgrim's Pride marked the beginning of a new economic life. Indeed, complaints of interest-rate manipulation, below-market prices, feed-arrival problems, the sudden requisitioning of poultry stock, lack of professionalism, *caudillismo* (heavy-handedness), etc. virtually disappeared. On another level, because Mexico's private banking industry does not see small-scale rural producers as a secure and profitable sector, the state has had to step in with creative funding programs administered through private industrial groups, like Pilgrim's Pride, who guarantee the loans.[16] The reason for this, according to one state official who oversaw these credit programs in central Mexico, is that the private banking sector views *ejidatario* producers as "a bankrupt sector with past-due bills, without resources, without collateral, and with a complete lack of continuity." Continuing, he emphasized,

> When you consider that rural Mexico has to modernize and mechanize [to compete] you find that those who are in rural Mexico are further behind and require more resources than we think. Remember that globalization is the key because if you don't mechanize you lose. The problem is that the price of technology is increasing while the price of primary products is going down. It's a vicious circle [begins drawing an imaginary circle with his hand] because if you don't have technology you can't compete, if you can't compete you can't get credit, if you can't get credit you can't invest, and if you can't invest you can't buy technology. . . . You throw in a devaluation, high interest rates and you begin to see a real problem.

Because state financing was insignificant (perhaps 1%) compared to Pilgrim's Pride financing schemes, the company's role in production relationships (i.e. "the credit it offered") compelled both small producers and the State to view companies like Pilgrim's Pride as a positive element in Mexico's larger development picture. It's interesting to note that while each producer in this category recognized the economic and legal aspect of their relationship, their commitment to and support for Pilgrim's Pride was largely personal. For these and other reasons, these producers expressed a willingness to absorb hidden costs and work longer hours with little or no pay. In the end, these dynamics convinced many that Pilgrim's Pride offered "economic salvation" and led many to believe they owed the company personally for helping them move beyond negative experiences.

Producer Relations as Economic Base

In the case reviewed here (producers with between 30,000 and 60,000 birds per farm), we found that providing Pilgrim's Pride with poultry was just one of several sources of income. Like those who saw Pilgrim's Pride as their "economic salvation", this group also had problems with Banrural, but were more focused on immediate problems tied to the market (or lack thereof) and prices. In particular, those interviewed in this group felt that their contracts with Banrural, or other State agencies, hindered their efforts, because they were threatened with resource blackmail (no more medicines, food shortages, etc.) if they attempted to sell their product to other buyers. This blackmail led to years of little or no profit and, for this reason, years of stable and profitable business relations with Pilgrim's Pride have contributed to a sense of professional trust that is as much personal as it is economic.

Indeed, one producer, who was approached by Bachoco—Pilgrim's Pride's primary competitor in Mexico—to produce for them, explained that he had no interest in what they had to offer. When he was asked about the specifics of Bachoco's offer, he said he did not allow the conversation to get that far because he felt his relationship with Pilgrim's Pride was based on confidence and professionalism, and that "there was no need to waste . . . time on something that wasn't going to happen." When asked about the "possibility" of Bachoco having a better offer, he simply said the confidence and trust built up over the years with Pilgrim's Pride was something he did not want to lose. In conclusion, while this group viewed Pilgrim's Pride as an integral part of their economic livelihood, their sense of commitment at the time was as much moral and personal as it was legal and economic.

Producer Relations as Economic Agreement/Convenience

In the final group of *aparceros* we looked at, there is no doubt that size (owning enough hatcheries to produce 60,000 birds or more) and knowledge (a better understanding of the poultry market) makes the producer relationship more legal and market-oriented than personal. For example, while it was noted that most small producers do not always require contracts (because they trust Pilgrim's Pride), larger producers will ask for contracts sixty days in advance. Here we found that larger producers had developed a more distant or professional approach to their production relationship, and a self-interested commitment to the business of producing chickens. In order to understand why producers, large and small, continued to connect with Pilgrim's Pride, we asked several large-scale producers why Pilgrim's Pride has been so successful in recruiting partners. There were several responses.

One producer said that the size of Pilgrim's Pride made it a convenient to do business, especially after the 1994 devaluation. When asked why *small producers* with few resources would take Pilgrim's Pride up on their offer to build hatcheries and form producer associations, two reasons were given. First, small producers who link up with Pilgrim's Pride "don't know anything else." Second, he said that people were willing to secure credit through the official structures managed by Pilgrim's Pride, build hatcheries for Pilgrim's Pride, and work with the company because they did not really understand how long it would take to recoup their investment. After outlining how long it would take to start making a profit at current (late 1990s) prices, one medium-sized producer commented that small producers were "dumb asses . . . they're simply dumb asses."[17] After outlining how many small producers lacked knowledge of larger markets and networks, he finished by saying that information disparities between local partners and companies like Pilgrim's Pride put the company in the driver's seat. The end result is that, because they don't understand larger market dynamics, "they don't realize that they're making somebody else a lot of money" because they "are willing to work hard." In sum, large-scale producers, who see their relationship with Pilgrim's Pride in legal terms and as a matter of economic convenience, appear to have little loyalty or sense of personal commitment to Pilgrim's Pride.

Concluding Observations

During the early stages of market opening, the question often arose as to how Mexico would be able to create a competitive market-oriented environment in some of the more marginalized areas of the countryside. Perhaps the largest concern, for the State at least, was how to accommodate and integrate local and small producers from Mexico's rural communities, into evolving modern production processes. A secondary but no less important concern was how to entice internationally competitive industries to Mexico to facilitate the transformation of rural Mexico. These issues are linked with the stated goals and promises of open markets and NAFTA—that most everyone will benefit as foreign direct investment and competition are enticed to bring new jobs and competition to Mexico. In our research, we have found that while many small producers have been forced out of the poultry industry because of high costs and difficulty with technological advancement, many individuals and small producer groups have seen their production capacity and facilities grow since they entered the poultry business with Pilgrim's Pride. Put another way, they have become productive and growing small entrepreneurs, as many promoters of open markets had hoped. However, as noted above, open markets and the promise of NAFTA had nothing to do with Pilgrim's Pride decision to invest in Mexico. In fact, Pilgrim's Pride decided to invest in Mexico well before Mexico's decision to join GATT in 1986 (a full thirteen years before NAFTA) because they saw opportunity in low per-capita poultry consumption, market-size potential, and their sense that Mexico's poultry industry was largely open to being organized.

While Pilgrim's Pride's decision to invest in Mexico had more to do with opportunity than market opening, our research nonetheless indicates that the arrival of Pilgrim's Pride helped to bring competition, opportunity for small producers, and (later) structure to the poultry market in several ways. For example, Pilgrim's Pride was able to help reorganize and restructure the poultry industry because it increased per-capita poultry consumption, which meant focusing on the consumer. To do this, Pilgrim's Pride strove to improve quality—while providing consumers with more options, and increasing the varieties of presentation. They were able to do this while keeping prices low, which impacted competitors and potential producer associates, by forcing them to invest in both technology and other areas of market research.[18] But more importantly, their presence helped to increase market demand that provided the rationale for reaching out to rural communities in search of producer partnerships. In the process, by seeking out producers from diverse socio-economic backgrounds, Pilgrim's Pride helped create opportunities for many small rural producers. It was in this area that we begin to understand the impact of Pilgrim's Pride on production and market structures in rural Mexico.

By forming alliances with Pilgrim's Pride, many small producers who were in weak or unstable positions found stability and security. Indeed, in the case of almost every small- and medium-size producer that we reviewed throughout central Mexico over a five-year period (1994–98), we found a sense of gratitude, if not relief, that "a company like Pilgrim's Pride will work with us." Today, while few small producers hope to reach production levels achieved by national giants Pilgrim's Pride or Bachoco, they at least can speak of becoming a regional power like Abrego in Querétaro. As well, by pushing others to compete on their level, Pilgrim's Pride has helped make the understanding of technology an integral part of any serious poultry producer in Mexico. To be sure, large domestic producers like Bachoco were pushing Mexico in this direction, but the arrival of Pilgrim's Pride insured this would occur across more regions, more quickly than otherwise anticipated. In a country which battled with literacy and education obstacles just thirty-five years ago, the premature push toward technological sophistication among Mexico's emerging small rural producers must be seen as a positive development (no matter how limited).[19] Finally, these factors contribute to an increasingly competitive and productive environment, characterized by local entrepreneurs who are now capable of working with transnational interests.

On the surface, this suggests that the State, or NAFTA, had little to do with advances made in this area of agro-industry. However, to suggest that the State's role in promoting development has been strictly peripheral would be misleading for three reasons. First, we need to keep in mind the fact that the State, via presidential administrations, opened Mexico's economy and made foreign capital welcome, which helped to facilitate other facets of production. This was the case for Purina initially, and for the Pilgrim's Pride Corporation after 1988. Second, while the State often did not provide needed resources and advice to local poultry producers during the 1970s and 1980s, the fact that they helped initiate various production projects in industries like poultry resulted in supplying local producers with infrastructure, knowledge, and basic training. Finally, and more recently, the State helped protect the Mexican poultry industry by arranging to put off NAFTA-mandated tariff reductions, which were scheduled for January 1, 2003. It is here that NAFTA begins to affect Mexico's poultry industry, albeit in a fashion not anticipated by NAFTA promoters.

As noted above, the introduction of Pilgrim's Pride to the Mexican agribusiness field was not affected by NAFTA negotiations because the company's decision to invest in Mexico had already been made before the arrival of the Carlos Salinas de Gortari administration in 1988. It is ironic then that the opening of NAFTA posed a threat to Pilgrim's Pride of Mexico, and the larger poultry industry in Mexico, because tariff reduction schedules were asymmetrical across products. For example, because corn (a primary component of feed for poultry) was not targeted for tariff reduction or elimination until 2008, the cost of feeding poultry in Mexico remained artificially high as a result of the tariff-laden corn costs in Mexico (Mexico is a net importer of corn). To be sure, because of demands in Mexico, NAFTA corn and dry beans have enjoyed special treatment, and have been allowed to be imported duty-free based on an annual (and slowly increasing) quota system. The problem is that, while the import tariffs have been rarely imposed, the quota system remains in place. This puts Mexico's poultry producers at a distinct disadvantage because imported corn is targeted for human consumption first. This is significant for poultry producers in Mexico because while the basic feed used to grow a three-pound bird is tied to a mixture of sorghum, soy products, and corn, Mexican producers are forced to use more sorghum and soy products (among others) than their U.S. counterparts.

This is important because U.S. producers not only have access to subsidized corn as their primary feed component, and state-subsidized programs to manage disease outbreaks, but more corn in the feed mix provides superior marketing advantages because of pigmentation (coloring) and its energy-producing components.

On the Mexican side, producers are forced to pay a higher price for nationally produced corn (when they can find it) and for imported corn, which adds to cost of competitive demand, transportation, and warehousing. This has a significant impact across the poultry industry in Mexico because more than 50% of costs associated with producing market-ready poultry are tied to feed. (Estimates of actual costs range up to 60% or more.) As a result, in spite of the fact that Mexico's poultry industry is *technologically competitive* with its U.S. counterpart, potential feed costs after January 1, 2003, would have buried the Mexican poultry industry and led Mexico to accuse the United States of dumping. For these reasons, the United States and Mexico agreed to return to 2001 tariff levels of 97.5% until 2008, when tariffs on corn are scheduled to be removed. In the end, and ironically, NAFTA's overall impact on Mexico's poultry industry is important in that it now protects rather than opens up Mexico's market.

What about the concern that transnational corporations do little more than undermine or displace local producers and communities while consolidating the role of producers who can afford to embrace technology? After speaking to producers at many levels, it appears that this argument is not well-informed. To be sure, there have been those who have left the market, but by and large, many of the small producers we interviewed five and six years ago have seen their facilities and production capacity increase significantly. Other larger groups have spun off from their Pilgrim's Pride contracts and have found markets on their own, preferring higher profits, but, with reduced market security (which purchasing agreements with Pilgrim's Pride offered). Is this a positive or negative development? We believe the answer depends on whether one is an advocate of modernization and neo-liberalism, or is more concerned with the dislocating effects globalization has on local communities. In the end, early reports from the field suggest that, while more work needs to be done, there is no doubt that the poultry industry in rural Mexico is dynamic, maturing, and generating positive outcomes for many small entrepreneurs.

Endnotes

1. For an excellent review on the dynamics and history behind NAFTA, see Robert Pastor's, *Toward a North American Community: Lessons from the Old World for the New*. While the broader economic impact of NAFTA is debated, there is little doubt that the political impact of globalization has fundamentally altered the Mexican state. From market opening (joining GATT in 1986) to the full embrace of market-oriented policies under Carlos Salinas de Gortari (1988–94) and Ernesto Zedillo (1994–2000) administrations, there is little doubt that—barring some unforeseen event—future Mexican presidents will find it difficult to undo Mexico's current market focus.
2. Agriculture has changed drastically since the early 1900s, when almost all agricultural activity took place on the farm. The term *agribusiness* was coined by two economists in the late 1950s, John Davis and Ray Goldberg, to identify and embrace these processes. Davis and Goldberg believed the term *agribusiness* was more suitable to describe the gamut of all these enterprises that now take place outside the farm, which include bringing products from the field to the consumer.
3. For example, critics argue that agribusiness is so interesting in Mexico (and Latin America) because new and modern agriculture processes are absorbed by smaller producers, creating new "enclave" centers of production in the process. Rivaling past "plantation economies" in terms of their scope, importance, and impact, these centers are the product of the new industrial revolution that emanated from the United States after World War II.
4. From authors' interview of Rodolfo del Toral, former Purina employee, in Queretaro on April 25, 2001. Other references to del Toral are from the same interview.
5. For example, Cirilo Colonel was a successful merchant who went from selling chickens from a small stall to raising chicks, and eventually established his own farms and moved to large-scale production. Many of Cirilo Colonel's descendants continued in the poultry industry, as is the case with other families, like the Alvarez and Vázquez families, who continue to sell poultry in the city of Querétaro.
6. Purina's website notes that with the Marshall Plan leading the way after World War II, they recognized that agriculture ventures, in general, and Ralston Purina in particular, could become the beneficiaries of the United States' global economic leadership. Purina's founder, William H. Danforth, understood the worldwide possibilities created in the post-war era and began to look beyond original marketing and production facilities in the United States. While Danforth would not live to see the internationalization of the company, Ralston's International Division was formed on October 1, 1956, and opened in Mexico in 1956: www.purina.com/company/profile/timetable.asp.
7. Many producers got their start when the federal government initiated a series of programs designed to increase the participation of local populations in their own development. To do this, various programs, like PIDER (*Programa Integral para*

el Desarrollo Rural—Essential Program for Rural Development), provided resources for the development of small- and medium-sized businesses which were managed by small producers like local peasant (*ejidatario*) groups. PIDER was created by the federal government in 1973 under the name *Programa de Inversiones Publicas para el Desarrollo_Rural* (Public Investment Program for Rural Development) and was designed to integrate various rural development programs that overlapped and lacked coordination. The program from 1973 to 1977 focused primarily on public works projects and improving access to jobs and education. In 1977, PIDER began to focus on increasing the participation of local populations in their own development. On this, see *Programa Integral para el Desarrollo Rural, PIDER: Memoria, 1977–1981* (Secretaria de Programación y Presupuesto: Gobierno del Estado, 1982).

8. In the 1950s, many small farmers in the United States were at least self-sufficient because as small producers they could produce basic milk, pork, poultry, and honey, among other things, for home consumption.
9. For example, in Querétaro the State established a facility in Ajuchitlán, Colón as part of the *Granjas de Fomento Avícola* program. A lack of technical assistance, proper feed, and financial assistance led to the eventual collapse of the project as disease and a lack of technical knowledge undermined its success.
10. See Miguel Angel Centeno (1994).
11. Just in the area of ventilation, advances have been made in knowledge of how fresh-air flows, drafts, regulated temperatures, heat moisture, odors, and gases impact production. Dealing with these dynamics has helped shape techniques for producing inlets, fans, insulation, ventilation controls, bypass panels, fogging systems, etc. In this manner, while an increased understanding of genetics has helped, knowledge of nutrition and the environment (i.e. process management) has also contributed to quicker production cycles.
12. See Pilgrim's Pride Company website: www.pilgrimspride.com/company/story/pt3.html.
13. We argue that after the economic crisis of 1994, when many local producers were absorbed by Pilgrim's Pride, a new structure of production began to take shape. Here we begin to see that while profit levels may have been reduced (for local producers), a new production structure evolved where risks associated with securing product, feed, commercialization, protecting against diseases, etc. are also reduced or assumed by Pilgrim's Pride.
14. The categories listed here and the case studies highlighted are a product of several Working Papers prepared for the Pilgrim's Pride Corporation. They were done in one-month intervals, over a period of three years, in the central Mexican states of Querétaro, San Luis Potosi, the Federal District, and Guanajuato. Interviewees included state officials, private non-ejido producers, ejido producers, and company officials from Pilgrim's Pride. The total number of interviewees numbered approximately seventy-five individuals, with the majority being poultry producers or workers. See Mark A. Martinez and Gaspar Real (1994, 1995, and 1997) for specific cases, numbers, and methods.
15. See note 6.
16. For example, the Bank of Mexico's *Fideicomisos Instituidos en Relacion con la Agricultura,* or FIRA, provides funds to private banks who then loan money to private companies like Pilgrim's Pride. These companies, in turn, are responsible for the bank loan, must find creditors, and then administer repayment. For a more specific overview of FIRA and its functions see Mark A. Martinez and Gaspar Real Cabello, *Producer Associations and Shared Risk* (1997).
17. Here it is important to note that there were conflicting views on how long it might take to recover original investments. For example, the longest period we were told

was 14 years. The shortest period was four to five years (under current conditions). Because the authors were not told how costs were calculated (although market prices and profit-sharing were explained) it is difficult to say with any degree of certainty whose figures were more reliable. However, it was obvious that smaller producers were more confident about recovering their investments in a shorter timeframe than were larger producers.

18. Because non-production activities—such as design, distribution, and services—became more significant, the importance of production declined as a share of total costs. This suggests that low-cost producers may have lost some of their competitive advantage in the larger poultry market. On the significance of this in other markets around the world, see Robert Gilpin, *Global Political Economy* (2001): 135–36.
19. It should be noted that Pilgrim's Pride has regularly set up basic education classes (and even built a school in one rural community in Querétaro) to help with literacy and other areas where workers need educational assistance. While no official numbers were made available to us, we estimate that many hundreds have benefited from these efforts.

Bibliography

Barquin, David, and Blanca Suárez. *El fin de la autosuficiencia alimentaria.* Mexico City: Ed. Nueva Visión , 1982.

Castro, Abel. Former Purina veterinarian, with a specialization in poultry-related diseases and health (interviews, 2001–02).

Centeno, Miguel Angel. *Democracy within Reason: Technocratic Revolution in Mexico* University Park: Pennsylvania State University Press, 1994.

Centro de Estudios Estratégicos. *Entendiendo el TLC.* México: FCE/ITESM, 1995.

Feder, Ernest. "The New Bank Programme for the Self-Liquidation of the Third World Peasantry." *The Journal of Peasant Studies* 3, no.3 (April 1976).

Featherstone, Michael. *Global Culture, Nationalism, Globalization and Modernity.* London: Sage Publications, 1996.

Flores, Victor, and Manuel Gómez Cruz. "Agroindustria, conceptualización, niveles de estudio y su importancia en el análisis de la agricultura." *Revista de Geografía Agrícola* 11–12. México: Universidad Autónoma de Chapingo, 1987.

Gilpin, Robert. *Global Political Economy: Understanding the International Economic Order.* Princeton, NJ: Princeton University Press, 2001.

González, Laura. *Respuesta campesina a la Revolución verde en el Bajío.* Mexico: Universidad Iberoamericana, 1992.

Ianni, Octavio. *Teorías de la globalización.* Mexico: Siglo XXI-UNAM, 1997.

Kearney, Michael. "The Local and the Global: The Anthropology of Globalization and Transnationalism." *Annual Review of Anthropology* 24 (1995): 547–65.

Macridis, Roy C., and Bernaard E. Brown. *Comparative Politics: Notes and Readings*, 6th edition. Chicago: Dorsey, 1986.

Martinez, Mark A., and Gaspar Real Cabello. *Producer Associations and Shared Risk: Issues and Challenges for Pilgrim's Pride in Rural Mexico*, Research Report presented to Pilgrim's Pride of Mexico, 1997.

Maya, Isaac. Former Purina employee and current partner in local producer group with Pilgrim's Pride (interviews, 2000–02).

Palerm, Juan Vicente, and Ignacio Urquiola. "A Binational System of Agricultural Production: The Case of the Mexican Bajio and California." In *Mexico and the United States: Neighbors in Crisis*, edited by Daniel G. Aldrich, Jr. and Lorenzo Meyer. (A U.C. MEX-US Book, *Great Issues of the Day*, No. 6.) San Bernardino, CA: Borgo Press, 1993.

Paré, Luisa. *El proletariado agrícola en México, ¿campesinos sin tierra o proletarios agrícolas?* Mexico City: Siglo Veintiuno Editores, 1988.

Pastor, Robert. *Toward a North American Community: Lessons from the Old World for the New.* Washington, DC: Institute for International Economics, 2001.

Programa Integral para el Desarrollo Rural (PIDER): *Memoria, 1977–1981*. Secretaria de Programación y Presupuesto: Gobierno del Estado, Querétaro, 1982.

Purina Corporation, profile history at www.purina.com/company/History.aspx

Rama, Ruth, and Raul Vigorito. *El complejo de frutas y legumbres en México.* Mexico: Ed. Nueva Visión, 1979.

Real, Gaspar. *El Campo Queretano en Transición.* Center for U.S.-Mexican Studies, University of California, San Diego, 1997.

Sanderson, Steve E. *La transformación de la agricultura mexicana: Estructura internacional y política del cambio rural*. Col. Los noventa: Consejo Nacional para la Cultura y las Artes-Alianza Editorial Mexicana, 1990.

Teissier, Francisco. Director of Production, Pilgrim's Pride de Mexico (interview in Querétaro, Mexico, 1997).

Valenzuela, Juan Samuel, and Arturo Valenzuela. "Modernization and Dependency." In *Comparative Politics: Notes and Readings,* 6th edition, edited by Roy C. Macridis and Bernard E. Bornan. Chicago: Dorsey, 1986.

Urquiola, Ignacio. "Querétaro: Aspectos agrarios en los últimos años de la Colonia." In *Historia de la Cuestión Agraria Mexicana, Estado de Querétaro*, vol. II., edited by Juan Pablos. Mexico: 1989.

Wallerstein, Emmanuel. *El moderno sistema mundial*. Mexico City: Siglo Veintiuno Editores, 1987.

Zúñiga, Pascual. Former employee for both *Purina* and *Sabropollo* (Aguascalientes) who specialized in the construction of hatcheries (interviews, 1999)

Chapter 4

Sweet Protectionism: State Policy and Employment in the Sugar Industries of the NAFTA Countries

Gerardo Otero and Cornelia Butler Flora*

IN THIS CHAPTER, we compare and contrast the intersection of international and State policies and their impact upon employment in the three NAFTA-member countries. We argue that prevailing trade policies have varied according to the relative power exercised by various groups in sugar production: cane or beet growers, industrial processors, workers, secondary industries that use sugar as the main raw material, and final consumers. Of course, each nation's perceived political and geopolitical interests have also played a key role. Primarily, sugar processors and the State's geopolitical and foreign policy interests have shaped U.S. policy. In Mexico, the populist legacy of the revolution (1910–1920) determined that the State would try to cater to a wider diversity of interests, including those of organized labor in sugar mills, organized peasant sugar cane producers, consumers, and processors. In Canada, by contrast, sugar policy has been shaped by a free-trade regime, and only occasionally have beet growers been offered some form of subsidy, but this policy ended in 1996. Thus, the main beneficiaries in Canada have been secondary industries (which use sugar as an input) and, to a lesser extent, consumers. We suggest ways to coordinate NAFTA-region sugar policies to maximize employment benefits.

Sugar is a particularly interesting example of the intersection of the conflicting demands of national policies and the superimposition of international policies. Its production in the Americas was initially driven by colonial powers seeking cheap inputs for capital accumulation, as inexpensive sugar keeps domestic food prices down. States must grapple with a diversity of domestic and foreign interests in the shaping of national policies on sugar production. In the United States, for example, the exemption of sugar from free trade has lasted longer than for any other agricultural product under NAFTA. By comparing the three NAFTA countries' responses to changing international rules for this privileged agricultural product, we can ascertain dimensions of power and labor impacts.

With respect to employment, one might imagine NAFTA negotiations evolving to enhance the complementarities of the three countries involved. Although Mexico employed close to half a million people in the sugar industry

* We wish to thank Oscar Contreras, Rachel Parker, David Orden, David Runsten, and Peter Singelmann for their thoughtful comments and to Rod Ralph for contacts in Agriculture and Agri-Food Canada which afforded useful data. Otero's research has been funded by the Social Sciences and Humanities Research Council of Canada and a grant by El Colegio de México, which he thankfully acknowledges.

before the start of NAFTA, its sugar prices have been, at most, on a par with, but traditionally lower than, those in both the United States and Canada. Sugar-production employment in Canada was lower than 2,000 and in the United States it was below 18,000, and nearly all this employment was seasonal. Yet, employment seems to have been the factor lowest in the priorities of NAFTA negotiators. If there were any concern for employment, it was to "liberate" more workers from Mexico's countryside to make them available for employment in other sectors. Expanding the labor force in this manner would guarantee Mexico's "comparative advantage" of cheap wages to lure foreign investment. As one of the negotiators on the Mexican team told us, "We went in [to the negotiating table] as if we had marbles in our pockets, and some of them had to be traded for others." It seems like the sugar industry "marble" was one of those most susceptible to being sacrificed by the Mexican team. And many of the sugar workers and small farmers thus liberated migrated to the United States for the seasonal work in the sugar harvest. In fact, Mexico has been the world's champion in expelling workers from 2000 to 2005, when two million migrated north. China and India, with populations over ten times larger, expelled 1.95 million and 1.75 million respectively during the same period.

Before plunging into the core of our subject matter, the next section offers some background information on sugar production and trade regimes. We then provide a section on each country with a description of how its respective sugar industry has evolved since the 1960s. The focus of this account is the groups shaping policy and employment issues. The concluding section highlights the main similarities and differences in State policies (as well as their key beneficiaries) and addresses employment and labor issues. We also offer a macroeconomic analysis of exports and imports of sugar-related products in 1994, 2000, and 2005, as the main results of each nation's policies throughout the period. We suggest ways in which the three NAFTA countries could find better ways to coordinate their sugar policies in order to maximize the employment benefits of this industry. But of course, if the public interest is to be served, then maximizing good jobs in sugar production should not be achieved at the cost of highly inflated food processes or environmental damage.

Politics, Sugar Production, and Trade

In general, most agricultural interests in different countries have resisted the current worldwide movement toward neo-liberalism. In fact, agriculture has been a major obstacle to both the Uruguay Round of GATT (1987–93) and NAFTA. These agreements, with their emphasis upon open borders and dependence on market forces, are part of the neo-liberal onslaught that promotes capitalist globalization. NAFTA is an example of such a trend pushed by selected multinational interests (Orden 1994). Since significant aspects of the neo-liberal reform have taken hold in most Western countries, the traditional groups that enjoyed protection by sugar policies have begun to lose the battle. In the end, more agricultural groups in the United States supported NAFTA than opposed it, primarily because they saw it as favoring their short-term interests. As with many neo-liberal policies, free trade is verbalized by authorities of developed countries and urged upon those of developing countries. Yet it is not implemented across the board within the developed countries, particularly in the United States, Japan, and the European Union, where the State is acting with increasing heavy-handedness to re-enforce existing vested interests in some sectors (*The Economist* 2002a; 2002b). In the case of sugar, NAFTA did not affect the highly protected U.S. sugar market for the initial seven years (until 2000), and then protection only gradually declined during the following eight (until 2008).

During the past four decades, sugar sold on the world market has had a residual character: a very small proportion of world sugar production actually enters the world market, as nation-states use control of sugar as an important lever for bilateral and internal relations (Gitli 1994). Most sugar produced worldwide is consumed domestically, often at government-controlled prices, and a large portion of world sugar trade is conducted under bilateral agreements and preferential terms—such as the European Community's Lomé Convention with ex-colonies in Africa, the Caribbean, and the Pacific (1975–2000) and the Cotonou Convention (2000–2020). Slight shifts in total world production or government policy can have a large impact on world prices, which, under the new international trade regimes, increasingly affect protected and supported domestic prices. Governments can block exports in times of scarcity and dump surpluses in times of excess production. Price variability, in turn, increases risk, particularly to producers who do not have mechanisms for smoothing out price variations.

Because sugar can be produced in both tropical climates (sugar cane) and temperate climates (sugar beets), developed and developing countries compete in international trade. Some differences in the nature of the production of sugar cane and beets, however, make each process distinctive. Sugar cane can be grown in monoculture continuously on the same ground, with constant addition of nutrients and pesticides to control the many pests that affect the cane plant. Sugar beets, on the other hand, must be rotated with other crops, as the nematodes that attack the roots are not susceptible to pesticides. Both these regimes of monoculture and chemical use have environmental implications. Both sugar cane and sugar beets quickly lose their sugar content after harvest. Thus, proximate and immediate processing (or cold storage, in the case of sugar beets) is critical to maintain value. Processing equipment is capital intensive, requiring coordinated value chains between growers and processors. Different mechanisms for coordinating those value chains, such as cooperatives, vertically integrated firms, contracts, and spot markets, are present in the three NAFTA countries.

Sugar processing requires enormous capital investments. Growers cannot process sugar individually, except at very inefficient levels (as in *trapiches*, which make *panela* in some developing countries such as Colombia). Thus, there is no market for either sugar beets or sugar cane unless there is a processor who, by the nature of the enterprise, is generally a corporate capitalist or a cooperative. Both sugar beets and sugar cane are relatively "heavy" crops vis-à-vis their value and must be processed prior to sale, even to wholesalers. Cane and beet growers both depend upon processors not simply to add value to their crop, but to sell it at all. Thus, power in the sugar industry is centered in the hands of the extractors and processors. The amount of labor used in sugar processing varies enormously, depending upon the age of the plant. After cane is processed into raw sugar, it is further refined.

In all three North American countries a variety of policies have been applied to either provide a safety net to agricultural producers, industrial processors and/or industrial workers, or to provide basic food to urban populations at subsidized prices. These sets of policies are now under assault by increasing integration into the international free-trade regime and the application of neoliberal rules that are geared to maximize the free flow of capital, goods, and services.

NAFTA's Provisions on Sugar Trade

The tremendous resistance placed by the sugar lobby in the United States, before the vote in the U.S. Congress on November 17, 1993, resulted in a last-minute executive negotiation that substantially modified the original sugar agreement. Thus, the sugar provision is more overtly protective of U.S. interests than those of other agricultural products. Under the NAFTA negotiation, Mexico's U.S. import quota would increase from 7,250 to 25,000 tons during the first six years (1994–2000), and to 250,000 tons in years 7–14 (2001–08). Thereafter, all barriers to trade between the two countries will be eliminated, including the quota system for domestic and international purchase of sugar. In the original formulation, Mexico was to be able to export any surpluses of sugar to the United States, duty-free, as long as it was able to cover its domestic demand. Beginning in 2001, Mexico would have been able to export duty-free to the United States the full extent of its projected surplus for that year, under either of two conditions: " . . . if 1) Mexico has been a net surplus producer for any two consecutive marketing years (including years 1–6 of the agreement), or if 2) Mexico has been a net surplus producer during the previous year and is projected to be a net surplus producer that year" (Buzzanell and Lord 1993, 12). Mexico's exports to the United States would be purchased at the U.S. preferential price, if that price preference were still in place.

The "side agreement," however, contained a formula to calculate Mexico's surplus which links the measurement of Mexico's self-sufficiency in sugar to its use of high-fructose corn syrup: it stipulates that high-fructose corn syrup (HFCS) must be included on the *consumption side only*. With this formula, Mexican sugar production would have to exceed consumption of both sugar and HFCS if Mexico is to be considered a net surplus producer, even if part of the HFCS is produced within Mexico (USDA-Economic Research Service 2000, 48). In addition, the rules of origin were redefined to prevent Mexico from importing sugar cane—possibly from Cuba—refining it, and then exporting it to the United States. At the time of the agreement, HFCS was imported from the United States at a price competitive with Mexico's domestic sugar prices. This made it more difficult for Mexico to be considered a net surplus producer and thus eligible to export more to the United States at its protected prices. Mexico's access to the U.S. sugar market was as follows: 7,258 tons duty free until 2000, even if it was not a net surplus producer; then, for the amount of its surplus as measured by the formula, up to 250,000 tons duty free from 2000 to 2007. The minimum duty-free access would remain at 7,258 through 2007, regardless of whether Mexico produced a surplus or not (USDA-Economic Research Service 2000, 48).

As of the 2008 complete border opening for sugar in NAFTA countries, Mexico stands to lose up to 1.4 tons of sugar used by the soft drinks industry, as it could replace most of its sugar with HFCS from the United States, produced with subsidized corn. Another irony that has resulted from this side agreement, signed only by the trade representatives of Mexico and the United States, is that the United States has ended up exporting more refined sugar to Mexico than the other way around. This result is due to a reciprocal allowance in NAFTA to export refined sugar to either country made from raw sugar produced in the other country. Because of the government's strategy to force the recently privatized mill owners to modernize, Mexico became largely self-sufficient in raw sugar. Nevertheless, Mexico imported 219,000 tons of refined sugar from the United States in 1991 and 97,000 tons in 1992. The figures dropped to 27,347 tons in 1996 and to 27,882 tons in 1997 (USDA-Economic Research Service 2000, 49).

With NAFTA, Mexico imposed import barriers similar to those of the United States. Yet prices of refined sugar in Mexico have been lower than those in the United States because of excess production and lower distribution and retailing costs. Up until 2000, Mexico maintained a high tariff rate of 48.586 cents per kilogram. Mexico was thus protected against world market sugar imports under NAFTA until year six. By Fiscal Year 2000, Mexico was required to have in place a tariff-rate quota (TRQ) system with rates applied to third countries at the same levels as those maintained by the United States. Thus Mexico, like the United States, is able to isolate its sugar industry from world market prices. In contrast, Canada's free-trade approach—Canada has usually had the lowest wholesale sugar prices in the region—has attracted several large confectionary processors from the United States to set up shop there. One example is Wrigley, the world's largest makers of chewing gum, which set up another plant in Canada in 2003. NAFTA instigated a declining high-tier tariff schedule for sugar imported from Mexico beginning in FY 2000. Instead of paying the former duty of just under 17 cents a pound, the raw sugar tariff is 12.09 cents a pound and the refined sugar tariff is 12.81 cents a pound. The raw sugar tariff drops about 1.5 cents each year, while the refined sugar tariff drops about 1.6 cents a year. Both rates will reach zero in FY 2008.

In January 1997, Mexico's National Chamber of Sugar and Alcohol Industries, the association of Mexico's sugar producers, charged that U.S. corn wet millers were exporting HFCS to Mexico at less than fair value. Mexico's trade ministry, SECOFI, initiated an anti-dumping investigation in February and imposed temporary (then permanent) tariffs on two (then three) grades of HFCS. In February 1998, the U.S. Corn Refiners' Association asked for a review of Mexico's anti-dumping actions under Chapter 19 of NAFTA. The U.S. Trade Representative (USTR) announced its intention on May 8, 1998, to invoke a WTO dispute proceeding to challenge Mexico's action. By January 27, 2000, the WTO ruled in favor of the United States. The following year, the Mexican Congress issued a law to tax industrial users of HFCS instead of sugar, thus avoiding any direct tariff or subsidy that would contravene NAFTA or WTO rules. President Fox unilaterally withdrew this tax for a few months, but Congress sent the issue to be resolved by the National Supreme Court of Justice (SCJN). In July of 2002, the SCJN ruled in favor of Congress, specifying that President Fox had acted unconstitutionally. The U.S. Trade Office did not say whether it would attempt to contest the tax in a NAFTA or WTO court.

Under the Canada-United States Free Trade Agreement (FTA), which went into effect in 1989, cane sugar was not treated as a product of Canada, given its strict rules of origin. A small concession in the FTA was that food products that contained ten percent or less of sugar from cane (by dry weight) could enter the United States duty free. On October 1, 1997, a new sugar agreement between Canada and the United States went into effect (BeeNews 1998). This bilateral agreement, which can be unilaterally terminated on six-months' notice, guarantees Canada access to the United States market for a limited quantity of refined sugar (10,300 tons) and sugar-containing products (59,250 tons). Canada can also compete on the remaining portion of the refined-sugar global tariff-rate quota (TRQ) of about 7,500 tons (BeeNews 1998). Under the NAFTA rules of origin, products shipped under Canada's allocation of these TRQs must be manufactured from Canadian sugar beets (Flores 1998, 3).

The Sugar Barons and U.S. Policy

Sugar production in the United States increased to record levels at the turn of the century (USDA-Economic Research Service 2000) largely due to the continued support from government policy. As we will show, the main beneficiaries since the 1960s have been "friendly" foreign countries and the U.S. sugar processors and producers of high-fructose corn syrup (HFCS). The latter have the benefit of bountiful harvests of subsidized corn. The latitude of the United States allows it to produce sugar cane in southern states and Hawaii, and sugar beets in northwestern and north central states, and California. Raw-sugar production from sugar cane has steadily increased since U.S. sugar production allotments were removed. Sugar beets are grown in many parts of the United States, including the following states: California, Colorado, Idaho, Michigan, Minnesota, Montana, Nebraska, North Dakota, Oregon, Washington, and Wyoming. Nominal production may also occur in New Mexico, Ohio, and Texas (Coalition for Sugar Reform 1999a). Sugar beets were important in Kansas in the 1970s, but then rapidly declined.

Up until the Cuban revolution of 1959, sugar plantations in Cuba were major suppliers for U.S. sugar consumption. Some were Cuban-owned while many were owned by U.S.-based companies, particularly sugar refiners. Cuban-grown sugar was preferentially imported and priced in the U.S. market, and U.S. growers were limited in the amount of sugar they could grow. With the suspension of the Cuban sugar quota in 1960, sugar allotments were taken off U.S. sugar producers, and only reimposed on July 1, 1993, and removed again in 1996 by the Federal Agriculture Improvement and Reform Act (Public Law 104–127), commonly referred to as "Freedom to Farm." Previous USDA authority from legislation to implement domestic sugar-marketing allotments was suspended by that legislation (Young and Wescott 2000). The highly protected price for U.S. sugar, as intended, expanded domestic sugar production between 1930 and 2000. That above-world-market price encouraged the production of corn sweeteners at the end of the 1970s. By the 1990s, HCFS had replaced sugar in a large number of products, soft drinks in particular, and outstripped sugar production by 1995 (Lord 1997).

U.S. imports of sugar were greatly reduced during the 1980s from 5 million metric tons to about 1.4 million metric tons by the late 1990s (USDA-Foreign Agricultural Service 2002). International production quotas were taken over by new or expanded domestic producers. The decline in sugar imports has hit heavily at countries which once counted on the United States as a preferentially priced market, particularly sugar-dependent countries in the Caribbean basin (Messina and Seale 1993, 177).

The major conflicts in the United States, where the State has provided a battleground through legislation and the courts, were between growers and sugar refiners. Tariffs on raw sugar imports have had very different impacts on sugar cane and sugar beet growers compared to sugar refiners. Refiners want to import raw sugar as cheaply as possible, while such imports provide competition for U.S. growers, who have thus resisted this practice.

The Sugar Trust, which dominated sugar production on the east coast of the United States at the turn of the twentieth century, focused on refining sugar and was dependent upon imports of raw sugar, particularly from Cuba and Puerto Rico (Eichner 1969). In contrast, sugar production on the West Coast of the United States was vertically integrated, including sugar cane production in Hawaii and sugar-beet production in the western states. State and federal antitrust legislation—and the attractive loopholes for eastern sugar interests—had the most impact on eastern sugar development, while the tariff was most important in the development of the western sugar industry (Roy 1995).

Tariffs are the traditional policy tool used by the U.S. government to protect sugar interests. Early exemptions from tariffs encouraged sugar production in U.S. protectorates such as Cuba, Puerto Rico, the Philippines, and Hawaii. In 1876, the United States signed a reciprocity agreement with the Kingdom of Hawaii, which permitted sugar to be imported duty free. The Spanish-American War (1898) added Cuba, the Philippines, and Puerto Rico—all sugar producers—to the American emporium. High tariffs imposed on sugar that did not come under unilateral quota agreements kept the cost of imported sugar well above the domestic price of around 26 cents per pound.

In the 1930s, sugar policy was primarily an income strategy for farmers as a part of general farm legislation. In the Cold War period of 1945 to 1989, tariffs were a tool of foreign policy, used to reward friendly countries by allowing them to export tariff-free, and thus enjoy the high prices received by domestic producers. Confectioners and other users of sugar consistently lobbied to have the tariffs reduced, which would have lowered the costs of producing soft drinks, candy, and other consumer products containing sugar. Well-organized agricultural lobbies, particularly from the powerful southern states, systematically resisted those pressures.

The provisions of the Sugar Acts gave the United States great international power. Countries defined as U.S. allies have been able to gain sugar quotas and export to the United States at its protected internal-market price. Those countries that have displeased the U.S. government in any of its policies were stripped of their sugar quota, which was then given to nations that better supported U.S. foreign-policy objectives. Cuba, greatly favored under early sugar quotas, lost all access to the U.S. market with the revolution of 1959. The United States redistributed Cuba's quota to governments, often dictatorships, who would stand firm against communism. The threat of losing sugar-related jobs and markets, combined with physical force, served to keep such rulers as Trujillo (the Dominican Republic) and Marcos (the Philippines) in power in the 1960s and into the 1980s. Sugar import quotas were established on the basis of historic U.S. imports. Thus there are countries which are no longer self-sufficient in sugar, such as Taiwan, and that buy sugar on the world market to sell to the United States under their tariff-exempt price, thus earning up to five times their initial investment in sugar from other countries.

The Food Security Act of 1985 mandated a price-support program for domestically produced sugar cane and sugar beets at not less than 18 cents a pound, which is over three times the world market price. The Dole Amendment to the 1985 farm bill, however, stipulated that the sugar program must be conducted at no cost to the U.S. Treasury. Commodity Credit Corporation forfeiture for unsold sugar against which a government loan had been secured, was not permitted, as is the case with such commodities as corn, wheat, cotton, and others. The same blockage to the federal treasury is in place for tobacco. Only these two commodity crops have federally determined supply controls. With the 1996 farm bill, the President is empowered to regulate commodity imports of only sugar and tobacco when such imports interfere with sugar or tobacco price support or stabilization programs of the United States. The cost of high prices to sugar producers is thus shifted from the federal government to consumers. The 2002 Farm Bill maintained the price-support loan program (18 cents a pound for raw cane sugar and 22.9 cents a pound for refined sugar) and the tariff-rate quota import system. It reinstituted flexible marketing allotments to control supply. Strong import controls are in place.

Estimates of the annual cost to domestic consumers of the U.S. sugar program ranged from $1.0 billion to $2.7 billion in the early 1990s (Messina and Seale 1993, 173). A 1998 report in *Time* magazine put this cost to Americans at midpoint—at least $1.4 billion in the form of higher prices for candy, soda, and other sweets. A GAO (U.S. Congress General Accounting Office) study, moreover, has estimated that nearly half the subsidy goes to large producers like the Fanjuls (*Time* 1998, 81). Alfonso and José Fanjul are two of the largest Cuban-American sugar industrialists, called "Subsidy Barons" by *Time* magazine because they receive State supports in the millions of dollars. According to a 2001 study by agricultural economists, if the sugar program were eliminated, with full passage of benefits to consumers, these would amount to $1.96 billion in 1998, with an additional benefit of $63 million to sugar cane refiners—who would have access to cheaper, imported raw cane (Beghin et al. 2001, 11). (All dollar figures in this chapter are given in U.S. dollars unless otherwise designated.)

The structure of the U.S. sugar industry was locked into place in July of 1993, when sugar marketing allotments were instituted. In that year, the United States reached the "trigger point", whereby its sugar needs were met by importing only 1.25 million tons of sugar. Domestic sugar production was capped and allocations given to current sugar processors based on historic patterns of production. (As mentioned, these domestic quotas were removed in 1996 however.) In 2002, with the reintroduction of sugar-market allotments, 45.65% are for raw cane sugar, and 54.35% for refined beat sugar.

The 1996 Farm Bill continued to support sugar prices through loans offered to sugar processors (not producers) and added the option of "non-recourse loans". Non-recourse loans allow the sugar processor to take the amount of the loan if market price does not reach the loan price, and forfeit the crop to the Commodity Credit Corporation (CCC). The CCC is a federally owned-and-operated corporation within the USDA, created to stabilize, support, and protect agricultural prices and farm income through loans, purchases, payments, and other operations. Unlike other non-recourse loans, which go directly to the producer (often the landowner), processors must pay a 1-cent fee on each pound of raw cane sugar and 1.07 cents on each pound of refined beet sugar forfeited to the CCC under the loan program. Those forfeiture penalties were removed in 2002. Thus, the non-recourse loan provides an important safety net to sugar processors against recent international trade agreements. Sugar processors, however, paid a marketing assessment, which is a fee per unit of domestic production sold in order to share the program costs with the government. That marketing assessment was increased by 25% in the 1996 Farm Bill, and was eliminated in the 2002 Farm Bill.

Field Labor in the United States

Both cane and beet sugar in the United States have been labor intensive, although there is increasing mechanization in the harvest and planting sugar cane, and in the thinning process of sugar beets. In a few parts of Louisiana and most of Florida, sugarcane is harvested by hand due to the fragile composition of the soil, which will not support large harvesting machinery, such as the combines used in Texas or the bulldozers and cranes used in Hawaii. Cane cutting is dirty, hot, and dangerous work. It is also relatively skilled work, as the ability to use a machete effectively takes time to develop. Almost all of the labor used to cut sugar cane is brought into the United States under special agreement with the Immigration and Naturalization Service, using specific laws passed for that purpose. Sugar growers have provided powerful pressure, in the face of Congressional investigation, to maintain an immigrant labor stream (Wilkinson 1989a). Generally, a contractor imports labor. Either the contractor or the plantation owner must provide housing for the workers, who then must leave the country when their contract is complete or their work is terminated. Workers are charged for a bewildering number of goods and services provided by their contractors and employers, often reducing their paychecks to nearly nothing.

Initially Puerto Rico, then Jamaica, and finally Haiti provided the bulk of the cane cutters for the United States. It is almost impossible to get U.S. citizens—who have other options for employment or at least access to public assistance—to cut cane under current wage rates and working conditions. Furthermore, the relatively low cost of this imported labor keeps growers from investing in mechanization or even urging research into it (Hayami and Ruttan 1985). Exposés of their working conditions reveal the exploitative nature of these labor relations (Wilkinson 1989a; 1989b).

After the conditions under which cane workers lived were investigated in the 1990s—motivated in part by the high rate of AIDS in sugar-worker towns—cane harvests have been largely mechanized in Florida. This has resulted in fewer, better jobs. Local African-Americans now operate the heavy equipment used in the harvest.

An active labor movement involving sugar workers exists in Hawaii, where sugarcane may be harvested almost all year long, with a very high yield per acre. Although the workers in sugar are still often immigrants (for example, Philippine women are the employees of choice for cane planting), their salaries are higher than those of cane workers on the mainland. Thus, in response to the relatively high wages and favorable working conditions of labor in Hawaii, a radical mechanization has occurred, as cane is bulldozed, then lifted by cranes to be taken to the sugar mills in large tractor-drawn wagons. This procedure decreases the sugar content of the cane, but losses are apparently offset by decreased labor costs. The high initial costs of the machinery were underwritten by generous investment tax credits for agriculture in the 1970s, furthering the motivation to reduce field-labor inputs.

Sugar-Mill Labor in the United States

Investment tax credits during the 1980s greatly encouraged the substitution of capital for labor in U.S. sugar cane processing mills, which became extremely capital intensive. In the late 1980s, the Commerce Department estimated that it cost $76,000 to save one job in the sugar industry. The high price of U.S. sugar has allowed producers to mechanize their field and factory operations, and sharply reduce their labor needs.

Sugar Production and Populism in Mexico

From its independence to the 1980s, Mexico was self-sufficient in sugar production, with some exportable surpluses. In the 1980s, sugar mills failed to modernize their plants and Mexico became a net sugar importer (Buzzanell and Lord 1993, 2). From the late 1970s, the State launched a nationalization policy of failing sugar mills in order to save jobs. By 1980, 54 out of 64 mills in Mexico were owned and operated by the State. Official Mexican government policies tried to satisfy a number of constituencies: sugar mill workers, whose union belongs to the *Partido Revolucionario Institucional* (Institutional Revolutionary Party, or PRI), which ruled political life at most levels from 1929 to 2000; sugar cane growers, whose two organizations also belong to the PRI; secondary industries for whom sugar is an important raw material (particularly the soft-drink and sweet-bread industries); and final sugar consumers, who have become accustomed to subsidized sugar prices.

With the onset of the debt crisis in Mexico in 1982, the State's financial ability to satisfy all these groups collapsed, as did its ability to efficiently operate the sugar mills. By the 1990s, sugar consumption increased both in absolute and per capita terms as a result of increased population growth, rising income levels, and attractive retail pricing. In the late 1990s, the growth of domestic consumption and production of sugar has been steady, and Mexico is once again capable of supplying its domestic market and having an exportable surplus. In the fiscal year 1997–98, Mexican consumption was 4,240,000 metric tons, and production in the same year set a record of 5,490,000 metric tons (Miranda and Ortiz 1999).

The key policy factor leading to the restructuring of production, in the fields and sugar factories, was the 1991 Sugar Decree (*Decreto Cañero*). New payment rules were set out in this decree, which led to increased milling efficiency and harvesting methods. It forced sugar mills to achieve a minimum level of efficiency in extracting sucrose (the technical name for sugar) from sugar cane by 1994. Sugar cane growers' payments are now based on cane sucrose content rather than simply on weight. Thus, quality both in the field and in the factory is compensated. If sugar mills were not able to extract the minimum sucrose content specified in the Sugar Decree, they would still have to pay cane growers according to sucrose content in their cane. In other words, the industrialist is responsible for extracting a reasonable amount of sugar from the cane, so as not to penalize growers for industrial inefficiency.

The growth in Mexican sugar production was, in part, fueled by a combination of increased sugar cane area harvested and recently instituted technological and producer-incentive measures, but the main factor for this growth has been the neo-liberal policies introduced in preparation for NAFTA. New technologies have increased the sugar recovery rates from 9.08% in 1992 to 10.77% by 1997. The effective milling season has been expanded from 130 to 175 days. This has led to a sharp competitive disadvantage for sugar mills which have not made the investments necessary to become more efficient. In the 1994 marketing year, Mexico produced only 3.8 million MTRV (metric tons, raw value) of sugar, while between 2000-2001 and 2004-2005 it averaged nearly 5.5 million MTRV (Haley and Ali 2007), including beginning stocks. By 2002–2003, the estimated production figure reached 6.238 million tons (USDA-Foreign Agricultural Service 2002, 13).

While U.S. policy has forced consumers to subsidize the sugar industry through high prices (the so-called "sugar tax"), the Mexican State has historically done the opposite. It has continuously subsidized consumption by maintaining artificially low sugar prices, at least in relation to production costs. As a result, sugar is very important in the Mexican diet. It is estimated that sugar provides 17 percent of caloric intake for Mexicans (García Chavez 1992; Otero 1992).

Mexico maintains import policies that support domestic sugar prices and isolates its sugar industry from the world market. In 2000, the domestic sugar price in Mexico was about twice as high as the international free-market price. The Mexican government also enforces marketing quotas. After a domestic consumption level has been estimated, the Mexican government and the sugar industry agree on marketing quotas to be assigned to all individual sugar factories in the nation. Production above the amount allowed into the domestic market must be exported or held in stocks (USDA-Economic Research Service 2000).

The major shifts in ownership of sugar cane land and sugar processing between private and public ownership were triggered by direct government intervention (Singelmann and Otero 1995; Chollett 1995). In contrast to the previous ownership pattern of sugar mills, which was centered on individual capitalists and government management, during the 1990s, mills were owned by nine large corporate groups. Given the sugar overproduction they generated, though, 27 mills were so heavily indebted with cane growers and other creditors that the government once again nationalized them in September of 2001 (SourceMex 2001).

The sugar industry in modern Mexico has been highly regulated and designated of national interest by a series of decrees. Price controls for sugar have been the norm since 1940, but the most interventionist policies began in 1970 with the formation of a series of government agencies to regulate the industry. In 1983, *Azúcar, S.A.*, was founded as a State enterprise to set prices, control the marketing of sugar, and generally plan national sugar production (Singelmann 1993).

Part of the dilemma for the Mexican State stemmed from trying to be on good terms with a multiplicity of social actors with divergent interests who participate in the sugar industry. According to Peter Singelmann (1993), Mexican State policy has moved along three main polarities, depending on which social group carried the most weight: free market or protectionism in foreign trade, sink-or-swim *versus* subsidies with regard to domestic producers, and domestic free market or State regulation with regard to consumer prices.

By the mid-1980s, cane growers were facing very unfavorable terms of trade with respect to industrial products (García Chavez 1992). Increasing costs and declining relative crop prices were squeezing them. At the same time, industrial processing was managed by political criteria and suffered from much corruption. The large number of mills was causing a substantial drainage of public funds. Sugar imports increased, as production did not keep pace with increased consumption. Thus, in a time of massive foreign debt, unsustainable public deficits, and a stagnant economy, re-privatizing the sugar industry became unavoidable. It was already written into the 1986 International Monetary Fund accord for Mexico's structural adjustment (Singelmann 1993).

Under the pressures of NAFTA, the WTO, and growing neo-liberal economic-policy emphasis, the Mexican government defined a new position with respect to the polarities posited by Singelmann. State interventionism was to be phased out of sugar policy. At least initially, the State chose free trade over protectionism in international trade, a sink or swim approach rather than subsidies with regard to domestic processors, and a free-market policy instead of regulation to determine domestic prices. A futures market, inaugurated on March 14, 1994, was established to provide a mechanism for risk management (or speculation). Azúcar, S.A. was dismantled in 1992, and private companies were allowed to buy and sell sugar on their own (including imports) between 1990–1992, leaving the industry without a regulated market or coordination of production and distribution.

Thus, the political context for the operation of NAFTA was one of withdrawal of the State from ownership of the means of sugar production. However, a government-controlled development bank for the sugar industry, *Financiera Nacional Azucarera SA* (FINASA) was estimated to hold over $1.3 billion of the Mexican sugar industry's debt by 1999. FINASA has provided extensive restructuring assistance to troubled sugar companies with high debt loads (Haley and Suárez 1999). After the expropriation of 27 mills in 2001, a new government management organization for these mills was formed, and its goal was to re-privatize the mills once their finances were back in shape. As well, a series of short- and long-term measures were planned to help the sugar industry. These included the granting of short-term loans to address the liquidity crisis of sugar mills, and the formation of an export cooperative, which would be 57% private and 43% government. This cooperative was the sole entity authorized to export approximately 650,000 million tons of sugar for the 2001–02 harvest (Flores 2002, 1). By the 2004–05 harvest, the new entity administering the remaining 23 nationalized sugar mills, *Fondo de Empresas Expropiadas del Sector Azucarero* (FEESA), managed a new sugar production record in 13 of the mills. The national harvest also broke the previous record established in 1997–98, with 5.65 million tons. The new record was attributed in large part to favorable rains (SAGARPA, 2005). In 2006, however, the Supreme Court reversed the expropriation and the government had not been able to recover its investment in the nationalized mills of 6,500 million pesos, or about $6 billion. According to Mexico City's newspaper, *Reforma*, this may have been the worst business investment of the Fox administration (*Reforma* 2006, 7F).

Field Labor in Mexico

Employment in the sugar industry was estimated at 420,085 workers in all the different aspects of cane production and processing as of 1998 (Lozano Gómez 1998, 9: see Table 1). Rather than decreasing, the number of sugar cane growers has actually increased in the past fifteen years, from about 130,000 in the mid-1980s (Otero 1991) to 143,763 in 1998 (Table 1). This phenomenon has to do with the fact that cane growers have access to Mexico's public health insurance, the *Instituto Mexicano del Seguro Social* (Mexican Institute for Social Insurance, or IMSS). Even though neo-liberal reforms have included the requirement that, in order to be eligible for IMSS membership, a cane grower must farm at least three hectares, it is very common to find children of older growers who get married and inherit one or two hectares (sometimes even less than one hectare), and still become members of IMSS. Its authorities have never attempted to enforce the rules of eligibility, for they know that it would cause a major social upheaval among cane growers, one of the best organized groups of rural producers (Otero 1998).

Cane cutters are paid by the kilogram. They perform the hardest part of the labor process and command the lowest wages in the industry. Day laborers manage to make the equivalent of one to two minimum wages in a day's work, which can hardly sustain the worker himself, let alone his family (almost all cane cutters are male workers). In the past, much cane cutting was left to migrant workers from rural areas that were more depressed than the sugar regions. In recent years, however, there has been an increasing surplus population within sugar-growing towns available for cane cutting. The proportion of migrant cane cutters has been reduced from about 30% of all cane cutters in the early 1970s to less than 10% in the 1990s. With the exception of a few that work for large sugar cane growers, who are affiliated to the CTM, a PRI-affiliated union, cane cutters are not unionized (Paré, Juárez, and Salazar 1987).

Sugar Mill Workers in Mexico

In contrast to cane cutters, the approximately 35,000 unionized workers in the sugar mills were relatively well protected until the privatization that began in the late 1980s. This is one of nine industries in Mexico whose industrial relations have been regulated through industry-wide contracts. These contracts were meant to unify working conditions in the country and were held in great esteem between the 1930s and 1970s, when there was a clear alliance between the official workers' organizations and the State. Thus, all sugar mill workers have been affiliated with the CTM (Workers Confederation of Mexico), or the CROM (Regional Confederation of Mexican Workers), both affiliates of the formerly ruling PRI. After the 2001 nationalization of 27 mills, the government intended to review the industry-wide contract agreement with sugar-mill workers. By 2007, the industry-wide contract had continued to be ratified on an annual basis as a collective agreement for all workers in the sugar and alcohol industries, as published in Mexico's *Diario Oficial,* where all new federal legislation is published by the government, on March 12.

According to the Mexican Ministry of Labor, most sugar mills had an average of 1.5 non-unionized workers for each 5 unionized in 1992 (Becerril 1993). An extreme case was a mill in the state of Veracruz, which reported 477 unionized workers and 232 non-unionized workers (*empleados de confianza,* or white-collar workers)—a ratio of one non-unionized worker for every two union workers. As of 1992, unionized workers were 78% of the labor force and received only 39% of the wages paid by the mills. In contrast, the non-unionized workers (clerical and managerial) were only 22% of the labor force and received 61% of the wages paid (Becerril 1993, 15). During the Vicente Fox (2000–06) administration, however, the industry's situation changed dramatically. With over 20 sugar mills directly managed by FEESA, the industry's operation was substantially streamlined, experiencing a sharp decline in employment to a mere 30 percent of what

Table 1
Employment in Mexico's Sugar Industry, 1998-2006

Activity	1998	2006
Cane Growers	143,763	77,575
Harvesters	81.076	n.a.
Day Laborers (cane cutters)	112,464	32,908
Transporters	29,444	6,504
Unionized Mill Workers	35,899	10,195
Non-Unionized Mill Workers	7,504	2,293
Retired Workers	9,935	n.a.
TOTAL	**420,085**	**129,476**
Economic Dependents	2,060,685	634,432
GRAND TOTAL	**2,480,770**	**763,908**

Source: for 1998: Lozano Gómez, Adriana. 1998. "Diez ingenios del país cerrarían por la fructosa." El Cañero Mexicano 3 (July): 9. For 2006: SAGARPA (2006) Sembrando soluciones. Año 1, núm. 28. Available at: http://www.sagarpa.gob.mx/cgcs/sembrando/2006/28-2006.pdf (accessed: 28/03/2008).

it was in 1998 (see Table 1 below).

Sugar Production and Free Trade in Canada

The Canadian sugar industry offers a sharp contrast to the way sugar industries developed in both Mexico and the United States. In Canada, the sugar industry developed since the mid-nineteenth century under a basically free-trade regime, driven by the differential in transportation costs between importing refined sugar versus importing it raw and then refining it. The cost difference lies in the fact that raw sugar can be imported in bulk, whereas importing refined sugar requires packaging and its transportation becomes more costly. From that time, State policy applied preferential rates to raw sugar, which further enabled the development of cane refining in Canada (Food Bureau 1999, 1). Law requires refinement of raw sugar—once imported—if it is to be sold in Canada.

The primarily free-trade regime in the sugar industry makes it exceptional also in the context of Canadian agricultural policy. In fact, State policy has involved a series of protective measures for agricultural producers. Policy mechanisms in Canada have been geared toward the stabilization of producer prices and incomes; the setting up of boards for marketing agricultural commodities; and the western grain-handling and transportation system which was subsidized by the federal government until recently. If the rule in Canadian agricultural policy has been protectionism of some kind (Skogstad 1987), then the sugar industry is actually an exception to this rule.

Initially the main locations for cane sugar refineries were ports, given the costs of transportation. Thus, several refineries were established in Vancouver, Quebec, and Ontario. Sugar from Canadian-grown beets became economically viable only in locations that were too distant from port cities with cane-sugar refineries. Beet refineries developed at some point in Alberta, Ontario, Quebec, and Manitoba. By 1999, however, only the Alberta plant remained in operation. The beet-sugar refineries had to face increasing cost competition from cane sugar, high-fructose corn syrup, and non-caloric sweeteners—although Canadian demand for sugar has remained virtually stagnant for three decades. In fact, total production of refined sugar was 1,154,310 tons in 1977 and remained at a very similar level twenty years later at 1,146,351 tons. During the 1990s, the most significant decline was experienced in beet-sugar refining. Sugar-beet acreage dropped from 56,733 in 1996 to 33,124 in 1997, after the closing of the Manitoba plant (Food Bureau 1999, 2). By 1999, however, the Taber, Alberta beet-sugar refinery had extended its operation, and acreage increased to 44,378 (Alberta Sugar Beet Growers Association 2000). Of Canadian sugar production for the domestic market, 18% is destined for the retail market for direct consumption and 82% goes to industrial users.

The Canadian industry has been facing continued competition from cheap U.S. high-fructose corn syrup, non-caloric sweeteners, and sugar imports, which are re-exported at a price much lower than that of the U.S. domestic price, as a result of a U.S. program established in 1983 (Coalition for Sugar Reform 1999b). Thus, the Canadian industry has always been under pressure to rationalize and consolidate. Employment has suffered in this process, having dropped from 2,803 jobs in 1976 to 1,540 jobs in 1996.

The consolidation process has resulted in the shake-up of several mills and companies. There were five companies operating seven plants across Canada in 1981, including two beet processors. By 1999, the number had been reduced to three companies operating only four raw-sugar refiners and one beet processor. As a result of rationalization, productivity—measured by value added per paid hour—increased by 20% between 1990 and 1997 (Food Bureau 1999, 3). Furthermore, the consolidation among several raw cane-sugar refiners, along with the modernization of the production process, account for the reduction of 77% of the labor force in the industry as a whole since 1988. Just in the period from 1990 to 1997, value-added per paid hour of labor increased by 20% (Food Bureau 1999, 3). Employment in both the cane-sugar and sugar-beet refining industries is declining due to increased capital investments and industry consolidation.

Most likely due to location and transportation-cost factors, Canada and the United States have been exporting sugar to each other over the past two decades at varying levels. Some prairie provinces produce beets for processing in U.S. plants. Yet, the value-added for Canadian sugar has remained stable at around 35% per year (Food Bureau 1999, 4).

Since confederation in the 19th century, the main goal of the Canadian government with respect to sugar has been to establish the conditions for self-sufficiency from domestic production, even if this involves the importation of raw sugar. According to University of Toronto political scientist Grace Skogstad (1987), the material basis for the conflict of interests that has shaped Canadian agricultural policy can be of two types: 1) conflicting interests between producers who want to export versus those who prefer to import—each will be interested in different types of tariff policies; and 2) those producing raw materials for another industry will be interested in commanding high prices for their goods, whereas the purchaser(s) will be interested in lower prices or in being able to import cheaper raw materials from abroad.

From this framework, the interests of raw-sugar processors have prevailed from the outset. Perhaps this accounts for the reason that sugar based on beets has always represented a small fraction of the total sugar supply in Canada. Beet growers and processors never had substantial State support to compete successfully with raw-sugar processors. During most of the past four decades, the share of beet sugar in Canada was around 10–15%. After NAFTA and the WTO, this share declined even further to about 8% by 1999, after one of the last two processing plants was closed down.

In the past, the Canadian government supported sugar-beet farming operations through direct payments to producers on a per-ton basis. Sugar beets, like many other agricultural products, have been part of a "tripartite price stabilization program" which shares the costs of subsidies equally among the federal government of Canada (25%), participating provincial governments (25%), and producers (50%) (Early and Westfall 1996). This cost-sharing among governments and producers' associations was a prevailing disposition of the Canadian sugar policy. New agricultural strategies put into place by the Conservative government in the late 1980s, however, resulted in phasing out such subsidies (Wilson 1990).

Considered in the context of overall Canadian agricultural production, sugar beets are a rather insignificant horticultural crop. Horticultural production makes up a mere 9.4% of Canadian agricultural production. But floriculture and vegetables take the lion's share of this percentage. They generated Cdn$800 million in 1996, whereas sugar beets accounted for only Cdn$40.6 million in the same year (Canadian Federation of Agriculture 1998, 8). Overall, sugar from beets makes up a very small proportion of agricultural production in Canada. Therefore, the most important State policy regards the free-trade regime prevalent in the importation of raw sugar for its refinement in Canada.

The largely free-trade regime in sugar has resulted in high-quality and low-priced refined sugar, representing an advantage to both consumers and food processors. In cases where "dumping" or other unfair trade practices are suspected, Canadian sugar refiners have the recourse to refer them to the Canadian International Trade Tribunal (CITT). The CITT may recommend the imposition of protective tariffs. Anti-dumping and countervailing duties have been imposed since 1995 on a number of sugar suppliers, including some from the United States and the European Union (Food Bureau 1999).

The government does get involved in health and quality standards, crop insurance and credit, research and information distribution, stabilization programs, and other areas (Loyns 1978, 18), which affect primarily sugar-beet producers. Even if this crop is not specifically targeted, beet growers can apply for support through the stabilization programs. Tighter forms of protectionism, such as tariffs, duties, and so forth are missing. In times of crisis, when market prices go down, the government compensates growers for the deficiency. Such compensation has been measured by the average prices in the previous ten years, with the government making up the difference to 90% of such average at one point, and to 80% in the more recent neo-liberal past, starting in the late 1980s. Only in the period between 1984 and 1986 did Canada feel the need to revise its sugar policy (Earley and Westfall 1996, 51), and this was in the context of one of the worst farm crises in North America since the Great Depression (Wilson 1990).

In sum, Canadian free-trade policy in sugar has worked well in meeting the goal of supplying the domestic market with internal production, even while importing raw sugar. The main beneficiaries have been sugar refiners and industrial sugar processors, but consumers have also benefited from lower prices in sugar-content foods. Beet farmers have never constituted a very large group and were among the least favored farmer groups in Canadian policy, receiving support only during exceptional circumstances. Employment is very low, at approximately 1,500 workers.

Conclusions: State Policy, Sugar Trade, and Employment

This paper has explored in detail three contrasting forms of State intervention and employment issues with regard to the sugar industries in the United States, Mexico, and Canada. While processors have been the group with the greatest political influence in the United States, Mexican policy has favored employment in both the cane fields and the industrial mills, and has tried to keep sugar prices low for consumers. Canadian policy has focused primarily on providing the lowest possible prices to industrial processors, who use sugar as a raw material, and to consumers, even if sugar beet growers have occasionally enjoyed some government support at times of acute crisis. Such supports, however, ended in 1996. Employment has not been a concern for either the U.S. or Canadian policies, but it has been central in Mexican policies.

The Role of the State in the Sugar Industry

As can be seen from the above discussion, State policy in the sugar industry is much more significant in the United States and Mexico than in Canada. Nevertheless, the different actors in sugar production in the three countries have successfully influenced State policy to favor their interests, according to each of their abilities to exercise power. The 14-year transition period allowed in NAFTA for the sugar industry, for instance, is the longest grace period (along with corn, its competition as a sweetener) given to any commodity and an indicator of the power of the vested interests in these countries—in the United States in particular. The sugar commodity group in the United States unanimously opposed NAFTA ratification (Orden 1994). Table 2 sums up the various interests and state policies that have prevailed in the three NAFTA countries until 1994.

Table 2

	Retail	**Wholesale**		**Retail**	**Wholesale**
Brazil		15	Russia	33	22
Australia	35		***United States***	***43***	***27***
EU	60		Japan	73	48
Cuba	8		South Korea		36
Thailand	13	12	Canada	30	16
Guatemala		22	Iran	NA	NA
South Africa		22	Malaysia	18	17
Colombia		27	Algeria		
Mauritius			Indonesia		
Mexico	23	21	Egypt	21	18

Source: Analysis in this paper.

U.S. sugar production has benefited from high levels of protection. The 1981, 1985, 1990, 1996, and 2002 Farm Acts have guaranteed relatively high prices and encouraged sugar production. Without the sugar program, U.S. prices would move in tandem with the world price but about 1.5 cents higher because of shipping and handling charges between the Caribbean (world markets) and the U.S. ports (Barry et al. 1990, 19). These prices would make growers much more vulnerable to world-wide price swings and would reduce sugar production (particularly cane growing in Florida, where it is most costly).

While the United States has tried to conform to the World Trade Organization's guidelines to remove protectionism from agricultural products, sugar remained as the most protected of all U.S. crops. The primary policy tools available to USDA to assist sugar cane and sugar beet producers are contained in the Farm Security and Rural Investment Act of 2002 (2002 Farm Act). The U.S. sugar program provides for USDA to make loans available to processors of domestically grown sugar cane at a rate of 18 cents per pound and to processors of domestically grown sugar beets at the rate of 22.9 cents per pound for refined sugar. The 2002 Farm Act allows processors to obtain loans for "in-process" sugar and syrups at 80 percent of the loan rate. The U.S. sugar program's effectiveness will be challenged in 2008 when all sweetener trade restrictions with Mexico are removed as part of the North American Free Trade Agreement. A provision in the House version of the 2008 Farm Bill would require the government to buy surplus sugar and sell it to ethanol producers for conversion into fuel alcohol.

Sugar producer groups managed to put in place important safeguards in NAFTA for sugar protection with a phase-out period of fourteen years. Only Mexican corn producers, who generally represent the weakest and most numerous farmers, share such protection. It is important to note that while corn growers in Mexico represent a very large and disadvantaged group of people, sugar growers in the United States represent a very small and privileged group of people.

Mexican sugar processors initially resisted the market liberalization introduced by the State, seeking continued subsidies. The neo-liberal regime countered by opening the borders to sugar imports in 1990–1992, bringing a shake-up and concentration in the sugar industry. Once industrialists saw the neo-liberal reform as inevitable, however, they generally supported NAFTA despite the crisis Mexico's sugar industry was undergoing in the early 1990s. Rodolfo Perdomo Bueno, then vice-president of the National Chamber of the Sugar and Alcohol Industry, stated that the industry would win out in NAFTA, and that Mexico's sugar industry was better off than that of the United States (Becerril 1993, 15). At the time, he did not know that HFCS would become a major competitor for Mexican sugar, and that the industry would be hit by an overproduction crisis at the turn of the century thanks to industrial restructuring and increased mill efficiency.

In fact, the main current challenge for Mexico's industry is its competition with HFCS— whether produced in the United States or in Mexico—which is

Table 3

Sugar Prices in the Leading Sugar-Trading Nations, 2000 (cents/pound)
NET EXPORTERS versus NET IMPORTERS

Interest Group	Canada	Mexico	United States
Consumers	Free trade	Subsidized prices	"Sugar tax"
Secondary Industries	Free trade	Subsidized prices	"Sugar tax"
Industrial Processors	Free trade	Subsidized prices	Subsidies
Cane/Beet Producers	Occasional subsidies	Subsidized prices/Tariffs	Tariffs, Subsidies
Mill Workers		Industry-wide Collective Contract	

Sources: USDA attaché reports, F.O. Licht, PROMAR International (reproduced in Coalition for Sugar Reform) Retrieved: 3 June, 2000; http://www.sugar-reform.org/sugpolic.htm.

based on subsidized corn. If corn subsidies were to decline in the United States, then HFCS might lose its competitive advantage against Mexican sugar. In this case, Mexican sugar would be the most competitively priced in North America. In fact, even with such competition, Mexico already has the best sugar prices for consumers of the three NAFTA countries; and they are among the most competitive world-wide (see Table 3). At 23 cents per pound, Mexico's prices are just above half of those in the United States (43 cents) and still well below those in Canada (30 cents). Canada, however, has the best prices for secondary industries at 16 cents per pound wholesale, compared to 27 cents in the United States and 21 cents in Mexico.

According to the Canadian Sugar Institute, which is a non-profit trade organization of sugar processors, Canada is the country with the lowest sugar tariff among the largest producers and consumers of sugar. As of 2000, a comparison of tariffs by equivalents in percentage puts Japan's tariff at close to 300%, Western Europe at 175%, the United States at 150%, Mexico at close to 100%, Brazil at about 40%, Australia at 25%, and Canada at less than 10% percent (Canadian Sugar Institute 2000). Sugar subsidies, on the other hand, continue to be prevalent in the wealthiest countries. The largest, once again, are Japan's at 55% of final price, the United States and the European Unions at 35%, Mexicos at 31%, and Australias at less than 5% (Canadian Sugar Institute 2000).

Sweets Exports and Imports in NAFTA Countries: 1994, 2000, and 2005

Comparing and contrasting the results of imports and exports of sugar-related products in NAFTA countries after this agreement took effect in 1994 is quite revealing. Data seem to indicate that economic actors in each country, particularly manufacturers of confectionary products, have been quite rational. They have moved their factories to those locations that have offered the best cost advantages to set up their export platforms. While the U.S. government continued to attempt to protect sugar processors, secondary industries simply looked elsewhere for better cost opportunities. This has resulted in declining confectionary exports for the United States, while both Canada and Mexico inverted their starting positions in 1994—from net importers of confectionary products, they have become vigorous exporters.

Let us start with a brief analysis of the overall trade change in relation to all sugar-related products—sugar beets, sugar cane, sugar confectionary, raw and refined sugar, as well as nectars. All these data come from the UN Food and Agriculture Organization (FAOSTAT) for the years 1994, 2000, and 2005. Our purpose is to assess the evolution of the sugar-trade situations for NAFTA countries. All three nations experienced dramatic changes, but with different contents and directions. Canada has always relied on the importation of raw sugar for the largest proportion of its raw and refined sugar, both for direct consumption and for secondary industries. Thus, the overall starting trade situation for sweeteners, including sugar confectionary, was at a deficit of almost $315 million. For the following years, however, Canada was able to substantially improve its trade situation, primarily on the basis of exporting new sugar-confectionary products: its sugar-related deficit declined to $164 million in 2000, and then further declined to just over $91 million by 2005.

For its part, Mexico also started the period with a deficit of almost $35 million in 1994, due primarily to its importation of sugar confectionary. By 2000, however, it had inverted its position to produce a surplus of just over $1 billion. This surplus was expanded to almost $1.6 billion by 2005. While Mexico was a net exporter of raw and refined sugar, as well as sugar confectionary during the entire period, its overall surplus in sweets was due to increased exports of sugar confectionary, which now account for about 40% of its sweets surplus. The rest of the surplus is accounted for by raw- and refined-sugar exports. Clearly then, some manufacturing jobs must have been created in sugar confectionary for this situation to have ensued. And yet, it is unlikely that they have compensated the sharp decline in direct employment in the sugar industry (as will be seen below).

For the United States, the sugar-related trade situation changed dramatically toward a greater deficit, due primarily to a worsening sugar-confectionary trade balance. While the United States exported a significant volume of refined sugar and sugar confectionary between 1994 and 2000, its imports were so much larger that its deficit worsened considerably. U.S. deficits in sugar-related products evolved as follows: they were almost $668 million in 1994, over $1 billion in 2000, and almost $1.6 billion in 2005. The largest part of this deficit is accounted for by sugar confectionary, whose proportion grew as follows: from almost 21% of the sweets deficit in 1994, to almost 49% in 2000, to nearly 56% in 2005. This evolution in the composition of the U.S. sugar-related trade deficit seems to confirm the interpretation proposed at the start of this section: economic actors, particularly heavy users of sugar in the secondary industries, have skirted the U.S. protectionist policies by moving some of their plants to Canada and/or Mexico. The specific ways in which these moves have affected employment in each nation is the topic of another study, but our suspicion is that, at least for Mexico, it has not compensated the heavy losses in the sugar industry itself.

Labor: The Employment Issue

Labor in the sugar industry has two distinct categories: field workers and industrial mill workers. Workers in these two sectors traditionally have had very different working conditions and compose different labor markets. While mechanization has reduced the number of both sets of workers, it has generally had greater impact on field workers. Field workers have historically been most disadvantaged and have been much more likely to be seasonal migrants in both Mexico and the United States. Sugar cane is not grown in Canada, so fieldwork is limited to sugar beet production. In the past, this required quite a bit of migrant labor, including Mexican migrant workers, particularly for "hand thinning". Beet production now uses chemical thinning, but some migrant labor is still used for harvesting. One of the main groups of migrant workers is Mennonites from Mexico, many of whom have dual citizenship. The Mennonite Central Committee of Alberta (MCCA) estimates that about 2,000 families have migrated from Mexico in the past decade (Fehr 2000).

The overall employment situation in Mexico, after NAFTA, has actually deteriorated. Mexico has become the largest exporter of labor power, surpassing Asia and the rest of the Latin American countries (Muñoz Ríos 2000).

Considering the direct employment generation in the sugar industries of the three NAFTA countries (about 17,000 jobs in the United States, about 1,500 in Canada, and well above 400,000 in Mexico), jointly modifying State policy to allow Mexico to be the main supplier of sugar would have tremendously positive employment effects for the NAFTA region as a whole. With the increased efficiency in Mexico's sugar industry, and without the subsidized competition from HFCS, Mexico could supply much of North America's sugar needs at adequate prices for most stakeholders, including Canadian direct consumers.

Canada could continue to supply its secondary industry from refining imported raw sugar, as long as its prices are lower than Mexico's. In the United States, the possible negative direct effects on sugar employment could be more than offset by the generation of additional jobs in secondary industries that use sugar as the main raw material, as they would have greater incentives to expand production from access to cheaper sugar. Similarly, more Mexican workers would have a greater incentive to stay in their own communities rather than having to migrate to Mexican cities or even further to "*El Norte*".

It is obvious that State policies have displayed a tremendous ability to shape the sugar industry. The question is what social groups' interests should be addressed. We suggest that a large majority of people would be benefited if Mexico were to become a large supplier of sugar for the entire region.

Bibliography

Barry, Robert D., Luigi Angelo, Peter J. Buzzanell, and Fred Gray. *Sugar: Background for the 1990 Farm Legislation*. Staff Report No. AGES 9006. Commodity Economics Division, Economic Research Service, U.S. Dept. of Agriculture, 1990.

Becerril, Andrea. "Necesario, Definir un Esquema de Comercializacion del Azucar." *La Jornada* (May 15, 1993).

BeeNews. "Canadian-U.S. Sugar Agreement." (1998). Retrieved February 3, 2000. http://www.albertabeekeepers.org/beenews/articles/a03_0198.htm.

Beghin, John C., Barbara El Osta, Jay R. Cherlow, and Samarendu Mohanty. "The Cost of the U.S. Sugar Program Revisited." (Working Paper 01-WP 273, March). Ames, IA: Center for Agricultural and Rural Development, Iowa State University, 2001.

Buzzanell, Peter, and Ron Lord. "Sugar and Corn Sweetener: Changing Demand and Trade in Mexico, Canada, and the United States." Washington, DC: USDA/ERS, *Agriculture Information Bulletin* 655 (April, 1993).

Canadian Federation of Agriculture. Commodities Agriculture in Canada. Canadian Federation of Agriculture. (March,1998). Retrieved June 29, 1999. http://www.cfa-fca.ca/commod.htm.

Canadian Sugar Institute. (2000). Retrieved June 3, 2000. http://www.sugar.ca/.

Chollett, Donna (1995) "Restructuring the Mexican Sugar Industry: Campesinos, the State, and Private Capital." In *Mexican Sugar cane Growers: Economic Restructuring and Political Options*, Peter Singelmann, Ed., Transformation of Rural Mexico series, Number 7, Ejido Reform Research Project. Pp. 23–39. La Jolla: Center for U.S.-Mexican Studies.

Coalition for Sugar Reform. (1999a). "The U.S. Sugar Industry." Retrieved June 2, 2000. http://www.sugar-reform.org/industry.htm.

———. (1999b.) "Sugar Import Quota Chronology." Retrieved June 2, 2000. http://www.sugar-reform.org/import.htm.

Earley, Thomas, and Donald Westfall. "International Dynamics of National Sugar Policies," *FAO Economic and Social Development* Paper 135 (1996). Food & Agriculture Organization of the United Nations. Rome.

Eichner, Alfred S. *The Emergence of Oligopy: Sugar Refining as a Case Study*. Baltimore: Johns Hopkins University Press, 1969.

Federal Agriculture Improvement and Reform Act of 1996 PUBLIC LAW 104-127,Section 156. APRIL 4, 1996 http://www.nationalaglawcenter.org/assets/farmbills/1996.htm.

Fehr, Abe of the Mennonite Central Committee of Alberta, Telephone interview conducted by Gerardo Otero on June 8, 2000.

Flores, Dulce. Sugar Market Country Report, Semi-annual report, Mexico. (Sept. 30, 1998). Retrieved June 29, 1999. http://www.sugarinfo.co.uk/Sugar_Report_Mexico.htm.

———. "Mexico Sugar: New National Sugar Policy 2002." USDA-Foreign Agricultural Service. Global Agriculture Information Network (GAIN) Report #MX2031 (February 27, 2002).

García Chavez, Luis Ramiro. "Perspectivas de la Agroindustria Casera de Mexico ante el Tratado de Libre Comercio." In *La Agricultura Mexicana Frente al Tratado de Libre Comercio,* edited by Jose Luis Calva, Luis Rey Carrasco L., Salvador Dias C., et al. Mexico: Universidad Autónoma de Chapingo, 1992.

Gitli, Eduardo. "El TLC y las perspectivas de la producción Azucarera." *Comercio Exterior* 44, no.7 (1994): 640–48. Haley, Stephen and.Mir Ali. 2007. *Sugar Backgrounder* Economic Research Service, USDA. http://www.ers.usda.gov/publications/sss/Jul07/SSS249/sss249.pdf

Hayami, Yujiro, and Vernon W. Ruttan. *Agricultural Development: An International Perspective*. 2nd Edition. Baltimore: Johns Hopkins University Press, 1985.

Lord, Ron. U.S. Sugar Consumption Continues To Grow,. *Agricultural Outlook,* AO-238, U.S. Department of Agriculture, Economic Research Service, March 1997. Economic Research Service/USDA Moving Toward the Food Guide.

Loyns, R.M.A. *Understanding Canadian Agriculture*. Toronto: Canadian Foundation for Economic Education, 1978.

Lozano Gómez, Adriana. "Diez ingenios del país cerrarían por la fructosa," *El cañero mexicano* (Organo informativo de la Unión Nacional de Productores de Caña de Azúcar-CNC) 3, no.1 (July 1998): 8–9.

Messina, William A., Jr., and James L. Seale, Jr. "U.S. Sugar Policy and the Caribbean Basin Economic Recovery Act: Conflicts Between Domestic and Foreign Policy Objectives," *Review of Agricultural Economics* 15, no.1 (1993):167–80.

Miranda, Sergio, and Martha E. Ortiz. "Caída en la demanda y sobreoferta bajaran, aún más los precios del azúcar en México: Tres empresas manejan más del 50% de la capacidad de molienda." *Excelsior* (1999). Retrieved September 7, 1999. http://www.excelsior.com.mx/azucar.html.

Muñoz Ríos, Patricia. "El país, primer lugar como exportador de mano de obra." *La Jornada* (2000). Retrieved June 5, 2000. http://www.jornada.unam.mx/2000/jun00/000605/eco4.html.

Orden, David. "Agricultural Interest Groups and the North American Free Trade Agreement." Working Paper No. 4790. Cambridge, MA: National Bureau of Economic Research, Inc., July, 1994.

Otero, Gerardo. "The Differential Impact of Biotechnology: The Mexico-United States Contrast." In *Biotechnology: A Hope or a Threat,* edited by Iftikhar Ahmed. London: MacMillan, 1992.

———. *Farewell to the Peasantry? Political Class Formation in Rural Mexico*. Boulder, CO: Westview Press, 1999.

———. "Survey of Cane Growers in Los Mochis, Sinaloa." Unpublished survey, 1996.

Paré, Luisa, Irma Juárez, and Gilda Salazar. *Caña Brava: Trabajo y Organización Social entre los Cortadores de caña*. Mexico City: Universidad Nacional Autónoma de México and Universidad Autónoma Metropolitana-Azcapotzalco, 1987.

Reforma. 2006 ¿Negocio del siglo? *Reforma* 16 April, p. 7F. Taken from SAGARPA's *Síntesis informative*, 16 April 2006, available at: http://www.sagarpa.gob.mx/cgcs/sintesis/sintesis/2007/abril/ss_16.pdf (accessed: 28/03/2008).

Roy, William G. *Socializing Capital: The Rise of the Large Industrial Corporation in America*. Princeton, NJ: Princeton University Press, 1995.

SAGARPA (2006) *Sembrando soluciones*. Año 1, núm. 28. Available at: http://www.sagarpa.gob.mx/cgcs/sembrando/2006/28-2006.pdf (accessed: 28/03/2008).

SAGARPA (Secretaría de Agricultura, Ganadería, Desarrollo Rural, Pesca y Alimentación) (2005) "Producción record de más de 5 millones 650 mil toneladas de azúcar en el presente ciclo." 15 June. Coordinación General de Comunicación Social. 2005. Available at: http://www.sagarpa.gob.mx/cgcs/boletines/2005/junio/B174.pdf (accessed: 28/03/2008).

Singelmann, Peter. "The Sugar Industry in Postrevolutionary Mexico: State Intervention and Private Capital." *Latin American Research Review* 27 no. 1 (1993): 61–88.

———, and Gerardo Otero. "Campesinos, Sugar and the Mexican State: From Social Guarantees to Neoliberalism." In *Mexican Sugar cane Growers: Economic Restructuring and Political Options*, edited by Peter Singelmann. Transformation of Rural Mexico Series, no. 7. La Jolla, CA: Center for U.S.-Mexican Studies, UCSD, 1995.

Skogstad, Grace Darlene (1987) *The politics of agricultural policy-making in Canada*. Toronto: University of Toronto Press.

SourceMex. "Mexican Government Seizes Control of 27 Sugar Mills." (September 5, 2001).

Sugar Online. Retrieved July 26, 2002. http://www.sugaronline.com.

The Economist. (2002a). "Cleansing the Augean Stables." (July 13, 2002): 12.

The Economist. (2002b). "Europe's Farms." (July 13, 2002): 42–43.

Time. "Sweet Deal: Why Are These Men Smiling? The Reason is in Your Sugar Bowl." Special Report on Corporate Welfare. (November 23, 1998): 81–82.

USDA-Economic Research Service. *NAFTA Commodity Supplement*. Washington, DC: United States Department of Agriculture, Economic Research Services. March, 2000.

USDA-Foreign Agricultural Service. "Sugar: World Markets and Trade." United States Department of Agriculture, Foreign Agricultural Service, Circular Series FS 1-02, May, 2002.

Wilkinson, Alec. *Big Sugar: Seasons in the Cane Fields of Florida*. New York: Alfred A. Knopf, 1989(a).

———. "Sugar Cane—Parts 1 and 2," *The New Yorker* (July 17 and July 24, 1989) (b).

Wilson, Barry K. *Farming the System: How Politicians and Producers Shape Canadian Agricultural Policy*. Saskatoon, Saskatchewan: Western Producer Prairie Books, 1990.

Young, C., and P. Westcott. (2000). "How Decoupled is U.S. Agricultural Support for Major Crops?" *American Journal of Agricultural Economics*, 82: 762–67.

Chapter 5

Multinational Agribusiness and Small Corn Producers in Rural Mexico: New Alternatives for Agricultural Development

Juan M. Rivera*

In the 1990s, Mexico embraced a development path characterized by economic neo-liberalism, open markets, and free trade. The new economic policies have caused a deterioration of the social and economic conditions of the Mexican rural poor. In a search for new development alternatives, this research studies two examples of associations between agribusiness firms and small agricultural corn producers in Mexico. It is expected that the lessons learned from these successful development experiments could be replicated with other products or in other regions of the country or the developing world.

This chapter discusses the characteristics of corn production in Mexico in the context of NAFTA and the economic policies of the Mexican government. It will then turn to concepts which cover contract farming and the potential benefits for the parties participating in this type of association. Following this, the fifth section documents a contract-farming experience between corn producers and a wet-mill manufacturing business in Mexico. The characteristics of another case of association between producers and agribusiness are presented in the sixth section. Summary and concluding comments are reviewed at the end.

The Unique Situation of Corn Production and Markets in Mexico

Measured by the volume of surface planted, the value of its annual harvest, and the number of agricultural producers, corn is the single most important crop in Mexico. In 1990, the production of corn in the country accounted for 33% of the total value of agricultural products, which included a total of 222 goods, and the seven million hectares planted are equivalent to 30% of the arable land in the country.[1] Corn is indigenous to Mexico; it is the principal food staple, and it is heavily engrained in national culture. In retrospect, at least in the recent past,

* This study has been possible thanks to financial support from the University of Notre Dame Program of Multinational Managers and Developing Country Concerns, and to travel funds from a Title VI federal grant from the Helen Kellogg Institute of International Studies at the University of Notre Dame. The author acknowledges the research help in the field provided by Kenny Miller and Anne Maria Golla, both graduate students from the University of Texas in Austin. The cooperation of the management teams of Almidones Mexicanos, S.A. and Monsanto Mexicana, S.A. who shared valuable information about their agricultural development projects in Mexico is also acknowledged and appreciated

one cannot easily find economic or technical comparative advantages for this heavy inclination to corn production in Mexico. Most of its production is of the seasonal, rain-dependent type, with 86% of the total amount of corn produced in the spring-summer cycle, with the harvest season between September and January; four Mexican states contribute a little more than 50% of the annual production (Mexico, Cámara de Diputados 2000, 56–57). It is important to state that these numbers (and the trade-related quotas) correlate to both white and yellow corn; for the purposes of quotas and production, some consider them perfect substitutes, although this remains a topic of debate.

Within the NAFTA region, the United States is also a main producer of corn (it is the most efficient corn producer in the world). The United States produces 14 times as much corn as Mexico, at an average yield of 7.1 tons per hectare. Compared to this, Mexico's corn yield per hectare is, on average, around 2 tons, and sometimes 3.7 in the best regions and years, the latter being about the average for the world as a whole (Ibid., 54–57).

The majority of corn producers in Mexico are small farm holders, usually working on parcels that used to be ejido or communal land. The 2.7 million corn producers out of a total of four million farmers in Mexico are classified into two groups:

a) Small agricultural producers with parcels of less than five hectares; this represents two-thirds of the total corn producers. Their average yield is a meager 1.8 tons per hectare, and they use 57% of the harvest for self-consumption.

b) The remaining corn producers have plots of over five hectares, with an average yield of 3.2 tons per hectare. They use 13.6% of their harvest for self-consumption.[2]

The trade liberalization that NAFTA brought, the decreasing agricultural protection that Mexico experienced, and the little competitive advantage that corn production manifests, are good reasons for Mexico's corn production to improve or restructure. One would have expected that part of the 2.3 million corn producers with parcels of less than five hectares on average would leave the market, or that some of the 4.7 million hectares of planted corn would be switched to alternative crops. Instead, total production of corn in Mexico has increased, from the 10.5 million tons in 1988 to 18.3 million in 1999, the latter a number very stable during the NAFTA years since 1994. Still, the production is not sufficient to match the domestic demand.

One of the assumptions made by the negotiators of the NAFTA accord was that crop liberalization in Mexico and open markets in the region would cause a switch of agricultural production in Mexico toward those products with more export potential and significant comparative advantages—namely, vegetables, fruits and nuts, coffee, and tropical fruits. These are products with more labor-intensive components that hold an attractive value in the U.S. and other foreign markets. This process could have reduced rural population or reallocated it to more profitable activities. However, the traditional concentration on corn farming increased rather than decreased. Moreover, a major effort to concentrate on horticultural production would face market constraints (considering the higher production costs and capital required for vegetable farming and processing), because the saturated North American market could no longer absorb further volumes (Nadal 2002, 16–37).

Corn, for Mexico, receives special treatment within the NAFTA agreement. In principle, NAFTA classified products into various categories, depending upon the timing needed for the gradual elimination of trade tariffs (in other words, if not immediately made duty free, then 5, 10, or 15 years for final duty-free status). Corn was one of the very few agricultural products with a long (15-year) transition period to liberalized free trade. Corn was also one of the products included in the novel regime of tariff-rate quotas that the Uruguay Round of GATT (General Agreement on Tariffs and Trade) had recommended. According to the NAFTA protocol, Mexico could import 2.5 million tons of corn from the United States duty free, and the volume would increase at an annual rate of 3% from 1994, until finally reaching 3.67 million tons in 2008. Concurrently, for any imports of corn that were above and beyond the annual duty-free level, the Mexican government could impose import tariffs. The duties levied on the excess to the tax-free quotas imported were substantial, starting at 215% for the year 1994, a percentage that would decrease at an annual 4% rate for the following six years. Afterwards, for the last nine years of the phasing-in of NAFTA, the annual decrease in the import duties was spread evenly before going to zero duties in the year 2008.

The reality of the Mexican market in the NAFTA years is that the demand for corn has outpaced the Mexican production, and imports from the United States have consistently exceeded the duty-free threshold. Thus, the annual demand for corn in Mexico is at an average of 23.5 million tons and the country can only produce 18.3 million per year. Consequently, the deficit of 5.2 million tons has to come from abroad, namely, from its NAFTA partner the United States. Interestingly enough, in comparing duties imposed on corn derivatives or byproducts, except for corn flour, no other processed corn good is required to pay an import tax into Mexico. A 15% progressively declining duty was imposed on corn flour for the first ten years after NAFTA implementation, but it has been duty free since 2004.

Given that the importation of corn in Mexico has been significant, the imposition of import tariffs on the excess over the duty-free quota would have generated substantial funds during the past ten years of NAFTA, enough to help with credit or to aid in transferring those Mexican farmers who remain in the cornfields. However, the Mexican government has opted not to impose the corresponding duties during all the years that NAFTA has been in place and for the quantities that have exceeded the duty-free threshold. A commission composed of several government agencies and representatives of the corn importer industrialists made the decisions about imposing or foregoing the corresponding tariffs.[3]

Cost and Opportunities for Associations between Agribusiness and Small Agricultural Producers

One can certainly predict that, with exporting corn farmers in the United States consistently receiving government subsidies and other financial support, the prospect for success in corn production by Mexican farmers is rather bleak. As the current support given by the U.S. government to its agricultural producers is expected to continue, and as the flow of corn in the NAFTA countries will become totally free (under the NAFTA agreement) in 2008, Mexican corn farmers have no alternative but to seek support from the federal government and other links in the production and consumption chain. Regardless of any support or preferences the Mexican corn producer might receive, however, he still has to negotiate very difficult markets. In all, there are two truisms that surface like buoys in the sea of economic uncertainty: being and staying competitive is a necessary condition for agricultural units to survive, and technical progress is a necessary condition to being and staying competitive. It is also natural that the new open-market environments have favored the highly intensive, technically advanced, export-oriented plantations in the developing world and one has to recognize the coexistence of these agricultural corporations alongside the small family-owned rural farms. But, at the same time, one has to accept that it is improbable or inappropriate that the same general solution would be valid for these two different types of agricultural producers.[4]

In the present research, we look at ad-hoc alternatives that could improve the competitive potential of the small agricultural producers in Mexico, units that can be typified as small family farms.[5] These are the units most affected by the persistent imperfections of the markets in areas of credit, crop insurance, technology, improved production inputs, and market information. They are the type of agricultural producers with limited or no access to basic markets, or that face significantly high transaction costs to make their activities economically attractive.[6] This is where creative links between agribusiness processors and small agricultural producers at the local or regional level can overcome those market imperfections; it is here that tested mechanisms, found to be beneficial for all participants, can be replicated or reproduced in other agricultural regions.[7]

In general, benefits and costs occur when there are contracting agreements between the agribusiness firms and the small agricultural producers; one has to find the appropriate middle point where everybody wins. Among the advantages cited by the business people who participate in these contractual agreements are: passing the production risk to another party; avoiding problems derived from salaried labor; eliminating the risk of holding capital and land assets; and receiving government incentives for promoting development. Among the benefits frequently mentioned by small agricultural producers are: an assured market at preestablished prices for their contracted product sales; technical assistance; use of extended family labor with more intensity; incorporating products with a higher market value; possible access to credit; and the potential use of agricultural machinery (CEPAL, Economic Commission for Latin America 1998, 48–50).

Agribusiness Firms and Their Potential Role in Agricultural Development

The need for more active participation from the agricultural private sector is essential in helping the Mexican rural poor. Through the agricultural development plan, the government can concentrate on designing macro-level agricultural policies to improve agricultural output within the framework of the neo-liberal, market-driven model now in place. It has been proven that at the micro level of the small agricultural producers (or their associations), past government policies have been either very limited in scope and results, or equally inefficient. As Glade and Tavis have argued (1997, 1219), in the long run, multinational enterprises are more likely to influence development at the local level—which needs almost any help that is tendered—than at the national level where company programs tend to get lost in the labyrinthine structures of government and politics. Given this scenario, the government should work on promoting development indirectly by providing incentives to agribusiness units and agricultural producers, improving marketing and distribution infrastructure, and supporting improvements in technology and education to their rural citizenry.

The possibility of agro-industrial firms helping agricultural producers with credit, improved production inputs, technical services, etc. has been studied by Key and Runsten (1999) when analyzing the various forms of contract farming in Latin America. In view of the governmental economic reforms that curtailed credit, crop–price guarantees, input subsidies, and extension programs, the option of contract farming could be a "private" alternative for promoting rural development. By definition, contract farming is an intermediate institutional arrangement that allows firms to participate in, and exert control over, the production process without owning or operating the farms (Ibid., 383). Contract farming can thus become a viable institutional response to imperfections in credit, production inputs, and insurance and information markets.

By analyzing an array of factors such as local sources of credit, level of technical expertise of local farmers, and degree of risk aversion by local agricultural producers, Key and Runsten studied the agribusiness firms' choices for contract farming with small farmholders (mainly *ejido* farmers) or large-scale, plantation-like agricultural producers.[8] The contract farming can thus take place in three (sometimes overlapping) forms, namely, market specification, resource provision, and product management. Each type of farming has an increasing degree of the agro-industrial firms' control over the production process of their agricultural producer counterpart.

In the case of contract farming via market specification, the agribusiness unit enters into purchasing contractual agreements with the agricultural supplier. Typically, the pre-planting agreement that binds the firm and the local farmers specifies a particular set of conditions for the product such as price, quality, quantity, and time of delivery. (This model of market specification applies in the case of the contractual agreement studied in this research and discussed later in this chapter, Almex Corporation).[9] The only variation is that, rather than directly engaging with the local small agricultural producers, the company uses an intermediary as a link between the supplying producers and the purchasing firm. *Almex* still guarantees the future price of corn arranged with the intermediary representing the farmers, and, as is normal for these agreements, the success of the transaction depends heavily on the satisfactory compliance with product delivery at harvest time by the participating small agricultural producers. In this case, some elements of the other types of contract farming are present in the Almex–corn producer's association, particularly the ones that allow the agribusiness firm to monitor production. Almex, directly or through the intermediary, checks on the corn-production cycle to assure the characteristics and yields of the corn delivered meet their starch processing specifications.

Reardon and Barrett (2000) have also studied the contribution that agro-industrial firms could make in agricultural communities in developing countries. They suggest that agribusiness units can be both agents of and responses to globalization and institutional changes. The key is to identify those activities of agribusiness firms that can favorably impact employment, reduce poverty, and at the same time preserve the ecology in the countryside. The Almex case is one where the contract-farming practices, if extended to more agricultural producers, could fulfill those objectives. Conversely, the other case included in this research documents the activities of another multinational corporation engaged in helping selected groups of poor agricultural corn producers in Mexico. Seven years ago, Monsanto Corporation (of the United States) started the "*Monsanto Campo Unido*" (United Farms) program. This program is a direct way to improve farm productivity with the help of tried and tested technology, and is helping small farming units (mostly *ejido* landholdings) in two rural regions of Mexico. Although not strictly a contractual exchange, but instead a promotional effort at the input side in the corn-production process, Monsanto has promoted business associations with small agricultural producers for the mutual benefit of the program participants.

The shift of agricultural production in developing countries toward those products where there is comparative advantage—such as frozen vegetables and fruits—is always an option, but requires substantial capital and management expertise.[10] Still, one of the most prominent and widespread changes observed in the agricultural sector is the rise of contractual exchanges between agro-industrial firms and agricultural producers. These liaisons have facilitated the introduction of better technologies, improved seeds, and other agricultural inputs, and have raised the quality and safety standards of the agricultural crops. Plantation-corn processing-for-export enclaves—such as were owned and run by Unilever and Del Monte—characteristic of the 1960s and 1970s, have given way to the input-supply global firms like Monsanto and Pioneer and the multinational food-processing units such as Nestlé and Gerber. When the individual farm producers integrate with these agro-industrial firms, they might gain access to credit, production inputs, improved technology, and extension services. For their part, the participating farmers are contractually bound to deliver a certain quantity of product, at an agreed upon price, at a future date, meeting specific quality and safety standards.

Contract Farming for Corn Processing: The Almex Case

Almidones Mexicanos, S.A. (Almex) is a 50-50 joint venture of Staley Manufacturing Company (a subsidiary of Tate & Lyle of England) and ADM (Archer Daniels Midland Company of the United States). Located in Guadalajara, Mexico and operating for over 40 years, the company is a corn wet-miller that produces starches, corn sweeteners, corn oil, and feed ingredients. It has a capacity to mill 1,600 metric tons of corn per day and employs 400 people.

Six years ago, Almex started a type of contract farming with small corn producers of the La Barca region in the state of Jalisco. As an industrial processor of corn that is at the center of the production chain, Almex contracts the purchase of corn from local agricultural producers at the beginning of the production cycle—the pre-seeding time. For the 2000 planting season, Almex agreed to buy 22,000 metric tons of corn, promising to pay an "indifference price" based on the future price of the grain in the commodities markets at the expected time of delivery, plus the equivalent costs of freight and insurance F.O.B. Guadalajara, Mexico. The quantity thus contracted in 2000 represents only 5% of the company's annual needs of half a million metric tons of corn and is equivalent to about 3% of the spring-summer production in the region.[11] Almex would like to increase the local purchases, but the supply in Mexico is mostly of white corn, with limited quantities of the much needed yellow variety. The company imports the rest of its demand from the United States. Arancia, a subsidiary of Corn Products International (of theUnited States), is a local corn processor and competitor of Almex that also participates in similar purchase agreements with local regional producers at the rate of 38,000 metric tons per year. Altogether, the quantities of corn thus purchased represent a small portion of the two million metric tons of yellow corn needed for industrial use in Mexico, but both companies are eager to extend this program to bring in more agricultural producers. The processors' preference is for yellow rather than white corn since the yellow variety has better characteristics for milling and processing for industrial uses.

The region of La Barca in the state of Jalisco is a fertile valley of 726,000 hectares where corn has been the main harvest for many years. The majority of the land is of the ejido type, with parcels averaging 8 to 10 hectares, and with 95% of production dependent on seasonal rain, which, at about 700 millimeters per year, is quite dependable in that region. The production cycle is in the spring-summer, with harvests from November to early January.

By engaging in contract-growing yellow corn primarily in the state of Jalisco, the Almex management feels it can prove to government officials, the financial community, and the Mexican farmers, that, with the right seeds, agronomics, and appropriate cooperation, Mexico can compete with U.S. producers at international prices. Almex guarantees to purchase a fixed quantity of corn at a price equivalent to its "indifference" or "shadow price."[12] The purchase agreement is signed before the seed is purchased and sown; for the participating farmer this eliminates the uncertainty of selling his corn at an unknown "spot price" at harvest time. Since international prices are normally higher in the future and the agricultural producer has a certainty of the sale before planting, the corn producer is in a better position to obtain credit for the seed, fertilizers, pesticides, and other production inputs. Although Almex does not finance the peasants directly but only contracts to buy, the arrangement enables the small agricultural producers to obtain credit elsewhere.

Almex started the contract farming of yellow corn in 1997 at low volumes of purchases, and it was only in 1999 that the program matured and had successful results for both contracting parties. Almex identified a group of yellow-corn producers through the corn producers' association of the state of Jalisco, whose president, a farmer and businessperson, is also a part owner and director of (Agroferretera (a small business located in the town of La Barca, Jalisco that distributes seeds, pesticides, and other inputs to the farmers in the region). The project consists of selecting a certain number of hectares from a group of ejido farmers to plant yellow corn for sale to Almex in Guadalajara. The small corn producers receive financing, a technology assistance package, herbicides, and seeds through Agroferretera. Agroferretera is thus the key link that acts as an intermediary between Almex and the small agricultural producers; furthermore, the area where the corn is planted occupies an extension of 30,000 hectares. Important multinationals represented by Agroferretera, such as Novartis from Switzerland and FMC from the United States, back Agroferretera with financial and other support.

Almex selects the seed for yellow corn for the production. Besides Jalisco, there are small productions of yellow corn in Chihuahua and in the Southeastern region of Mexico. Still, it is very expensive to transport the corn from those locations. However, it is also expensive to transport the yellow corn from the United States, which is why Almex managers have looked for a closer source of supply. In addition to the Jalisco project, in the year 2000 they contracted additional quantities of yellow corn produced in the state of Nayarit. In that case, Monsanto served as the intermediary between the small agriculture producers and Almex, and supplied the production inputs to the corn producers. Almex does not finance the producers but only contractually promises to buy directly from the intermediary who represents and contracts with the individual corn producers. Since the corn producers have the customer and the price guaranteed, it is easier for them to obtain financing.

Producing yellow corn in Mexico is feasible and profitable, and Almex management thinks that there will be more hectares of yellow corn every year. In 1999, Almex was successful because the future contracts entered with the local corn producers were fulfilled completely, with excellent crop yields of a minimum of 6.0 tons per hectare, and up to 7.5 tons per hectare in Nayarit. They estimated that they could get 8 tons per hectare for the December (2000) crop in Jalisco.[13]

The transaction is structured so that when the contract is signed, Almex agrees to pay the intermediate contractor, who represents the participating corn producers, the future price of the corn at international markets (which means at mid-bridge Laredo). To do so, they use the quoted future price for the date when the crop is expected to be delivered—plus other expenses that include transportation and incidentals from Laredo to Guadalajara—to arrive at a price FOB the Almex plant.

Almex hedges the purchase commitment with future sales contracts of equivalent volumes in the Chicago commodities exchange market. In contrast, their competitor Arancia, which also buys yellow corn, enters into an option to buy the corn from the local farmers at an international price, but asks the producer to hedge the transaction on his own. The federal government helps subsidize risk insurance and hedging of future prices through a government program called ASERCA (*Apoyos y Servicios de Comercialización Agrícola*— Support Services for Agricultural Marketing) but that option has been expensive and the local producers rarely, if ever, insure their future crops through this mechanism.

Almex has had positive experiences in using Agroferretera as the intermediary with these contracts, because Agroferretera pays the producers the total contracted price according to the hectares planted by each farmer. Agroferretera does not charge fees or commission for its intermediation, nor does it charge interest for the credit extended to farmers on the purchases of production inputs. The agreement between Almex and Agroferretera's director, who represents the corn producers, is possible because Agroferretera benefits as a distributor of seeds, fertilizers, pesticides, and other inputs to the local farmers, who then benefit by locking up the quantity and price of their corn through the arranged future contracting. By committing to the sale of their crops from the time the seeding takes place or earlier, the small corn producers can receive interest-free credit for seeds, fertilizers, and other inputs from Agroferretera's distribution business. Thus, benefits for the farmers are tangible, as there are few alternative credit lines available for small agricultural producers from either the Mexican government or from private financial institutions. The farmers can pay back the amount for the inputs used in the production cycle after the delivery of their harvested corn and the collection of the contracted price. This novel program referred to as "selling before planting" has been tried for more than five years with success and win-win outcomes.

The benefit that Almex seeks is a more direct, reliable source of yellow corn for its manufacturing process. Currently, Almex and other similar cornstarch producers have to import approximately 90% of their corn raw material, mainly from the United States. The production of corn in Mexico is not sufficient to supply all the existing demand, which is heavily weighted towards white corn. The production of yellow corn in Mexico is very limited, and Almex is trying to expand it by participating and encouraging programs such as "selling before planting." Almex also feels a moral commitment to help the small corn producers of the region become more efficient and self-sufficient.

According to Agroferretera's data, the Mexican corn producer needs an investment of 1,450 pesos per hectare and if the yield only reaches 3.5 tons per hectare (that is, the national average for the Mexican corn producer), the producer would not reach an income equivalent to the minimum salary in Mexico.

In La Barca, a region in east-central Jalisco, the average size of a plot is 3.5 hectares per producer, but there are areas where a plot of 6 hectares per farmer is not unusual. Even though the area depends on the seasonal rain for the production of corn, there is usually a good yield when compared to the average corn yields in the rest of Mexico. La Barca has very good temperatures and soil, fertile land, and enough humidity to reach yields of 6 tons or more per hectare. In addition, as real-income diversifiers, many of the local agricultural producers benefit from the dollar remittances from family members and close relatives who reside and work in the United States.

The production of corn in the state of Jalisco reaches two million tons a year compared to 400 million tons of yellow corn produced in the United States.

In the year 2000, the average farmland per peasant in Jalisco was six hectares. Taking into account the direct costs of production of 4,500 pesos per hectare, a yield of six tons per hectare and a sale price of 1,500 pesos per ton would bring a net income of 27,000 pesos per year, an amount that is much better than the minimum salary in Mexico, which was 12,000 pesos in Mexico City in the year 2000.[14]

A series of interviews were conducted with agricultural producers in the La Barca region.[15]The participants in this contract farming with Almex were very pleased with the program and its results. The sizes of their plots, all ejido land, varied from three to 20 hectares per farmer. The local corn producers who had not been participating in the program with Almex expressed general discomfort with the uncertainties in the market prices of corn, complaining that it was generally very low. Most of the farmers of the region have diversified sources of income, including some trade wages earned by members of their extended families, and very frequently, remittances from relatives working in the United States.

Technical assistance from Agroferretera was another benefit received by the participating farmers. Several farmers interviewed stated that by having technical advice and good inputs, the yields that they obtain from corn production are much improved.[16] Their region has relatively good soil, excellent climate, and normally reliable rain, though very little or no irrigation. In order to use water from the subsoil, they would need to incur costly expenditures in pump equipment, and the cost of electricity in Mexico is also very high.

There are some *ejidatarios* in the La Barca region who own up to twenty hectares. The agriculture in the region is highly mechanized and some of the farmers own or rent combines to do the corn planting and harvesting. Very few tasks, such as applying pesticides with applicator tanks, are done manually. Even some airplanes for hire in the region aerially spread herbicides or pesticides if needed. Because of the change to Article 27 of the Mexican Constitution, the ejido land has reached a stage where every ejidatario can have title to his/her parcel, so they can use, sell, lease, or mortgage their parcels if they so wish. Some of the ejidatarios are now practically small proprietors and act as such. They can hire local daily workers during the time of herbicide application. The collection of crops is done mechanically with the use of combines that even frees the corn grains from their husks.

Altogether, this is a well-managed operation and a win-win situation for all parties involved. There is always the risk of losing the harvest and that risk is insurable, though nobody is known to buy such insurance. This is probably because they have not had any catastrophic event in many years. In addition, the cost of insuring the harvest is very high and, if there was a catastrophic event, the farmer can only receive compensation based on an average yield of about 3.0 tons per hectare.

Monsanto *Campo Unido* Project

The *Campo Unido* project that Monsanto Corporation started in Mexico in 1997 is part of its Global Reach program, and is intended to increase the food supply in the developing countries and improve the economic and social conditions of the small agricultural producers. It is a unique and comprehensive approach to improving the various steps of the corn-production cycle, from the pre-planting stage to the placing of the harvest in the market place. It is not simply a case of technology transfer, although this is an important component. It is a project that helps the small corn farmers organize themselves in producer associations, teaches them to use better crop management techniques, provides them with expert advice on fertilizer application and pest controls, and even helps them to find available credit and insurance for their crops.

The project is currently operating in two areas of Mexico: the high valleys in the states of Puebla and Mexico and part of Chiapas, and the tropical zone in the southern part of Veracruz. These are areas with a large concentration of small and poor agricultural producers. In Mexico, approximately 30% of the arable land is planted with corn and 92% of the 2.7 million of Mexican corn farmers operate in plots of five hectares or less. These are the poor agricultural producers that the *Campo Unido* project tries to reach, and Monsanto Corporation in Mexico has assigned about 45 people (project manager, field supervisors, promoters, and agricultural technicians) to this program. The Monsanto group works closely with "solidarity groups" that are associations of corn producers who decided to join in the *Campo Unido* project in the two main regions mentioned above.[17]

From the start, the company saw that the agriculture sector in Mexico is represented by 20% of the rural population that is sufficiently prepared with inputs and land to be economically self-sufficient. The other 80% is represented by poor agricultural producers who depend mainly on corn, and who have limited or no technical production means and hold small parcels, normally of the ejido or communal type. The *Campo Unido* project is targeted at this segment of the rural population, the poor farmer in the central and southern regions of the country with plots of five hectares or less, and with limited means to buy the more technical ingredients that would improve their productivity. For Monsanto, this is a project with heavy emphasis on rural development and social work. The project, initiated in 1997, had a close collaboration with *Fundación Mexicana para el Desarrollo Rural* (FMDR), which is a non-governmental organization specializing in agricultural development. In the long term, Monsanto expects to reap the benefits of an enhanced market of 80% of Mexican farmers that currently do not use or use very little of the herbicides, pesticides, improved seeds, and other agricultural inputs that Monsanto produces and distributes. Monsanto believes that they can succeed, by doing what they know best, to increase the productivity and yield of the crops in order to raise the standard of living of the poorest peasants in Mexico and elsewhere.

The small corn producers from central and southern Mexico have been considered as the best candidates to develop and implement this project. It is true that some of the poorest peasants in Mexico live in the states of Guerrero and Oaxaca and should have been part of the target for the *Campo Unido* project. However, some cultural barriers impeded the start of the project there. For instance, the agricultural producers in Oaxaca only plant in sets of 21 furrows with one meter of space in between each line. Monsanto technicians suggested reducing the space to 80 cm. between furrows to intensify the planting. This was not acceptable to the local farmers, because the allocation of communal land in that part of the country is based on the number of furrows. The farmers simply did not want to give up part of their previous space.[18]

Monsanto's approach is a mutually beneficial strategy, in which both the company and the participating farmers are rewarded. The main objective is to improve the living standard of the peasants. This can be accomplished through a combination of approaches: increasing the use of improved seeds, because the indigenous corn seeds only yield an average of 1.9 tons per hectare, while with the hybrid seeds, four tons or more per hectare can be obtained; applying the dosage of fertilizers appropriately; proper handling and use of herbicides and pesticides; a proper agronomic handling or management of the crops; searching for available and inexpensive credit; and looking for attractive and secure outlets for the product at the end of the harvests.

In principle, Monsanto's *Campo Unido* program helps peasants achieve the various links of what Monsanto calls the "Circle of Success," which involves all of the following:

a) organizing the participating farmers in solidarity or cooperative associations to strengthen the program and increase the potential for more participants; (This is probably one of the most important factors because, by grouping the agricultural producers together, their power to negotiate prices, obtain credit, and serve as solidarity guarantors, etc., multiplies.)
b) providing the best available technology and training to the farmers;
c) finding ways to help farmers obtain credit for acquiring the improved production inputs; (The technological package includes improved hybrid seeds, pesticides, and fertilizers.)
d) following up to ensure increased crop yields;
e) providing training and extension services to farmers in the various production and marketing activities; and
f) using marketing and promotion to seek the best available sales otions.

The Monsanto *Campo Unido* project is complex and has difficult objectives. Credit availability is always a challenge because the private financial institutions in Mexico are not interested in investing in projects for social development. In addition, the government's support funds for agriculture are either gone or are fairly exhausted, since, in Mexico, the government does not provide much financial backing to agricultural producers (This is quite different from governmental policy in the United States).[19]

Monsanto looks hard at the steps of the process to make it a successful operation. They have helped organize the corn farmers in producer groups for the benefit of the project. Monsanto people feel that rather than applying the available formulas for their legal association, it is more important that the participating members of *Campo Unido* share a sense of belonging, cooperation, cohesiveness, and group identity. This is particularly important in the processing of credit loans for the agricultural producers. The group negotiates the loan as a unit for the benefit of each of its members, but each individual is jointly responsible if anyone in the group fails to pay his/her share.

The *Campo Unido* Project works closely with the small corn producers as a mechanism to initiate the use of better inputs and to facilitate the provision of resources or performance of tasks that are crucial in the production process. Monsanto aims for a more comprehensive approach to corn farming—different from a contract-farming or production-association approach that other programs or corporations have used. Through this *Campo Unido* program, Monsanto encourages its promoters to reengineer the agricultural development process and to seek alliances with government agencies, non-governmental organizations, and even private corporations. It uses pilot demonstration parcels for cultivation of corn, and it provides technical assistance on the correct use of fertilizers, herbicides, and pesticides. It focuses on improving the key steps of the production process, progressively introducing the appropriate technology or making the recommended changes in the process. These changes are made gradually so that the farmer is not overwhelmed or resentful. In a way, Monsanto tries to respect the peasants' traditional forms of cultivation. Above all, the *Campo Unido* promoters are aiming to prepare the small agriculture producers to become successful farmers.

The premise of *Campo Unido* is that, using hybrid seeds and with proper care of the crop, one can raise corn yields in comparison to corn produced from indigenous corn seeds. The participating farmer is not forced to switch to improved seeds for the parcel all at once. In fact, it is recommended that if a farmer has three hectares of land, the hybrid corn be planted on only one of them, using traditional domestic varieties of corn on the other two. This domestic variety of corn can be stored for a longer period and can be used for personal consumption. The results of the two types of planting would be evident from the yields of the demonstration parcel. This approach makes it possible for the *Campo Unido* farmer to commercialize only the corn coming from the better yields and thus automatically increase the farmer's family income.

A pilot project was started in 1997 with 450 small corn producers that were organized with the help of the *Fundación Mexicana para el Desarrollo Rural* (FMDR). Based on that initial experience, Monsanto decided to expand the project. For the year 2000, the project reached 14,200 hectares of planted corn. The results have proven beneficial to the participating corn farmers who have seen their corn yields improve from 3.7 tons to 5.5 tons per hectare on the average, and their incomes increase from $48 to $240 per hectare.[20] Monsanto expected to expand the coverage of *Campo Unido* and to bring in more participants with a projected 17,800 total hectares for the year 2001. Along with the improvements in production volume, good practices of soil conservation and environmental control are emphasized. Thus, farmers are taught not to slash and burn their plots prior to sowing, and to avoid using paraquat or similar herbicides that are inappropriate for the environment.

One of the unique features of this *Campo Unido* project is its approach—fostering the cooperation of various agents in the process, and seeking workable solutions to difficult problems in the corn-production cycle. For instance, obtaining credit has been a difficult challenge for the small agricultural producers in Mexico. In this area, *Campo Unido* has relied on available funds from the FIRA, a federal trust fund that earmarks moneys for agricultural production. Funds from the government FIRA have to be administered through a financial institution (usually a commercial bank or equivalent), and the final recipients of the credit must provide loan guarantees. Here, *Campo Unido* has been successful in using a few mechanisms that have allowed for the allocation of these loan funds to the solidarity corn producer groups in the program. Thus, FIRA financing to small holders is done through a commercial bank, or through a *parafinanciera* (financing facilitator), an entity authorized by the Central Bank to act, as a bridge, to carry the farmer's account like one of its customers. Channeling of loan moneys can be also done through a *Procrea* (Program of Agricultural Credit) unit, a non-government organization that services the FIRA debt and receives a fee for its participation. Lastly, the same independent distributors of Monsanto products can act as the responsible links between the FIRA agency and the *Campo Unido* corn producers and carry part of the loan credit on their books. On the side of the participating farmers, besides paying the loan, their responsibilities include contributing the receipts of the Pro-Campo subsidies towards the minimum 10% of the loan guarantee. In addition, they are required to buy insurance (equivalent to 10% of the value of the loan) to pay for it in case of catastrophic crop losses. Interestingly, the farmers benefiting from these credits do not receive cash but rather the corresponding production inputs like improved seeds and fertilizers that are essential for their farming.

The benefits of the project for the participating farmers are expected to appear on the third year from its inception. It is Monsanto's intention that the project becomes jointly "owned" by their technicians and the agricultural producers and that both work together to make it a successful enterprise. The stages that the project goes through during the three years of maturation are:

1) first year—implementation of the program with no substantial gains predictable, yet;
2) second year—development of the program to increase the number of participating and committed farmers; and
3) third year—working of the program at full capacity, with economic gains expected to occur.

Monsanto is very interested in making *Campo Unido* a feasible and profitable undertaking and has engaged an outside evaluation team to measure its benefits and determine its continuance. The benefits should derive not only from the use of improved seeds, but also from the opening of market channels for the expected incrementally increased volumes. The main benefit for the agricultural units is the reduction of crop costs per ton of corn produced, achieved from yields improved by the use of better technology and guided extensionism. Monsanto is not a buyer or distributor of corn and cannot do anything about the price of corn in the market. It can only help the *Campo Unido* farmers search for good outlets to place their corn at harvest time.

It is logical that Monsanto seeks business goals for itself too. For Monsanto, there is the potential of an expanded market of small corn producers who traditionally have not used much technology in their production processes. If those small corn producers start using Monsanto products, find them useful, and become accustomed to their brands, it can be expected that their business relation with Monsanto would be enduring. To reach this target market, the company has reconfigured some of its marketing strategies. For instance, one strategy is to modify the product presentation. This has been applied to the herbicide "Round Up," a Monsanto brand, which is considered environmentally friendly and is normally sold as a liquid in large containers. It is now distributed as powder in packages that can be used with backpack applicator machines. This permits the herbicide to be purchased in small quantities by poor farmers with limited resources, and to be used only for the annual production season. This way, the farmer buys only what is needed and does not have to store excess herbicide for the following season.

In principle, the *Campo Unido* program is intended to help the small corn producers who have practiced traditional farming methods of planting native seeds with limited or inefficient use of chemical inputs and technology. Specifically, the objectives of *Campo Unido* are to increase small farmers' understanding and familiarity with modern agricultural techniques, to show the advantages of using Monsanto products, and to provide financing arrangements so that farmers can purchase these inputs. Improving market channels for small producers is another goal of the program and Monsanto is constantly searching for contract-farming opportunities and/or cooperative marketing arrangements. To achieve these goals, Monsanto helps to organize solidarity groups of farmers that typically have five to ten members though there is not a set membership limit.

On reflecting about the role that a multinational corporation can play in helping to improve the conditions of the rural poor in Mexico, the Monsanto managers in the field believe that progress is possible. The Monsanto *Campo Unido* proponents feel that for many years the Mexican government, through its programs, institutions, and personnel, did not appropriately address or closely follow the myriad of problems affecting the small agricultural producers in the country.

Often, government programs do not respond to the needs of the agricultural producers, and though the new administration appears to follow a more cooperative approach to problem-solving, progress is still slow and piecemeal. Witness the fact that the national agricultural development plan for 2002–06 in Mexico was finalized at the end of 2001 and its specific programs were not published until 2002. It is true that the resources that the federal government allocates to agricultural programs are dependent on an outdated tax system and that the slowing in the economy directly affects the available funds, but the needs of the small agricultural producers do not disappear. It is precisely in this role of helping the small corn producers of the poorest regions of Mexico where Monsanto feels it complements what the federal government policies have overlooked. It is here that Monsanto sees it can help with rural development and improve its potential market reach in the process.

Summary and Concluding Observations

The NAFTA years have brought to Mexico a 180-degree change in its approach to economic development, and to government influence and administration, not to mention a sudden shift in political control. The Mexican government has had to build and maintain the structural mechanisms that the NAFTA framework requires, while at the same time it has had to reluctantly withdraw from its previous role of first and foremost engine of economic change.

Within the new economic environment that NAFTA helped create, not all the expected economic and social benefits trickled down to the poor masses of the population, especially those rural farmers still engaged in low-scale production in small family plots.

It is in response to the less active participation of the State, as a sponsor of development, that the private enterprise can provide viable and promising alternatives to economic progress, especially in those areas of the rural countryside where the benefits of the open markets rarely reach. The role of business, especially in the context of Mexican agriculture, is even more critical in view of the comparatively disproportionate support that the farmers in the United States receive from their own government.

Some formulas for engaging the cooperation of agribusiness firms with local small agricultural producers have been tried and tested in the past. One can revisit these alternatives and assess their challenges and opportunities as a means to improve the economic conditions of the small farmer in rural Mexico.

In the process of reviewing corporate-sponsored alternatives for agricultural development, this study has documented two cases for analysis. These two multinational corporations currently participate in agricultural-production programs with small corn producers in Mexico. In one of the projects reviewed, Monsanto Corporation seeks to improve the production yields of corn through the distribution and use of improved technology in two regions of Mexico. The other project reviewed describes the association of a corn-mill processor with ejido farmers in the state of Jalisco to guarantee the supply of corn for industrial processes. Notwithstanding the fact that these are programs with limited regional coverage and product-specific scope, they serve as examples to replicate or sponsor in other parts of the country. In the end, they represent the type of activities where all participants in the process of agricultural development can benefit.

One can argue that the government can still rightfully provide the general path to economic and agricultural development within the framework of a free market, export-oriented environment.[21] Ultimately, a system of checks and balances in a truly functional democracy can empower the citizenry to approve or

Endnotes

1. Recent data put the area of corn cultivation in Mexico at 8.8 million hectares which is ostensibly many times larger than the 350,000 hectares dedicated to horticultural products that have a better appeal for export markets (Nadal, 37).
2. Figures used in this part are from Mexico, Cámara de Diputados, several pages.
3. As of December 31, 2000, the Mexican Congress had authorized the Executive Branch of the Federal government to administratively impose a maximum duty of 30% on the importation of corn from the United States, applicable to the quantities exceeding the duty-free quota. As it turned out, the Office of the President never issued any executive order to introduce this duty and none was imposed on further imports before the full implementation of NAFTA took place in 2008 when those restraints on the importation of corn were to expire.
4. CEPAL (1998).
5. A prior analysis of the characteristics of the 2.2 million family agricultural units in Mexico identified 64% of them with four hectares of land or less and at or below the subsistence level. Only 9% of these units of twelve or more hectares in size showed the potential to generate excess income beyond grains for self-consumption, replenishment of production inputs, and reserves for uncertainties (CEPAL 1989).
6. The market constraints are the reasons that preclude the small agricultural producers of corn and dry beans to switch to non-traditional crops that are more attractive to agribusiness processors. For instance, the total costs to produce corn in Mexico were close to 2,500 Pesos per hectare in 1995, compared to 9,000 Pesos for broccoli, 14,000 for potatoes and 30,000 for strawberries (R. Marsh and D. Runsten 1994, 9).
7. It is difficult to find references to success stories involving agribusiness units and small rural producers, not necessarily because there are few, but simply because they are rarely documented. One worth citing is the supply of vegetable crops by previous corn producers (ejido farmers) to an agribusiness firm called EXPOHORT in the Valley of Amealco, in Mexico (G. Dutrenit and A. Oliveira 1991, 16). Also, the Economics and Agriculture Research Center of Universidad Chapingo has documented a good sample of agribusiness and producers' associations in Mexico. The projects studied—of a medium to large size—involved the participation of smallholders (ejidatarios or community farmers) but took place before the NAFTA years when direct government support to the agricultural sector in Mexico was a very important component. See Universidad Autónoma de Chapingo (1994).
8. They study in detail the case of frozen-vegetable contracting in Mexico, specifically in the Bajio and Zacatecas region.
9. Almidones Mexicanos, S.A. is a 50-50 joint venture between Archer Daniels Midland (ADM) and Tate & Lyle, which produces corn starches and derivatives in Guadalajara, Mexico.
10. In Mexico, the tomato agro-industry has been cited as an example of this alternative. See M. A. Barron and F. Rello.
11. For the year 2000, the expected production volume for the state of Jalisco was equal to 732,700 tons—698,500 from seasonal rain crops and 34,200 tons from irrigated lands.
12. This price is equivalent to what it would cost Almex to import and bring the yellow corn directly from the United States to its plant in Guadalajara.

change those general government policies. However, at the level of the indivi(ual production units operating in the market place, the participating individu als and firms are the ones who can better join efforts in agreements and trade that could benefit all. They are the ones who (as the examples of Almidones Mexicanos, S.A. and Monsanto Mexicana, S.A. here demonstrate) can design new formulas for helping the small agricultural producers reach the sustainable levels of development that they have sought for so long and that they so much deserve.

13. For the 2000 production cycle, the contract between Almex and AgroFerretera called for 23,500 tons of yellow corn at an average price of 1,470 Pesos per ton, with actual prices varying depending on the future date contracted for delivery. Almex has continued to expand the contract farming model and is working with one more intermediary. In the cycle crops of 2001 and 2002, they contracted purchases of 35,000 tons and 50,000 tons of yellow corn, respectively, from local producers.
14. The cost of production numbers are based on estimates provided by agricultural producers from the region where this study took place.
15. Among the ejidos visited were El Nuevo Refugio in Tototlán, Jalisco; Ejido San Joaquín in Atotonilco; Ejido San Miguel de La Paz in Jamay; and Ejidos Portezuelo, San Francisco de la Cal, La Laja de Gómez, and Santa Elena in La Barca.
16. In addition, Almex owns and maintains a small plot of planted corn for demonstration and agricultural extension services in the neighboring state of Guanajuato.
17. These small-producer associations are scattered in the two areas of Mexico where the project operates. In the year 2000, the project included 300 of the farmer solidar ity groups representing 3,800 families. Our field research included visits to some of these families in the communities of Frailesca, San Cristóbal, Tapachula, Tuxtla Chico, Frontera Hidalgo, and Villa Flores in Chiapas; and those of Acayucan and San Andrés Tuxtla in Veracruz.
18. In addition to these barriers, the corn-producing areas in Oaxaca and Guerrero are devoid of accessible roads and strategic communications to reach the main markets.
19. For the sake of comparison, in the year 2000, the U.S. federal government distributed $28 billion of direct payments to U.S. farmers, accounting for half of the money earned by them. There have been many instances when the U.S. farmer receives over $100,000 for not making any money on what is grown, and $50,000 for taking other land out of production (*The New York Times*, December 24, 2000).
20. For 2000, the increase in production yield was from 2.5 to 5 tons per hectare in the area of the tropics, and from 5 to 7 tons per hectare for the high valleys.
21. On this subject, the Mexican Government has published its National Development Plan for the six years of the Fox regime. While the plan sets general objectives and strategies for the various sectors of the economy, a detailed mapping of the government policies and procedures for agriculture in Mexico appeared only in 2002. See Presidencia de la República. *Plan Nacional de Desarrollo*, http://pnd.presidencia.gob.mx.

Bibliography

Andrews, E. L. "Rich Nations Are Criticized for Enforcing Trade Barriers," *The New York Times,* September 30, 2002.

Barron, M. A., and F. Rello. "The Impact of the Tomato Agroindustry on the Rural Poor in Mexico." *Agricultural Economics* 23 (2000): 289–97.

CEPAL (*Comisión Económica para America Latina*—Economic Commission for Latin America). "Agroindustria y Pequeña Agricultura: Experiencias y Opciones de Transformación.) In *Agroindustria y Pequeña Agricultura: Vinculos, Potenciales y Oportunidades Comerciales.* Santiago, Chile: CEPAL/FAO/GTZ, 1998.

———. *Economía Campesina y Agricultura Empresarial: Tipologia de Productores del Agro Mexicano.* Mexico: Siglo Veintiuno Editores, 1989.

Dutrenit, G. and A. Oliveira. "Factores de Éxito y Fracaso de las Asociaciones de Empresarios Agropecuarios y Productores Rurales en Mexico: Analisis de Casos." In *Agroindustria y Pequeña Agricultura.* Mexico: CEPAL, 1991.

Egan, T. "Falling Farmers Learn to Profit from Federal Aid." *The New York Times,* December 24, 2000.

Glade, William A. and L. A. Tavis. "Actualizing the Development Response of Multinational Corporations: The Case of Agribusiness in the Mexican Countryside," *Journal of International Economic Law* 18 (1997): 1211–34.

International Fund for Agricultural Development (IFAD). *Rural Poverty Report 2001: The Challenge of Ending Rural Poverty.* London: Oxford University Press, 2001.

Key, N., and D. Runsten. "Contract Farming, Smallholders, and Rural Development in Latin America: The Organization of Agroprocessing Firms and the Scale of Outgrower Production." *World Development* 27, no. 2 (1999): 381–401.

Marsh, R., and D. Runsten. "From Garden to Exports: The Potential for Smallholder Fruit and Vegetable Production in Mexico." (paper presented at the 18th International Congress of the Latin American Studies Association, Atlanta, GA, March 10–12, 1994).

McDonald, J. *Agribusiness Concentration, Competition and NAFTA.* Research Paper. Washington: Economic Research Service, U.S. Department of Agriculture, 2001.

Mexico, Cámara de Diputados, LVII Legislatura, Comisión de Agricultura. *Cuanta Liberación Aguanta La Agricultura? Impacto del TLALCAN en el Sector Agroalimentario.* Mexico, 2000.

Mexico, Presidencia de la República. *Plan Nacional de Desarrollo.* Mexico, 2001. http://pnd.presidencia.gob.mx.

Murphy, S. *Managing the Invisible Hand: Markets, Farmers and International Trade.* Canada: Institute of Agriculture and Trade Policy, 2002.

Nadal, A. *The Environmental and Social Impacts of Economic Liberalization on Corn Production in Mexico.* A Study Commissioned by Oxfam GB and WWF International. London: Oxfam GB, 2000.

Narayan, D., ed. *Empowerment and Poverty Reduction: A Source Book.* Washington, DC: The World Bank, 2002.

Reardon, T., and C. B. Barrett. "Agroindustrialization, Globalization, and International Development: An overview of Issues, Patterns and Determinants. *Agricultural Economics* 23 (2000): 195–205.

Rostow, W. W. *The Stages of Economic Growth: A Non-Communist Manifesto*. London: Cambridge University Press, 1960.

The New York Times. "Falling Farmers Learn to Profit from Federal Aid." *The New York Times*. National News Section, December 24, 2000.

United States Department of Agriculture, Economic Research Service. *International Agriculture and Trade Reports: NAFTA*, WRS-99-1, August, 1999.

Universidad Autónoma de Chapingo, CIESTAAM. *Modalidades de Asociación e Integración en la Agroindustria Mexicana*. Chapingo, Mexico: 1994.

Wiesebron, M. L. "Transformation in Latin America." In *Competing for Integration: Japan, Europe, Latin America and Their Strategic Partners*, edited by K.W. Radke and M. L. Weisebron. New York: M. E. Sharpe, 2002.

Chapter 6

Transnationals and Agriculture by Contract: The Case of Three Frozen-Food Companies in Mexico

Elia Patlán Martínez and Juan de Dios Trujillo Félix*

THIS CHAPTER, DERIVED FROM FIELD RESEARCH in the Mexican regions of the Bajío and of the north of Guanajuato, analyzes the relationship established between companies and producers that engage in agriculture by contract. In order to do this, the study will include the cases of three businesses whose focus is the export of frozen vegetables: Bird's Eye, MarBran, and Expor San Antonio (see Table 1). The first of these is the oldest frozen-broccoli processing plant in Mexico and operates completely on foreign capital; the second, whose headquarters is located in Mexico, and which has experienced a period of expansion in the last decade, represents a business that has contracted a strategic transnational alliance; and the third is a locally financed business that is completely oriented toward exports, and—as is the case with all three companies—combines direct production with agriculture by contract.

Table 1
Principal Exporters of Frozen Vegetables

Company	Began Operations	City and State	Source of Capital	Current Owner	Orientation of Production
Bird's Eye	1967	Celaya, Guanajuato	North America	Argilink Foods	Export
MarBran	1980	Irapuato, Guanajuato	North American; National	Simplot (North American company, leader in frozen potatoes)/ Raúl Nieto Gómez	Export
Expor San Antonio	1990	Villagrán, Guanajuato	National	Enrique Nieto	Export

Seen from a historical perspective, transnational businesses were the basis for development of the frozen-food industry, but the market became steadily profitable and this caused producers with capital and knowledge in the area to move toward a more vertical arrangement. The development and consolidation

*The authors acknowledge and recognize the collaboration of Victor Sánchez Fabián, José Olvera Martínez, Honorato Cerón, and Iturbide Arce.

of this agro-industry took place during a period of 40 years, although its origin is much earlier.

Each of the three cases has its own peculiarities, and they range from those with an inclination toward larger producers to, as in one case, the tendency to contract with small ones. They also register differences in terms of the way they interact with the producers. The practice of contractual agriculture is rooted in the area of study and is not only practiced by transnational but also by domestic agribusiness firms.

This study is derived from a collaborative effort between CIESTAAM, Michigan State University, and the University of Notre Dame. Information was obtained from interviews and surveys conducted with 32 contract producers, and with five administrators or responsible technicians of the same during July 2000.

Business and the Development of the Frozen-Vegetable Export Industry

The Mexican frozen-vegetable industry is primarily centered in Guanajuato, although it is also present in other states including Aguascalientes, Michoacán, and Querétaro (see Table 2). The industry's development in the last three decades has been chiefly associated with the processing of broccoli and cauliflower. Fruit has also been important; for instance, strawberries originally formed the basis of the industry. Strawberry exporters experienced a period of growth until the 1970s, after which there was a decline. However, the frozen-food industry was able to consolidate itself by way of other crops.

This industry would not have reached its present level without the dynamic growth of the frozen-food market in the United States, which was associated with an increase in the income of the population, and the changing tastes of the consumer toward healthier foods. Additionally, vertical integration, especially of broccoli and cauliflower, led to increased processing capacity as a result of the establishment of more plants.

In a study by Cook, et al. (1991), the number of plants registered had risen to 30 by the early 1990s, 12 of which were located in Guanajuato. The industry went through a notable expansion, especially during the 1980s, that resulted in an increased number of plants. However, a readjustment occurred in the 1990s in which that number was reduced to 19. The number of plants in Guanajuato did not change, but the size of these operations did. Activity tended to become centralized and the dominant role of the transnationals declined. The frozen-foods activity showed greater resistance in this state than in other federal states in Mexico.

In 1988, Campbell Foods, which had been prominent in the processing of broccoli and cauliflower through contractual agriculture, withdrew from the area of frozen foods and decided to focus on its traditional line of canned soups with an orientation toward the international market. This decision was motivated by the economic crisis of 1982 and the depression in the internal market for its

Table 2

Frozen-vegetable Processors in Mexico (1998)

OWNER	COMPANIES	LOCATION	BEGAN OPERA-TIONS	ANNUAL VOL. PROCESSSED (x1,000 TONS)
Nieto/Simplot	MARBRAN-SIMPLOT	Irapuato, Gto. (2) Jaral, Gto. (1)	1980 1995	45
Nieto	EXPOR SAN ANTONIO	Villagrán, Gto.	1990	40
Agrilink	BIRD'S EYE	J. Rosas, Gto.	1967	28
Diageo	GIGANTE VERDE	Irapuato, Gto.	1983	27
Usabiaga	COVEMEX	Celaya, Gto.	1976	16
Arteaga	LA HUERTA	Aguascalientes	1976	15
Roiz	EXPOHORT	Querétaro	1985	14
Fox	CONGELADOS DON JOSÉ	León, Gto.	1985	11
Bours	CONGELADORA HORTÍCOLA SONORENSE*	Cd. Obregón, Son.	1990	11
Alvarado/Amerincs	ICEMARK	Aguascalicntes	1999	8
Covarrubias	FRESPORT	Irapuato, Gto.	1986	7
	CONGELADORA CEUTA*	Culiacán, Sinaloa	1990	5
Miranda	LA ESPERANZA DE MIRANDA	Dolores Hidalgo, Gto.	1990	5
Alvarado	FRIENDLY NATURE	Irapuato, Gto.	1996	4
Bimbo	FREXPORT**	Zamora, Mich.	1991	4
	FRUVEZA**	Zamora, Mich.	1988	4
Valdéz	EMPACADORA EL CELIO**	Jacona, Mich.	1985	4
González	PRODUCTOS FRUGO	Salamanca, Gto.	1989	3
León	CONGELADORA LA HACIENDA	Silao, Gto.	1991	3
				254

* Their primary activity is the freezing of bell peppers.
** Although they are primarily freezers of strawberries, the volumes indicated refer to broccoli and cauliflower.
Source: Echánove 2000.

products. This move resulted in transferring its producers to Bird's Eye. MarBran, a Mexican enterprise that first ventured into frozen vegetables in 1980, entered into an alliance with Simplot in 1992,[1] and thus acquired a leadership position in the Mexican export of frozen products, followed by Expor San Antonio (1990), leaving Green Giant and Bird's Eye in third and fourth place, respectively. The Bird's Eye plant, previously affiliated with Green Foods, was acquired by Agrilink Foods, a subsidiary company of the Pro-Fac Cooperative.

Mexico continued to have a high level of participation, although declining, in the importation of broccoli and cauliflower by the U.S. market. In 1989, for example, Mexico provided 93% of the imports of both products, but this decreased to 81% in 1999. A loss of 12 percentage points occurred during this period. This means that the U.S. market has become more competitive, and other countries have tended to gain in importance (such as Guatemala, with 14.3% of imports in

1999, and Canada, with 3.8%). Mexico has taken advantage of the growth of the market, but it has not been able to prevent the diminishing of its participation in the market (as seen in Table 3).

Mexico was attractive to the transnationals that were initially established in the Bajío region, especially in Guanajuato and Querétaro, because of: a climate favorable to the production of vegetables; an abundant cheap labor force; the availability of land and water, and the proximity to the U.S. markets. However, Mexico's comparative advantages in large-scale vegetable production are currently diminishing because of the relative increases in wages of workers compared to other countries in Central and South America; the scarcity of water in the region due to the overuse of water from the subsoil; and the problems with pest infestations. Furthermore, the readjustments occurring in the number of processing plants, as well as the pressure to introduce other products, suggest that the market has reached maturity—according to the expectations of some producers interviewed.

Table 3

United States Imports of Broccoli and Cauliflower from Leading Supplier Countries, by U.S. $ and Percentage, 1989–1999

Year	Mexico		Guatemala		Canada		Total	
	Value	%	Value	%	Value	%	Value	%
1989	86,748,300	92.8	5,165,276	5.5	935,135	1.0	93,494,839	100
1990	92,823,139	92.4	5,930,209	5.9	1,081,990	1.1	100,443,883	100
1991	92,733,736	90.2	8,755,521	8.5	957,547	0.9	102,855,558	100
1992	122,409,402	89.8	11,724,359	8.6	2,017,363	1.5	136,275,449	100
1993	112,045,714	88.5	12,014,594	9.5	1,886,347	1.5	126,594,249	100
1994	104,895,984	87.7	11,843,829	9.9	2,341,695	2.0	119,576,377	100
1995	103,769,756	84.3	17,486,813	14.2	1,847,421	1.5	123,166,235	100
1996	107,208,812	84.1	17,073,249	13.4	3,114,466	2.4	127,450,760	100
1997	116,012,044	83.3	15,161,326	10.9	7,875,328	5.7	139,291,449	100
1998	114,555,054	79.8	21,276,554	14.8	7,412,952	5.2	143,535,777	100
1999	138,053,453	81.4	24,278,706	14.3	6,420,500	3.8	169,618,500	100
Average annual variance per period								
1989–94	3.9%		18.1%		20.1%		5.0%	
1994–99	5.6%		15.4%		22.4%		7.2%	

Source: http://151.121.66.126/db/fatus/index.asp?Type=MC.

Companies' and Producers' Motivations

Given that companies need to be provided with raw materials and producers with a secure market for their crops, one can speak of a relationship of mutual benefit, although all parties may not gain equally. For producers, the frozen-food companies present the most secure option for the sale of their crops. According to responses to the surveys conducted, 62.6% of those interviewed cited selling security and the fulfillment of contractual agreement as reasons for staying with a company, in addition to being the best alternative for the marketing of its products.

The relationship between companies and producers transcends simple product supply—insofar as the companies are interested in exercising a certain level of control over the production process in order to assure the level and quality of the product which they need. Processing companies operate according to the demands and characteristics of the market, which often requires the adoption of "packages" of techniques and services that the producer must accept as part of the agreement.

In general, small producers tend to establish a relationship of greater financial and technical dependence on the company compared to medium-size and larger producers. This is due to their more marked need for credit and agricultural extension services. Of these producers, there may be those who achieve above-average production and deliver a product of superior quality as a result of their small, well-regulated work force or more personal attention to the entire production process. However, these producers require close technical supervision in order to assure compliance with the guidelines established by the company. Their ability to negotiate is minimal, but the administration of contracts may be more costly for the company.

The size of larger-scale producers affords a number of advantages, such as ease in supervision and fewer demands for credit and technical assistance. In addition, these producers have recourse to other sources of financing, or to methods for managing existing resources, derived from the planning of parcels of land or alternative activities. Other advantages include a greater endowment of infrastructure, machinery, and equipment, and their ability to handle larger volumes of produce. Furthermore, given the scale of their operations, these producers are in a better position to introduce innovations and to directly obtain their own technical assistance. In spite of their complaint that prices are established arbitrarily, the producers' greater ability to negotiate permits them to consider other options that may lead them to terminate their relationship with a company with which they interact. It is not uncommon to find producers in the region who at one time had contracted with the processing companies, but who now work independently in the export of frozen vegetables or fresh products.

Given the characteristics and conditions of the contracting relationship, one can understand why the companies have shown a bias toward medium-size and larger producers and why these corporations have not tried to exercise complete control over the production process. There is already a certain competition among companies to get the best providers, which results in better dealings for some in the assignment of land and no restrictions about working with other frozen-food companies or in the fresh produce market. This bias is not new; transnational companies, once established, have preferred to work with this type of producer.

Classification of Producers

Given the Mexican farming structure, substantially composed of farms that are under two hectares, and the type of producer with which the company is working, one might assume that there is little room left for the small producer. Nevertheless, companies classify their producers within their own context. Bird's Eye deals annually with 70 producers whose size ranges from 20 to 200 hectares; a tract of 50 or fewer hectares is considered small, while the larger ones are considered to be those over 100 hectares. In contrast, for MarBran, which works with a total of 800 producers and operates annually with 300 hectares of its own, the small producers would be those with fewer than ten hectares, a group that includes 70% of their providers. Those classified as large have more than 50 hectares each, a group which composes 10% of their present providers. *Expor San Antonio* works with 80 producers annually; it prefers those of more than 100 hectares, but also works with those who farm plots of less than the minimum limit established by Bird's Eye. A few of their providers work plots larger than 300 hectares (see Table 4).

Table 4

Classification of Producers by Size (Hectares Planted)

Type of producer	Bird's Eye	MarBran	Expor San Antonio
Small	20 to 50	4 to 30	5 to 50
Medium	51 to 100	31 to 50	51 to 99
Large	101 to 200	50 to 200	100 to 240
Average	**106.4 hectares**	**43.6 hectares**	**89 hectares**

Company Policies

The inclination toward a specific class of producers indicates the existence of different company policies. The Bird's Eye plant, like that of Green Giant in Mexico (both of which are subsidiaries of U.S. corporations), supply themselves solely through contract farming, which is not the case with MarBran, a joint venture with a North American transnational, and Expor San Antonio, which is solely owned by a Mexican family. These latter companies combine production on their own ranches with supplies from contractual agriculture, creating a situation that may imply a preference for their own crops and may provoke complaints from some of their providers. Until now, one basic element in their policies has been to strengthen the processes of vertical integration. In the case of Expor San Antonio, 40% of their marketed production comes from their own ranches; for MarBran that figure is one third.

Due to the brand recognition of Bird's Eye, its systems of distribution and a precise knowledge of the demand for its products, this company is better positioned than its competitors to plan its requirements. The minimization of costs in the plant, by way of adequate planning and control of the cost of raw material, reflect the coordination of their supply with the demand they expect to face. All this is fundamental for their continuing existence in Mexico, where they cannot overlook their transaction costs. From this perspective, Bird's Eye does not encourage financial dependence for its suppliers, since its policies show an inclination toward larger commercial producers with sufficient capitalization and a capacity for assimilating new technologies. In general, these producers can maintain a high level of control over their production processes.

The package offered by the company to its provider includes the following: supply of seedling; supervision and/or technical advice; adjustment in the price for not receiving financial support, or in compensation for greater distance; margin of tolerance; less inclination to totally reject the produce; effective payment one week after receiving the produce; and, flexibility to assume the plant costs in case of a disastrous weather event—although this is not established contractually. Delays result in a greater deterioration of the product and greater penalties to the producer for not conforming to the specifications.

Although the company does not encourage financial assistance, and tries to operate with the producers who do not demand it, it can be said that, in general, this is in exchange for the fact that producers receive a higher price at the time of harvest. On the other hand, the Bird's Eye plant, which represents around 3% of the total volume of Agrilink's sales, does not define the existence of this company, to such an extent that its capacity to adjust to the market is restricted by corporate policy.

MarBran has defined a policy of operation with small producers (in general, providing financing), a fact which has allowed it to control more closely the production process of its providers—who are, at the same time, recipients of technical assistance. This policy, although it may elevate the transaction costs, implies assurance not only of the harvest but of the providers as well, because—according to the agreement—they cannot deal with other frozen-food producers who may eventually offer a better price for the produce. Furthermore, this class of producer is more likely to tolerate the less favorable policies of the company, which benefits by a more labor-intensive production and the potentially better quality of harvested produce. As a substantial element of its strategic planning, the company has determined a movement toward organic products in the next ten years, such that, in order to adjust to the philosophy that this type of production implies, small family-type production will be encouraged.

Expor San Antonio, in turn, does not tend toward small producers nor fully accept the Bird's Eye model, but instead situates itself between the two extremes. Since it does not depend on a foreign parent company and works with a wider range of products, it has a more defined policy than Bird's Eye for taking the greatest advantage of its installed plant capacity all year long, and is not considering venturing into organic products. It combines direct production on its own farms with contractual production, and utilizes, to a greater extent than Bird's Eye, a system of financing for its providers.

In recent years, Bird's Eye has moved from an exclusive focus on its own brands to allowing production at the request of other companies who market the products under other brand names and specifications. This move is a result of the need to rationalize fixed costs. In this way, it has moved into the market that allowed Mexican companies to become strong, given their limited capacity for placing brand-name products.

The tendency toward larger producers, especially by Bird's Eye, has become stronger in the last decade. Changes in Mexico's agricultural policy that have encouraged this trend have taken away incentives for the production of grains, allowing producers to participate in the production of broccoli and cauliflower through contract growing. In the same way, all companies have had the opportunity to follow effective policies of selection of the best producers to bring about an increase in the average size of their suppliers. The rental of land has been the way that the size of the production units has increased.

For Bird's Eye, and to a lesser extent the other companies, the ideal is to adopt control mechanisms only over the planned supply, by using seedlings that, by contract, cannot be obtained in the open market nor grown in greenhouses by the producer. Furthermore, the allocation of land to the best providers of raw material eliminates the need to assert strict control over the operations of the production unit. The monopoly over seedlings has two types of justification: one is of a technical nature and involves inducements of the use of varieties that respond better within the specifications of quality and volume; the other pertains to the need for planning, since—keeping in mind the expected yield—planting dates and harvest by lots reduces the possibility of gluts in product delivered for processing at the plant. The company's planning is mainly influenced by orders from (and expected market trends in) North America.

Broccoli defines the pattern of specialization in the frozen-food industry of the Bajío region and the north of Guanajuato, although other options are also exploited. Around 90% of the production in the Bird's Eye plant is broccoli, with the remainder being cauliflower and zucchini. However, the level of differentiation for these products is such that this company operates with a range of 50 commercially distinct products. Expor San Antonio follows a less focused pattern with 80% broccoli, 15% cauliflower, 3% carrots, and 2% green and yellow squash. Mar-Bran incorporates alternatives such as carrots, yellow and green squash, sweet peas, onions, string beans, mangoes, and strawberries, among others.

Vision of Producers—Pattern of Specialization

Production destined for export has a long history and dates back to before the establishment of multinational businesses, which has played an important role in the introduction of new crops, such as broccoli, and in technologies and access to the U.S. market. Dating from the processing of broccoli, a pattern less inclined toward the harvest of products for the fresh produce market was adopted in this region. Now, whether for the frozen-vegetable industry or for the fresh-produce market, products such as broccoli, cauliflower, squash, peas, tomatoes, chili peppers, lettuce, asparagus, celery, garlic, strawberries, onions, and marigolds represent more important and profitable crops in the region.

For those producers involved in contractual agriculture, broccoli represents a high proportion of their income, especially when they do not follow a strategy of risk administration through crop diversification or participation in other economic activities. The bulk (83.3%) of the producers polled name this product as their principal option, and almost 39% have cauliflower and/or chili peppers as their alternative or second crop. Broccoli is considered a profitable option, while cauliflower is less profitable. The interest of brokers in this product and other crops from the Bajío region has increased in recent years. However, the fresh-produce market is still very small, which stimulates independent production in competitive conditions, aside from the demand of the companies.

As much as possible, given their resources, the producers interviewed tend to use contracting with industry as a mechanism for ensuring a stable income base for their production units, while engaging in more risky endeavors that may eventually become much more profitable, as is the case with products destined for the fresh-produce market. Contracting with industry can be an advantage, but it also restricts the possibility of increasing income, particularly because the industry assigns quotas of land usage in order to guarantee its supply.

As mentioned earlier, the willingness to make contracts has been stimulated by changes in agricultural policy that caused a dramatic decrease in the profitability of grains (corn, sorghum, wheat, and beans being the most important). These products play a role in crop rotation and in breaking the life cycles of pests, and continue to be used by the majority of producers though they are not sufficiently attractive options.

Among those producers contracted by the industry, in particular those of larger economic dimensions, a strategy of diversification can also be applied not only to crops, but to other activities as well (livestock, services, or production of dyes). According to information obtained in the field, it is probable that this diversification has been supported by a relationship with the industry. It is worth observing that 31.7% of producers have professional studies done so that their expectations do not preclude the possibility of an indefinite and stable relationship with processors.

Producers' Evaluation of Their Relationship with the Industry

More than 90% of frozen-food companies interviewed work with private producers. This collaboration remained consistent regardless of whether the producers' land was their own property, as long as they had guaranteed access to water (preferably from a well) and were well-equipped with machinery and agricultural equipment—in particular, a tractor with wide plowing capacity. To this effect, any producer of a certain income level who fits this pattern can be included, regardless of the size of the estate. In the assignment of land and volumes contracted, the companies evaluate the producer's performance record in terms of their fulfillment of contracts and their loyalty to the company. The type of producer with these characteristics is far from the image of the poor country farmer.

The average estimated farm size for the group of producers interviewed was 78.6 hectares, ranging from 4 to 240 hectares. However, as indicated earlier, these values are not the same for each company and change according to its policies. The producers' evaluation is that their relationship with frozen-food companies chosen is positive, but not overwhelmingly so. Some 65.6% of producers perceive improvements in their quality of life and economic standing, while the remaining 34.4% do not see any change. The reason to continue the relationship is based on the need for technical assistance, for supplies and fertilizer, for a secure income, and largely, because of the existence of a secure contract. Given the nature of Mexican agriculture and the co-dependence between each producer and its respective processing company, the agricultural producers identify the fulfillment of agreements and the lack of a better alternative as the most important reasons for not changing their partnering company.

In spite of what has been said earlier, it is useful to point out some problematic aspects of such relationships. First, producers are at a disadvantage in fixing the price of their crops because they are not organized for collective bargaining over their concerns. Most likely, a certain amount of collusion exists among businesses regarding the price that will be paid to the producer. There are no clear criteria for the way prices are set, so that producers are unaware of how they are determined. Conflict has not arisen over this point because the profitability of other options is very low and because yields per hectare have increased with sufficient speed to keep rising costs from devouring potential earnings.

For the year 2000, owing to an accumulation of inventory in 1999, prices for producers decreased and companies had to lower the amount of land programmed for planting. The old problem of poor coordination of the receiving of produce has not been resolved; long waits for delivery at the plants have hurt producers who complain that they are being penalized or that their produce has been refused due to deterioration of the quality of the produce. Furthermore, this favors crops coming from company-owned farms and elevates the quality requirement when the production rate is high.

There are producers who criticize the supervision and functioning of the agricultural departments and the method of turning in the plants. Smaller producers, especially, consider that if the supervision were more frequent and less biased toward those with larger farms, less of their produce would be rejected. Meanwhile, the more efficient producers favor the convenience of having more freedom to select the varieties to be planted because the material promised is not always delivered.

While the relationship between companies and producers has not been exempt from conflicts, these have rarely ended in litigation, given that informal relationships predominate. Both companies and providers value the existence of a stable relationship. As a result, companies are not always uncompromising and producers generally manage to fulfill the contract agreement, especially with regard to not selling the contracted produce to other buyers.

Strain on Resources and Modification of Farm Ecosystems

Broccoli and cauliflower came to modify the cultivation model since they offered, among other advantages, a greater turnover of capital. Another important effect was the increased pressure on resources due to their more intensive use. In the Bajío region, the phreatic mantle has diminished to the degree that agribusiness demands from its producers guaranteed access to water as a basic precondition for establishing a contract. Manuel Gómez (1989) states that in the 1960s it was normal to find water tables at 5 to 10 meters beneath the surface, but by the mid-1980s the norm was from 300 to 350 meters.

The decline in the quantity and quality of water and the greater pressure on its use in watering crops may lead to a greater deterioration in the quality of the ground because of high salt content and competition over resources of land and water.

The increase in the number of plants and of the land planted, in addition to the desire of companies to optimize the use of available plant capacity, contribute to extending the cultivation of the cruciferous vegetables mentioned to almost the entire year.[2] This has given rise to a new production specialization and also to mono-cultivation in a significant number of hectares. However, as a result of this practice, the life cycle of pests is left unbroken, with the consequent proliferation of pests. This increases the need to use more pesticides, with the corresponding increases in the costs of cultivation. In addition, the intensified use of the land has contributed to the appearance of resistant varieties of pests. For example, the Diamond-back Moth, which previously had not been considered a problem, became uncontrollable. In the search for greater pesticide effectiveness, the use of wide-spectrum "bombs" ended up harming populations of beneficial insects that were natural predators of the pests. The need to develop efficient methods of control led to the creation of COTECO, the General Technical Committee of the Association of Fruit and Vegetable Processors and Exporters (*Comité Técnico de la Asociación de Procesadores y Exportadores de Frutas y Vegetales en General, A.C.*), which was formalized in 1988 (Hoy 1999). This organization established a mechanism for the coordination and agreement between businesses and research institutions to incorporate integrated pest-management practices[3] in areas of production of cruciferous vegetables. However, Diamond-back populations continue to be a problem due to the increase in farmed territory (Hoy 1999).

In addition, the scarcity of water, which in the same interval has inspired the introduction of drip irrigation systems, continues to be a problem. The public preoccupation with the capacity for renewal of the phreatic mantle has led to the design of programs (subsidized by state and federal governments) for the adoption of more efficient water usage technologies and decreased waste through pipes.

Feminization of the Workforce, Child Labor, and Competition for Labor

In towns located near frozen-food plants, the companies have exerted an important influence on a generation of stable employees—especially for Bird's Eye, which has a low employee turnover rate. However, the companies have had a greater effect on the development of rural work markets through employment by the producers themselves, and the demand for support services. The indirect effect on the creation of jobs is not inconsiderable, given the importance of migratory processes in this territorial area.

Guanajuato is among those Mexican states that have most provided the North American economy with a migrant labor force. The development of the frozen-food industry, though not actually halting the migration process, especially of men, has to a certain degree slowed the process through the creation of local jobs, given that agricultural products require a large workforce. However, in the face of a scarce male labor force, women and children have been incorporated as paid employees in the plants and fields. The use of child labor is currently part of the existing problem in the region, and is a situation that has arisen from the need to harvest products demanded by the foreign market.

Considering the production process of broccoli, around 30% of the labor force is less than 18 years of age and earns below the minimum wage.[4] However, in the 1990s a new situation developed for the frozen-food industry regarding the workforce. Around the middle of the decade, the introduction of machinery in production zones caused a greater competition for labor, especially that of women. This trend exerts strong pressure on salary levels in the field, with possible negative effects on the future of the activity. Although producers connected to agribusiness and export have complained in previous years about the relative scarcity of labor due to emigration, there is now a new element which pushes toward a greater mechanization of some work in the field. There is increased competition between field and non-agricultural industries for the rural workforce, and it is likely that, in response to this competition, people from other poorer regions of the country will be coming, and thus aggravating the already precarious wage levels.

Technology Transfer and Agricultural Supply Market

In the contract-agriculture scheme, the transfer of technology toward producers is fundamental for achieving the quality and volumes required. According to information from the field, producer culture has been improving as a result of the contractual relationship between agribusiness and producers to such a degree that some producers point out weaknesses that they observe in the operation of the company with which they work. Likewise, there are more cases of producers that in reality do not need any technical supervision from the companies.

The transfer of technology related to those crops approved is important in the beginning of the relationship between the producer and business, but it decreases in importance as experience is gained. To this effect, the sources of innovation introduced by the producer may not come from the plant itself, but from the necessity of being more competitive, as is reflected in the introduction of innovations in irrigation, something which was not required by the companies.

From a technical standpoint, the key elements for the frozen-food businesses are: the types of suitable pesticides that are permitted; the respect of prohibitions; and the types of plants provided by producers. Regarding this last point, studies of agriculture are not conducted, but rather a seed company's product is approved for selection and delivery to its contracted producers.

One of the factors to influence the frozen-food companies is the development of the market for services and supplies for agricultural activity. The arrangements applied by some companies do not necessarily provide all the production inputs but concentrate primarily on the supply of plants. This situation has had the positive effect of motivating the private market toward other agricultural supplies, given that the providers of raw material are producers with buying power who understand the technological package and seek greater profitability.

Agriculture by Contract and Producers in the Bajío Region and the North of Guanajuato

Companies have resorted to contracts in order to deal with failures derived from the workings of the market (such as uncertain property rights) and in order to supply themselves with the raw material that they require. Furthermore, these companies have applied policies that try to reduce their transaction costs, leaning toward contracting with medium-size and large producers. Only the case of MarBran is an exception in terms of this preference, which is attributed to the characteristics of the organic product markets it is trying to develop.

Contractual agriculture has improved economic development in the Bajío region with a definite process of vertical integration (Rehber 1998). This integration occurs in the face of the businesses' need for direct production and in order to rationalize the investment in the construction of plants. These businesses were unable to place their product under their own brand names. In the consumer markets, however, the existence of claimants who marketed under their own label permitted its development. Furthermore, these businesses have enjoyed a situation of less threat in terms of the ownership of the land—given their national character and superior knowledge of the political and social contexts within which they operate.

As has been in the Bajío region, the type of relationship established between producers and businesses depends to a great extent on the efficiency of the judicial system, the type of producers (large, medium, or small—commercial or rural) and on the degree of monopoly that the company has in the market of products and supplies. On this point, the presence of a greater number of plants influenced the capacity to exercise market power and to gain a better bargaining position in the supply market.

In Mexico, contracts can include anything from technical requirements to economic obligations that bind both parties, and they are not always written contracts. Although they can become "leonine" (*leoninos*)[5] and weighed toward the interests of the companies, the cases of conflicts brought to court have been rare. From the point of view of the producer, the possibility of being excluded as a supplier of a company is a greater risk, and informal relationships become very important in the functioning of contracts. The normal procedure is that contracted producers receive their contracts for signing once the agricultural cycle is well underway. A relationship of trust is fundamental.

Conclusions

The contract-agriculture plan reveals a high degree of stability in the regions of the Bajío and the north of Guanajuato, and has been part of the functioning of established frozen-food plants, whether they are of transnational or national origin. Thanks to the prominent production of broccoli and cauliflower, the frozen-vegetable export industry has thrived in this part of Mexico.

Transnational companies have played an important role in the incorporation of this form of relationship between producers and businesses, and in the development of the frozen-vegetable industry. Yet neither the future of the industry in the region nor the future of the contracting activity is clear. Changes in plant ownership and alliances suggest the existence of a process of reorganization and adjustment to the food industry of the United States that may have repercussions for Mexico. The tendencies of the market for consumer goods and the products discussed here are not definite, but it is possible that it is already entering a state of maturity. If so, a readjustment in the number of companies involved in the activity can be expected, which will make it more concentrated. The need for diversification, the shift toward organic products (as MarBran is doing), and the gradual decrease of participation by Mexico in the U.S. importation of broccoli and cauliflower are trends that seem to support this prediction. While the regions considered are losing their historical and natural advantage, the characteristics of the producers involved in the industry and the new context of the country indicate a greater inclination to alleviate this loss by way of an increase in technological change. Diminishing resources and competition for labor may impose limits on the performance of the frozen-food industry if the constraints affecting its growth are not adequately addressed.

The frozen-food industry in the region studied illustrates more the agro-industrial chain than the industry of a small area, suggesting that its impact over employment is greater than that which is directly registered. This industry has been important for the development of horticultural activity, the introduction of new technology, and the development of agricultural services and supplies, yet it has done little to stop the flow of workers to the United States. It has also been a cause for the greater incorporation of women in the workplace and of the use of child labor.

The agricultural ecosystem has been seriously impacted by specialization in cruciferous vegetables and their exploitation during nearly the entire year.

Nevertheless, these crops have justified the adoption of integrated pest management and the introduction of technologies which have been less harmful for the environment in the second half of the 1990s.

Agriculture by contract has been considered a way of transferring technology to small producers and the Mexican experience is ambiguous in this regard. Transnational companies have opted to deal with the type of producer that is more cost-efficient for them in order to stay competitive and maintain their profit levels—and not to be an instrument of development for small producers.

Endnotes

1. J. R. Simplot, a private company with its headquarters in Boise, Idaho, is among the most rapidly growing companies in the American Union, with an annual income of around US$2.8 billion dollars, derived primarly from food-processing, fertilizer production, agriculture, and related businesses. Simplot employs close to 12,000 people in the United States, Canada, Australia, and Mexico, and in a growing number of other countries. Simplot considers itself a pioneer in food services and a leader in innovation in frozen potatoes since 1950, with 25 direct-processing plants or associates in the United States, Mexico, Canada, Australia, and China. The company defines itself as a worldwide provider of frozen french fries and many other foods, http://www.simplot.com.
2. In the region, broccoli and cauliflower are typically planted from August to April and harvested from September to June, which extends the growing period to almost 11 months. See Edelson (2000).
3. The basic principles of integrated pest management are: knowledge of pests; monitoring of populations in order to determine the thresholds of tolerance; and the efficient use of all available tools for the management and control of populations.
4. Surveys conducted assert that 75% of producers report paying from 60 to 70 pesos per day's labor. Regarding this, see the article by F. Martínez (July 31, 2000).
5. Tayde Morales Santos and Fco. Javier Ramírez Díaz (1994), 25.

Bibliography

Adam, M. "Les effets de l'integration des économies nordaméricaines sur l'organisation spatiale de l'industrie mexicaine: le cas su secteur de la transformation au Bajío guanajuatense." Master's thesis, Université de Montréal, 1998.

Allen, C. "Hog Cash Contracts: Advantages and Disadvantages." NebFacts NF 96-280. Nebraska Cooperative Extension, Institute of Agriculture and Natural Resources, University of Nebraska, 1999.

CEPAL. *Agricultura de Contrato en los Países en Desarrollo: Aspectos Teóricos y Análisis de algunos Ejemplos en México*. Santiago, Chile: CEPAL/GTZ/FAO (and Mexico: FAO/CAPAL), 1996.

———. *Agroindustria y Pequeña Agricultura: Vínculos, Potencialidades y Oportunidades Comerciales*. Santiago, Chile, 1998.

Cook, Roberta, et al. *NAFTA: Effects on Agriculture, Fruits and Vegetable Issues*. Park Ridge, IL: American Farm Bureau Research Foundation, 1991.

Echánove, Flavia , and Cristina Steffen. "Ejidatarios y Empresarios Hortícolas en Guanajuato: Cambios Recientes." Paper presented at the Congreso Nacional sobre El Ajuste Estructural en el Campo Mexicano, Efectos y Respuestas (March 1–4, 1998).

———. "Mecanismos de abasto de la industria hortícola: integración vertical y/o agricultura por contrato." Paper presented at the XX Seminario Internacional de Economía Agrícola del Tercer Mundo, Instituto de Investigaciones Económicas, UNAM. México, 2000.

Edelson, J. V. "La Eficacia de los Insecticidas en Función de la Temperatura en Noti-Crucíferas." Sistema Producto Crucíferas. Celaya, Mexico: INIFAP/SAGAR, 2000.

Feder, Ernest. *El Imperialismo Fresa: Una investigación sobre los mecanismos de dependencia de la agricultura Mexicana*. México: Editorial Campesina, 1979.

Gómez Cruz, Manuel Ángel. "Hortalizas Congeladas de Exportación: Situación, Problemática y Alternativas." In *Implicaciones del Progreso Tecnológico en la Agricultura de Países en Desarrollo*, edited by Rita Schwentesius Rindermann and Manuel Ángel Gómez Cruz. México: Humblodt Universität Zu Berlín/ CIESTAAM, 1992.

——— (coord.). "Informe de Investigación: Tendencias del Desarrollo Agroindustrial de México," *La Coyuntura 1982–87*. Mexico: Universidad Autónoma Chapingo/ SARH, 1998.

———, et al. "La Agudización de la Crisis y la Revolución Tenológica en la Producción del Bajío Guanajuatense." *Textual* 1 (1998): 24. **Gutman, G and Miotti, L.** Agricultura de Contrato en los Países en Desarrollo: Aspectos Teóricos y Análisis de algunos Ejemplos en México. Santiago, Chile: CEPAL/GTZ/FAO (and Mexico: FAO/CAPAL), 1996.

Hoy, Casey W. Conectando el Manejo de Plagas con el Manejo de Agroecosistemas. Celaya, México: INIFAP/SAGAR, 1999. Marañón Pimentel, Boris, and Ma. del Carmen Cebada Contreras. *Agricultura No Empresarial y Horticultura de Exportación: ¿Articulación viable?*. Paper presented at the Congreso Nacional sobre el Ajuste Estructural en el Campo Mexicano, Efectos y Respuestas

(March 1-4, 1998). Marín Jarillo, Antonio, and Rafael Bujanos Muñiz. *Enemigos Naturales de Plagas de las Cruciferas en el Contexto del Manejo Integrado de Plagas*. Celaya, México: INIFAP/PRODUCE, 1997.

Martínez, Fabiola. "Guanajuato: Empleo para Casi Todos, pero con Bajos Salarios." *La Jornada* (July 31, 2000).

Minot, Nicholas. "Contract Farming and Its Effects on Small Farmers in Less Developed Countries," *International Development Papers, Working Paper*, no. 31. East Lansing: Michigan State University, 1986.

Morales Santos, Tayde, and Fco. Javier Ramírez Díaz. *Contratos, asociaciones y sociedades en Modalidades de asociación e integración en la agroindustria mexicana*. Chapingo. México: CIESTAAM, 1994.

Morett Sánchez, Jesús Carlos, and Celsa Cosío Ruíz. "La Agricultura de Contrato en el México Colonial," *Geografía Agrícola* 11, 12 (July 1986, January 1987).

———. "Las Nuevas Modalidades de Acumulación de Capital en el Campo: La Agricultura de Contrato," Master's thesis, Universidad Autónoma Chapingo, 1985.

Muñoz Rodríguez, Manrrubio, and V. Horacio Santoyo Cortés. *Visión y Misión Agroempresarial: Competencia y Cooperación en el Medio Rural*. Chapingo, México: CIESTAAM, 1996.

Rama, Ruth, and Raúl Vigorito. *El Complejo de Frutas y Legumbres en México*. Mexico: Nueva Imágen, 1980.

Rehber, Erkan. *Vertical Integration in Agriculture and Contract Farming*. Storrs, CT: Food Marketing Policy Center, University of Connecticut, 1998.

Ruíz Ledezma, Javier, and Alejandra Hinojosa Rodríguez. "La Agricultura de Contrato de Producción de Hortalizas en el Bajío: Un Estudio de Caso." In *Implicaciones del Progreso Tecnológico en la Agricultura de Países en Desarrollo*, edited by Rita Schwentesius Rindermann, and Manuel Angél Gómez Cruz. Mexico: Universidad Autónoma Chapingo/Humboldt Universitat Zu Berlin, 1992.

Runsten, David. "Transaction Costs in Mexican Fruit and Vegetable Contracting: Implications for Asociación en participación." University of California, 1992.

Schejtman, Alejandro. "Agroindustria y Pequeña Agricultura: Experiencias y Opciones de Transformación." In *Agroindustria y Pequeña Agricultura: Vínculos, Potencialidades y Oportunidades Comerciales*. Santiago, Chile: CEPAL, 1998.

———. *Agroindustria y Pequeña Agricultura: Enfoques y Lineamientos de Política*. Mexico: FAO/CEPAL, 1996.

SECOFI. *Inversión Extranjera Directa en Alimentos, Bebidas y Tabaco*. México, 1999.

USDA (U.S. Department of Agriculture). *Farmers´ Use of Marketing and Production Contracts*. Farm Business Economics Branch, Rural Economy Division, Economic Research Service. Washington, DC: USDA, 1996.

Chapter 7

The Organic Farming Sector in Mexico: An Example of Resistance to Globalization

Laura Gómez Tovar and Manuel Ángel Gómez Cruz

ECONOMIC GLOBALIZATION IS CREATING exclusionary models of development for the poorest regions of the world. Some of the changes produced by this new world order include reduced State intervention, liberalization of the land market and labor, introduction of foreign investment, marginalization of low-income producers, and destruction of natural resources. In the social context, economic globalization is producing more migration and causing living standards in the rural areas to fall at an unprecedented rate.[1]

In Mexico, agriculture is experiencing a severe economic crisis. The free market is swamping the internal market with cheap goods. Producers must face international competition with minimal governmental support; subsidies, extension programs, and training have been drastically reduced. As a consequence of these changes, almost all agricultural sectors have experienced a drastic setback, and their future prospects are not favorable. In this context, a new technology, organic farming, has appeared as a mechanism of resistance and as a viable alternative for Mexican producers.

Organic agriculture by definition includes "all agricultural systems that promote the environmentally, socially, and economically sound production of food and fibers. These systems value local soil fertility as a key to successful production. By respecting the natural capacity of plants, animals, and the landscape, they aim to optimize quality in all aspects of agriculture and the environment. They reduce external inputs by refraining from the use of chemo-synthetic fertilizers, pesticides, and pharmaceuticals, by instead allowing the powerful laws of nature to increase both agricultural yields and disease resistance."[2]

This type of agriculture also prohibits the use of genetically modified organisms (GMOs), sewage, and food radiation.

The International Federation of Organic Agriculture Movements (IFOAM), which is the most important organic agriculture association in the world—representing some 760 member organizations in more than 100 countries—states that the main aims of this agriculture are these:

- to produce food of high quality in sufficient quantity
- to interact in a constructive and life-enhancing way with natural systems and cycles

- to consider the wider social and ecological impact of the organic production and processing system
- to encourage and enhance biological cycles within the farming system, in volving micro-organisms, soil flora and fauna, and plants and animals
- to maintain and increase long-term fertility of soils;
- to maintain the genetic diversity of the production system and its surroundings
- to promote the healthy use and proper care of water, water resources, and all life therein
- to give all livestock conditions of life with due consideration for the basic aspects of their innate behavior
- to minimize all forms of pollution
- to allow everyone involved in organic production and processing a quality of life which meets their basic needs and allows an adequate return and satisfaction from their work, including a safe working environment
- to progress toward an entire production, processing, and distribution chain which is both socially just and ecologically responsible.

Organic agriculture, as a technology, is an example of resistance to globalization. This alternative was not developed by the transnational agro-industrial complexes which gave rise to industrial farming and biotechnology, but rather by grassroots pioneers and idealists, who have a strong ecological and social consciousness. Subsequently, consumers who supported the same ideals began to buy organic products in cooperatives and farmers' markets. Currently the retail sales value of these products in the world totals more than $20 billion and continues to grow at a spectacular rate. In fact, organic farming has evolved in opposition to industrial farming, and against the dominant economic and political powers that rejected organic farming methods for being impractical and idealistic.[3] (All dollar figures in this chapter are given in U.S. dollars unless otherwise designated.)

The increasing demand for organic products (with a growth rate of 20% on average in the main consumer areas)[4] is a product of a post-materialistic worldwide trend in values, which promotes, besides other ideas,[5]health and environmental awareness. This global trend has created a demand for tropical organic products which cannot be cultivated by producers in developed countries because of agro-ecological conditions. At the same time, however, this trend has created an ideal opportunity for some producers in countries such as Mexico. Mexican producers who have benefited from this "green" demand are those located in regions where the chemo-synthetic fertilizers, improved seeds, and pesticides of the "Green Revolution" could not be easily obtained, and where traditional agriculture is still practiced.

Currently, the organic sector is the smallest in Mexican agriculture, but it is the most dynamic and has impressive growth rates. For the year 2002, more than 40 different products were produced, including coffee, corn, sesame, agave, vegetables, herbs, and mango—totaling more than 215,000 hectares. More than 53,000 producers were involved in organic agriculture, generating $280 million annually in foreign currencies.

Organic agriculture in Mexico has proven to be an alternative for Mexican producers. It is one of the few agricultural subsectors which can be considered successful and sustainable. It takes into account the protection and enhancement of natural resources, creates better incomes and conditions of work for producers, re-energizes the economy of rural communities, and makes use of traditional methods of production and social structures.

Organic producers are taking advantage of the possibilities offered by burgeoning world demand for organic food, including the area covered by NAFTA. At the same time, producers are creating local processes which put organic farming methods into practice with the use of local technology, local and natural inputs, and peasant and indigenous knowledge. In this way, organic farming enables producers and indigenous groups with scarce economic resources to avoid part of the exclusionary mechanisms of the globalization process.

In this chapter, various factors related to the organic farming sector in Mexico are explored. First, organic farming's international situation and its market are taken as a reference. This is followed by an explanation of driving forces for the emergence of organic farming in Mexico and mechanisms of resistance to globalization. Next, the current situation of the organic farming sector in Mexico and its importance are detailed, with particular focus on its economic and social importance, the type of products it generates, the producers and the markets, and the premium prices that they are able to obtain. This discussion leads to the subsequent analysis of the influence of NAFTA on the organic sector in Mexico. Finally, important elements for further development of the organic-farming sector are set forth and some conclusions are outlined.

International Situation of Organic Farming

Globally, there are about 23 million hectares cultivated with organic methods. The major parts of this area are: located in Australia (10.5 million hectares), Argentina (3.2 million hectares), Italy (1,230,000 hectares) and the United States (950,000 hectares). Mexico occupies the16th place in the word in relation to the number of organic hectares (see Table 1). This country is the fifth in importance in Latin America after Argentina, Uruguay, Brazil and Chile; it is followed by Peru (85,000 hectares), Paraguay (61,500 hectares), Ecuador (60,000 hectares) and Colombia (30,000 hectares).

In relation to the area under organic management, with respect to the percentage of total agricultural area, only eight countries use more than 5% of their agricultural land areas for organic production. These countries are Liechtenstein with 17% of its land being farmed with organic methods, Austria with 11.3%, Switzerland with 9.7%, Italy with 7.9%, Finland with 6.6%, Denmark with 6.5%, Sweden with 6.3%, and the Czech Republic with 5%.

All of these countries have experienced high organic growth rates (see Table 1) while conventional agriculture is currently growing at less than 2%

Table 1

Dynamics of Cultivated Organic Land in Selected Countries, 1990–2003

Country	*Organic Land 1990 (hectares)*	*Organic Land 2003 (hectares)*	*Growth Rate (%)*	*% of the Total Land*
Australia	5,293,723***	10,000,000		2.3
Argentina	116,519*	3,192,000	51.2	1.9
Italy	13,000	1,230,000	46.1	7.9
United States	370,000	950,000	8.1	0.2
Great Britain	25,000	679,631	31.6	3.9
Uruguay	—	678,481	—	4.0
Germany	100,000	632,165	16.6	3.7
Spain	8500**	485,079	49.8	1.6
Canada	163,843***	430,600	37.8	0.5
France	75,000	419,750	15.4	1.4
China	—	301,295	—	0.06
Austria	25,000	285,500	22.5	11.3
Brazil	100,000***	275,576	40.1	0.08
Chile	—	273,000	—	1.5
Czech Republic	110,756***	218,114	25.3	5.0
Mexico	23,265*	215,843****	37.4	0.5

* 1995; ** 1993; *** 2000; **** 2002

Source: Yussefi and Willer 2003, pages 16–17; and for Mexico, Gómez Cruz et al. 2003, 89–104.

annually, in fact, it is even falling in some countries. Organic growth rates are especially high, more than 25% per year, in countries such as Argentina, Spain, Italy, Brazil, Canada, Mexico, and the Czech Republic.

Demand for organic products has been growing at an exponential rate over the last ten years (more than 20% in developed countries). In 1997, the retail sales value of organic products in the main consumers' areas around the world was more than $10 billion, including $5 billion in Central Europe, $4.2 billion in the United States, and $1.2 billion in Japan. For 1998, this sum grew to $13.5 billion, and in the year 2001 it was estimated at $21 billion.[6] In Europe, organic retail sales reached EU$25 billion by the year 2005. This shows a progression from a market niche to mainstream status.[7] On average, organic retail sales by individual countries are less than 2.5% of total food sales, though this figure is also increasing very rapidly (see Table 2).

Organic products which have more demand on the international market are primarily fresh produce (vegetables and fruits), then cereals, and finally meat and dairy products. However, most all foods grown using conventional methods are also now available in organic form.

The Danish case stands out, due to its high percentage of sales for internally produced products. Some examples are rye flour at 22%, milk at 20%, oatmeal at 17.5%, and eggs at 13% (see Table 3).

Table 2

Retail Sales of Organic Products in Selected Countries, 1997 and 2000

Country	*Retail sales 1997 (million dollars)*	*% of total food sales*	*Retail sales 2000 (million dollars)*	*Expected % growth (mid-term)*
Germany	1,750	1.2	2,200-2,400	5-10
France	770	0.6	800-850	20
Great Britain	450	0.4	1,000-1,050	25-30
Netherlands	450	0.4	225-250	25-30
Switzerland	350	2.5	60-47060-470	30-35
Sweden	—	1-1.5	175-200	—
Denmark	300	2.5	350-375	30-40
Austria	—	2	250-275	—
United States	4,200	1.2	8,000	10-15
Japan	1,000	—	2,500	—

Source: International Trade Centre, 1999, and Dimitri and Richman 2002, and Cunningham 2001 cited by Gómez Cruz et al. 2002, 15.

This general overview of organic product sales at the global level provides an indication of the speed at which demand is growing. It is important to note that the countries with the largest markets are also those with the highest growth rates of organic land (Japan is an exception).[8] Favorable governmental policies (along with increased consumer demand) have accelerated the production of organic products.

In the United States, there are governmental programs for organic certification with low user fees (in some states, two-thirds of the certification cost is subsidized), plus financial assistance for research (a budget of $5 million for

Table 3

Market Share of Individual Products in Denmark, 1998

Product	% Internal market
Rye flour	22.0
Milk	20.0
Oatmeal	17.5
Eggs	13.00
Carrots	10-12.0
Wheat flour	11.0
Potatoes	7.0
Onions	3.0
Cheese	2-3.0
Butter	2.0
Beef	2.0

Source: The Danish Ministry of Food, Agriculture and Fisheries, 1999, 18.

organic-methods research in 2001), aid for exports, and a special insurance program for organic harvests. In addition, the final National Organic Regulation, which will standardize organic production, was approved in April 2001.

Currently, all countries in the European Union (E.U.) have support policies under the agri-environment program which defines organic production and promotes economic support for conversion and for continuing organic production.[9] The quantity of organic land in the E.U. increased by 80% during the last six years—principally as a result of this program. Support for organic production in the E.U. is based on the desire to fulfill various objectives: to satisfy internal demand, to conserve natural resources, and to control overproduction of conventional crops.

Support for organic agriculture in developed countries indicates that these countries are looking for self-sufficiency in organic products—at least for those which they can produce. Yet these countries still have to import organic tropical and out-of-season products from other countries (such as Mexico) that have comparative advantages due to natural conditions.

Driving Forces for the Emergence of Organic Agriculture in Mexico: Mechanisms of Resistance

Organic agriculture first emerged in the southern part of Mexico, in the state of Chiapas. The German-owned company, *Finca Irlanda,* initiated the practice of biodynamic agriculture,[10] due to their affiliation with the antroposophical movement in Europe. The first certification obtained for organic coffee was in 1967.

In the mid-1980s, some private coffee producers—*Rancho Alegre, Finca San Miguel, Finca La Granja, and Finca Montagua*—began to shift from conventional methods of production to organic farming. This shift was due to two main factors: a dramatic fall in coffee prices (as a consequence of the power exerted by multinational companies and processors over coffee producers), and a growing trend in developed countries to use organic farming.

Later, as a consequence of the success of private farms, the low price of conventional coffee, and the high demand for organic products, some small-scale, low-income producer cooperatives began to implement organic farming. This implementation was principally in cooperatives that were made up of indigenous people and producers with scarce economic resources (They had not yet incorporated the use of agrochemical products into their farming practices.). Among those who encouraged the conversion process were some Catholic advocates of the Theology of Liberalization and some foreign trading companies.[11] Some people interested in the well-being of the peasants were associated with trading companies or fair-trade groups in developed countries, and this connection gave the producers some credit on loans or outlets for their produce.[12] This facilitated the beginning of the process, and made the connection between production and the market.

The most important organic coffee cooperative of indigenous people, UCIRI, initiated the shift to organic farming in 1982 under a strong religious influence, along with support from a German trading company (GEPA) which imported the first "natural" coffee.[13] This cooperative obtained its certification in 1988 and began to assist other cooperatives with training and marketing in order to facilitate their changeover to organic technology.

To small-scale, low-income producers, organic farming has represented an opportunity to take advantage of their own agro-ecological, cultural, and social conditions. Organic producers have incorporated the aforementioned conditions into their farming practices as a means of defense against globalization's negative effects. The most important elements in this process are these:

- Organic producers take advantage of the fact that the Green Revolution and its technology was not adopted in the poorest regions of the country; therefore, the absence or limited use of fertilizers and pesticides has facilitated the conversion to organic farming methods.
- They utilize traditional methods of production, which has allowed producers to use their background knowledge, specifically peasant and indigenous knowledge, including "peasant technology", which are part of the Mexican agricultural culture. Traditional techniques, such as terraces, multi-cropping, rotation of crops, use of mulch, incorporation of organic materials, and other soil conservation practices have been easily and quickly adapted to organic technology.
- They take advantage of indigenous cosmovision, which includes the protection of Mother Nature (*Madre Tierra*) as part of the indigenous belief system. It has facilitated the adoption of organic farming by indigenous people because this technology is completely in agreement with their immaterial framework or way of thinking.
- They use the available resources in their own communities, such as natural local inputs, local technology, and family labor—hence, production costs are lowered. The investment cost involved in buying external inputs (seeds, fertilizers, and pesticides) is eliminated and, instead, natural materials—such as crop residues and manure for making compost or herbs with repellent properties for preparing natural pesticides—are used for production. The main cost of production in organic farming is the labor cost, but family labor is used because it is available.

The production of organic vegetables primarily rose out of the demand for healthy products in the United States. It began in 1985 with a small-scale, low-income producers cooperative called *Productores Orgánicos del Cabo*, with headquarters in San Jose del Cabo, Baja California Sur. Afterwards—some private and large-scale producers began to appear in Sinaloa, such as Salt Best—at the end of the 1980s, Agricola Crisantes in 1991, Alonso Campos in 1993, and others.

This was a direct consequence of both the difficult economic situation in the agricultural sector in Mexico and the growth in the organic market, which brought the establishment of mechanisms operated by trading companies for maintaining a better supply to consumers and obtaining better prices. These mechanisms include contracts that imply capital investment and financing for production in Mexico. For large-scale producers in the north of the country, this opportunity was a powerful reason for shifting to organic methods, because the conventional production that they had practiced before was not receiving governmental support, and national and private banks canceled credit for production, especially after 1994.

Another significant factor that led some large-scale producers to convert to organic farming was the possibility of reducing production costs, because 1) conventional inputs increased their costs and 2) the quantity of inputs used is higher than in organic farming methods.

In the 1990s, a large number of producers emerged. These new producers initiated not only the organic production of coffee and vegetables, but also of honey, bananas, vanilla, avocados, mangos, and cocoa. Governmental support for encouraging organic agriculture in Mexico was very limited. Only a few rural development programs, mainly in the states of Chiapas, Oaxaca, Chihuahua, and Mexico, have promoted courses and training in organic agriculture geared towards home gardens. In addition, between 1990 and 1993, the National Indigenous Institute promoted various organic honey projects in Oaxaca. And, under the Alliance for Agro in Oaxaca, there is an initiative to give a small subsidy to some organic coffee producers: $66.30 for certified producers and $52.60 for those in the process of converting to organic production.

The economic crisis in the Mexican agricultural sector contributed significantly to the emergence of small-scale and large-scale organic producers in the 1990s. As a consequence of reduced governmental support, low product prices, high input prices, increased agricultural imports, and reduction of tariffs, Mexican producers began to look for viable alternatives with the purpose of obtaining a better income and better prices. In this context, organic farming represented an excellent alternative due to the premium prices received (20%–40% over conventional products; some though in some cases these figures are higher) and increasing international demand.

The Organic Sector in Mexico and Its Importance

Table 4

Economic Importance and Growth Rate of Organic Agriculture in Mexico

Year	1996	1998	2000	GR	2002*
Acreage (hectares)	23,265	54,457	102,802	44.98	215,843
Number of producers	13,176	27,914	33,587	26,35	53,577
Employment	3,722,400	8,700,00	16,448,000	44.98	34,534
Foreign currencies ($)	34,293,380	72,000,000	139,403,992	41.99	n.a.

Source: Statistics based on fieldwork, 1996, 1998 and Gómez Cruz, et al. 2001, pag.11.

* Projections for 2002: Gómez Cruz et al. 2003, 89–104.

The organic agriculture sector is the smallest in the Mexican agricultural industry (less than 1% of the total acreage), but it is the most dynamic. It has shown spectacular growth in the last years. The growth rate (GR) in acreage was 45% between 1996 and 2000, while the number of producers grew by 26%, employment by 45%, and foreign currencies by 42% (see Table 4). Projections for 2002 were also very promising with more than 215,000 hectares, 53,000 producers, and more than $280 million generated in foreign currencies.

Mexico is internationally recognized as an organic export producer more than as a consumer. There are 262 zones of production in 28 of the 32 Mexican states. The total acreage in the year 2000 was almost 103,000 hectares, which was mainly distributed in the states of Chiapas (42%), Oaxaca (27%), Michoacan (5%), Chihuahua (4%), and Guerrero (3%). The remainder is distributed across the other states.

Types of Products

The organic acreage is cultivated with more than 40 different products. The most important product by acreage cultivated is coffee with 70,838 hectares (69%). In second place is white and blue corn with 4,670 hectares (4.5%). There are 4,124 hectares cultivated with sesame; 3,831 with vegetables (tomatoes, chilies, squashes, cucumbers, onions, garlic, peas, eggplants, melons, etc.); 3,047 with agave (for production of honey); 2,510 with herbs (basil, mint, ginger, and others); 2,075 with mangos; 1,849 with oranges; 1,597 with beans; 1,444 with apples; 1,171 with papayas; and 911 with avocados. With less acreage, there is the production of soybeans, bananas, cocoa, oil palm, vanilla, peanuts, pineapples, hibiscus flowers, lemons, coconuts, nuts, litchis, chickpeas, safflower, passion fruit, and peaches. Also, it is possible to find production of honey, and marginal quantities of milk, cream, cheese, candies, and cosmetic products (see Table 5).

While it is true that only a small percentage of total cultivated land in Mexico is used for organic farming (less that 1%), the acreage cultivated with some organic products in comparison with the same products cultivated with conventional production methods is significant. Some 14.5% of all the area cultivated with vanilla is organic; 10.4% of coffee; 8.7% of papayas; 7.1% of sesame; 4.5% of oil palm; 2.7% of litchis; 2.4% of nuts; 2.4% of apples; and 1.4% of mangos. These figures demonstrate that organic agriculture is gaining a foothold in Mexico.

Types of Producers

In the year 2000, there were more than 33,000 organic farmers in Mexico. Illustrating an interesting duality, these farmers can be divided into two types of producers: the small-scale, low-income producers (peasants and indigenous people who are grouped together in cooperatives), and the large-scale producers (private enterprises that operate independently). The former are characterized by many features of the approach followed by "puritans" of the international organic movement (use of "peasant technology", indigenous knowledge, local inputs, support by NGOs, and Fair Trade). The large-scale producers are guided by the logic of the "industrial organic systems of production" and the profit potential of this technology.

Table 5

Organic Land by Product Cultivated in Mexico, 1996, 1998, And 2000

	Organic Land (hectacres)		
Product	**Total** *1996*	**Total** *1998*	**Total** *2000*
Coffee	19,040.00	32,161.00	70,838.09
Corn (blue and white)	(n.a.)	970.00	4,670.50
Sesame	563.00	1,895.00	4,124.75
Vegetables	2,387.00*	4,391.00*	3,831.00
Agave	(n.a.)	(n.a.)	3,047.00
Herbs	(n.a.)	(n.a.)	2,510.90
Mangos	(n.a.)	284.00	2,075.00
Oranges	(n.a.)	(n.a.)	1,849.90
Beans	(n.a.)	1,241.00	1,597.00
Apples	380.00	2,010.00	1,444.50
Papaya	16.00	73.00	1,171.50
Avocado	85.00	307.00	911.00
Soya Beans	(n.a.)	n.a.	865.00
Bananas	300.00	500.00	826.00
Cocoa	(n.a.)	252.00	656.00
African Palm	(n.a.)	(n.a.)	400.00
Vanilla	150.00	1,203.00	331.00
Piña	(n.a.)	(n.a.)	329.00
Others	353.00	9,170.00	1,323.75
Total	***23,273.00***	***54,457.00***	***102,802.38***

* Includes herbs. , n.a. not available. Source: Statistics based on fieldwork, 1996, 1998; and Gómez Cruz et al. 2001, 14.

In the group of small-scale, low-income producers are found the most marginalized and poorest peasants of the country—the indigenous people. They comprised 53% of all the organic producers in the country in 1996.[14] Indigenous groups that participate in the organic sector are: Nahuas, Otomies, Tepehuas, Mixtecos, Cuicatecos, Chatinos, Chinantecos, Zapotecos, Tojolabales, Tzotziles, Tzeltales, Mayas, Amusgos, and Totonacos.

Small-scale, low-income producers have a small quantity of land (2.25 hectares on average) and slender economic resources. These conditions have encouraged the formation of cooperatives, which enable these producers to certify their production at a lower cost,[15] to amass higher production quantities, to export, and to obtain better prices for their products.

Organization in cooperatives has also permitted the development of community benefits that would not otherwise be possible. Examples of such benefits can be found among the cooperatives that belong to The Oaxacan State

Coffee Producers Network, which has established a wide array of community programs, including a health program that promotes the use of alternative medicine through courses and advising;, a women's program that creates integrated farms with minor animal production and home gardens; and a credit union in which some producers save their money and others obtain loans at low interest rates. Another example is The Union of Indigenous Communities of the Isthmus Region (UCIRI), which has various interesting projects. In its health project, advocates of natural medicine not only offer courses in personal hygiene, they build rural bathrooms and show how to use plants as medicines. As part of this project, a Central Health Clinic has opened in the headquarters of the cooperative, where a specialist in homeopathic medicine treats producers and their families. The Ironmonger's Store Project sells agricultural instruments, building materials, and home utensils with a 20% discount to cooperative members. The credit and savings fund is a community fund, which cooperative members build up by contributing a portion of their income from coffee sales. Additionally, The Center of Peasant Education is a rural training center that educates those who will serve as trainers for members of the cooperative in the future.

Large-scale producers have a considerable quantity of land (between 100 and 2,000 hectares, with the average being close to 150 hectares), hire labor, do not collaborate with other producers for production, have an independent certification contract, and sell their products in an independent way.

For the year 2000, the small-scale, low-income producers comprised 98.6% of the total number of producers, farm 84.1% of the total organic acreage, and generate 68.8% of the foreign currencies earned. On the other hand, large-scale producers represent only 1.4% of the total producers, cultivate 15.9% of the land, and generate 31.2% of the foreign currencies (see Table 6). Large-scale producers cultivate the most profitable crops (mainly vegetables and some fruits, such as mangos and bananas), obtain higher productivity than small-scale, low-income producers, and are more directly related to the market. In spite of small-scale producers being the majority in the sector, the trend is toward an increase in large-scale producers, with a concomitant increase in the share of economic benefits in this sector. In this context, the role of the government should be to

Table 6

Typology of Producers in Organic Agriculture in Mexico, 2000

Type of producer	*Number of producers*		*% of acreage*		*% of currencies generated*	
Year	1996	2000	1996	2000	1996	2000
Small-scale, low-income producers	97.5	98.6	89.0	84.1	78.0	68.8
Large-scale producers	2.5	1.4	11.0	15.9	22.0	31.2

Source: Statistics based on fieldwork, 1996 and Gómez Cruz, M., et al. 2001, 21.

generate better conditions for small-scale, low-income producers, in order to assure that benefits will accrue to a larger number of producers.

Market for Production and Premium Prices: Exports

Conversion to organic farming methods did not imply that only producers shifted to this technology. Also, as in the case of small-scale, low-income producers, they became both organized farmers and exporters, due to the demands of the international market for their products and the low development of the national market.

The organic sector is represented by a large group of producer-exporter cooperatives. The largest produce-export associations in this sector are these: the Union of Indigenous Communities of the Isthmus Region (UCIRI) with 2,395 members; the Ecological Federation of Chiapas (FIECH) with 2,030 members; Indigenous Peoples of the Motozintla Sierra Madre (ISMAM) with 1,243 members; S.S.S. Yenin Navan with 974 members; Union of Ejidos La Selva with 921 members; Majomut Union with 785 members; and Tiemenlonla Nich K′lum with 594 members. Other important exporters are Organic Producers "Del Cabo," and The Oaxacan State Coffee Producers Network.

The majority of the country's organic production is grown for export (between 80% and 85%). Organic product exports generate more than $280 million in foreign currencies every year, which represents 8.5% of all exports in the agricultural sector.[16] This amount is larger than that generated by some traditional export products such as *cocoa*, citrus juice, cotton, strawberries, and tobacco.

Foreign currencies generated by some individual organic products are significant in relation to the total conventional export value. In 2000, organic vanilla, for example, generated 23.4% of the total exported, safflower 21.9%, coffee 4.6%, and sesame 4.1%.

Table 7

Destination of the Organic Products Cultivated in Mexico, 2000

Product	*Export Destination*
Coffee	United States, Germany, Netherlands, Switzerland, Japan, Italy, Denmark, Sweden, Spain, Norway, France, Austria, Great Britain, and other countries.
Vegetables	United States, Canada, Japan, and Great Britain
Honey	Germany, England, United States, and Italy
Sesame	United States and Europe
Vanilla	United States and Japan
Pineapples	United States
Agave honey	Germany
Herbs	France, Unitied States, Italy, and Germany
Mangos	United States, Canada, Japan
Bananas	United States, Japan
Corn	United States, Canada, Japan
Cocoa	Germany, United States

Source: fieldwork, 2000.

Mexican organic products are destined for the United States, Europe, and Japan (see Table 7). The former can absorb more fresh products because of the shorter distance travelled. Almost all organic products are sold as raw materials. Therefore, the aggregated value is earned in developed countries leaving even less benefit to the national producers.

Premium Prices

Premium prices obtained are higher for vegetables. Some examples are squash (with a 219% increase over the conventional price) and tomatoes (with a 75%–133% increase). Other products which gain a high percentage of premium prices include mangos with 100%–150%, and avocados with 133%.

Products that obtain medium-range premium prices (25%–50% on average) in the organic sector are vanilla and sesame. In the case of coffee, the average premium is 25% more than conventional coffee. However, cooperatives trading in *Fair Trade* can obtain premium prices greater than 100% over the conventional price. Honey receives between 12% and 22% and agave honey between 20% and 25% more than conventional products.[17] It is important to point out that part of the premium price that consumers are paying is to avoid negative externalities, such as contamination of food, soil, and underground water sources. These benefits are not incorporated into conventional methods of production. Organic products internalize the environmental costs—i.e., these products give a value to those elements provided by the ecosystem, while conventional products do not.

Internal Market

The internal market is in an incipient stage, with less than 5% of the production traded as organic in health food stores, specialized organic stores, cafeterias, and weekly food deliveries in the largest cities: Mexico City, Monterrey, and Guadalajara, in tourist areas, and in cities close to important zones of organic production. Some 10% of the total production, which is not exported, is traded on the national market, but as conventional product. The lack of development of this market is due to various factors, including lack of information to consumers, high premium prices, and lack of availability in the common market structures.[18]

There are few people in Mexico who know exactly what the terms *organic* and *ecological* mean. Surveys with people of the upper and upper-middle class in Mexico City (1,600 people were interviewed) and Querétaro (200 people were interviewed) revealed that more than 88% and 83% of the people, respectively, do not know the meaning of these words. Some people associated them with fruits and vegetables (without paying attention to the system of production) and others with the classification system of garbage (organic and inorganic materials).[19]

The premium prices of organic products is another factor in limiting demand, because the per capita income in Mexico is low ($4,296) in comparison to developed countries ($27,174).[20] A large percentage of the population is unable to cover their basic needs; therefore, the type of product put in their mouths is unimportant. Even with these arguments, the surveys of the upper and middle classes showed that when people knew characteristics of organic products, 70%

in Querétaro and 35% in Mexico City were in agreement with paying a premium price of 10%.[21] A few organic stores offer organic coffee, fruits, vegetables, herbs, honey, milk, and tea. Premium prices received are variable (10%–100%). Prices received for organic products in the internal market respond to various factors. These factors include the costs faced by producers in the transition period while the production system is stabilized; high costs of certified production; increasing costs of labor; costs of technical advice, training and infrastructure; and high costs of distribution and marketing of products because of the small quantities traded. Some of these aspects can be improved, mainly those which are related to the commercialization process. It simply created more direct commercialization channels between producers and consumers for avoiding high costs of distribution—for example, farmers' stores, networks of consumers and producers, and organic clubs. Also, it is possible to establish networks between producers for supplying higher quantities of production to supermarkets, thus eliminating intermediaries. The latter can be encouraged to reduce premium prices and make these products more available to the Mexican population.

In summary, development of the internal market in Mexico is vital in reducing constraints in the marketing of organic products. It will not only remove the dependence of this activity on the external market, but will also offer Mexican society the opportunity to enjoy these high-quality healthy products, instead of chemically grown products while at the same time preserving natural capital.

The Organic Farming Sector and NAFTA

The primary role of Mexican organic production in the NAFTA region is to complement the organic production of the United States and Canada. The Mexican exports are those products which cannot be produced in these countries, such as winter-grown vegetables (mainly tomatoes, squashes, cucumbers, eggplants, onions, peas, and melons), tropical products (coffee, cocoa, vanilla, mangos, pineapples, and bananas), and labor-intensive products (such as sesame).

Organic Mexican products have to fulfill the same requirements as conventional products, including regulations for quality and safety standards, plus organic certification. Exports to the United States require certification by an agency approved by the USDA through the National Organic Program (NOP). In this case, Mexican producers have to produce according the National Organic Regulation of the United States, which was approved in April 2001. In terms of Canada, on September 2, 2006, the federal government released its proposed "Organic Products Regulation" a draft regulation that, by the time of this writing, was still being negotiated in Parliament regarding its implementation as a national regulatory policy.

In the NAFTA accord, there is no specific mention of organic products. None of these three countries has created harmonized trade codes for organic products. The impact of NAFTA on the organic sector is similar to that on the conventional sector. In the United States, products in the organic sector have to first pass all USDA requirements for quality and safety, as well as organic certifications depending on the market they enter. In addition, NAFTA eliminated non-tariff barriers, quotas, and tariffs for organic products, allowing for increased competition and greater access to new markets. However, the market for organic products is very different than that for conventional products in the United States and Canada, with demand still rapidly growing for organic

Table 8

Premium Prices of Organic Products in the United States, 2002

Product	*Place*	*Non-organic ($)*	*Organic ($)*	*Premium (%)*
Carrots, box of 22 kg	DA	13.00	31.00	138%
Broccoli, box with 14 pieces	BH	10.00	40.00	300%
Apio, cja de 24 pieces	DA	14.00	16.90	21%
Small lettuce, 1.5 kg	BH	6.00	6.50	8%
Lechuga de hoja, box with 24 pieces	DA	10.50	18.50	76%
Romaine lettuce caja de 24 pieces	DA	10.50	29.40	180%
Onions, box with 48 pieces	DA	12.00	23.80	98%
Grapefruit, box with 18 kg	DA	16.50	26.00	58%
Oranges, box with 17kg	DA	13.00	24.50	88%
Apples "Golden Delicious", box with 18 kg	DA	24.00	35.50	40%
Cherry tomatoes, 12 x 450 g	DA	12.75	21.00	65%
Bananas, box of 22 kg	SX	9.50	16.50	74%

Source: "Market News" USDA, July 31, 2002, cited by Bertinuson and Castillo, 2002; SX= San Francisco; DA=Dallas; BH=Boston.

products (more than 20% each year), while many of these products still receive high price premiums (see Table 8).

Measures such as safety regulations, which are a non-custom barrier, will more seriously affect the export of fresh products, particularly vegetables. Producers have to make large capital investments to comply with such regulations, particularly in terms of infrastructure. The latter allows large-scale producers to become involved in growing organic vegetables in Mexico, giving fewer opportunities to small-scale, low-income producers. With other products, such as fruits, less strict safety regulations will enable small-scale, low-income producers to take a leading role in this area. The same applies to products such as coffee and cocoa.

Important Factors for Further Development of the Organic-Farming Sector

Further development of organic produce will depend on various factors, such as continuing consumer demand for these products, development of the internal market, and governmental support for this type of agriculture.

The growth of organic-product demand in developed countries has been a significant factor in the development of organic produce in Mexico. If this trend continues, organic farming methods used for growing products demanded abroad will increase as export demand increases. However, this trend will not affect products that are not demanded by the external market. In that case, it is important to consider that other developing countries are increasing their organic tropical produce exports, which can limit the market and increase competition in the future. The latter point means that it is necessary for Mexico to maintain the high quality of its organic products in order to retain its current export markets.

To increase organic production, development of the internal market in Mexico is vital. This will also end the dependence of this sector on the external market and give Mexicans the opportunity to consume these high-quality healthy products, instead of chemically-grown products—while at the same time preserving the natural capital of the country.

The growth of the internal market should include the active participation of producers, national trading companies, retail and wholesale channels, government, and consumers. Some initiatives that could facilitate the development of this market include the following:

- Promotional campaigns on the national level to inform the public of the meaning of *organic food*. Simultaneously, a National Organic Logo could be promoted. This would contribute to consumer confidence, because Mexicans would come to see products bearing this label as regulated by a reliable and trustworthy system. In addition, this campaign could help to motivate additional small-scale and large-scale producers to put this technology into practice, thus ensuring the increased supply for future demand, increasing the areas used for organic production, and leading to sustainability in the rural areas of the country.
- The creation of commercial spaces for selling organic food. The establishment of regional networks between producers and consumers is an efficient way of reducing premium prices and distribution costs. As well, it is necessary to encourage supermarkets to offer these products, which will stimulate a rapid growth in the internal market, as the international experience has shown.

In order to increase governmental support for organic farming in Mexico, it is necessary for the government to recognize organic agriculture as a technology useful for reaching sustainability in the country. This technology presents more advantages than other technological options such as biotechnology, because the latter depends on foreign technology while organic agriculture uses local technology. Biotechnology can be adopted only in some areas of the country, mainly those where producers have more economic resources. In this sense it is an exclusive technology, while organic agriculture is an inclusive technology because it presents opportunities for all types of producers and uses local resources. Moreover, organic technology can increase social welfare, especially in the poorest areas of the country—particularly indigenous and peasant regions.

The government can take advantage of this promising alternative because it can contribute significantly to solving the nation's various social, economic, and environmental problems. Organic agriculture can help reduce poverty, increase social welfare in rural areas, decrease migration, improve rural producers' income levels, generate more foreign currencies, reach environmental sustainability, and solve environmental problems.

The role of society is vital for facilitating government involvement. If society pushes the government to increase organic production and to protect the environment, organic technology could be fostered more easily. In Europe, for example, consumer interest in these products has encouraged governmental support of this technology.

Concluding Observations

Negative effects of globalization caused a debilitating economic crisis in the agricultural sector in Mexico. The increasing demand for organic products in developed countries—a product of a post-materialistic trend in values—was the driving force for Mexican producers looking for an alternative means of production. It was in this way that organic farming emerged in Mexico.

Organic producers in Mexico have incorporated their own agro-ecological, cultural, and social conditions into their farming practices, therefore generating unique local processes on 215,000 hectares. These include taking advantage of the fact that conventional agriculture, with its high chemo-synthetic inputs, never gained much of a foothold in the poorest regions of the country; using traditional methods of production including peasant and indigenous knowledge; and utilizing local inputs and family labor in order to reduce production costs. These actions have enabled producers, especially poor and indigenous producers, to avoid the negative forces of globalization. However, the booming international market for organic products and the weakness of the internal market led organic farmers to become export producers as part of this process.

Mexican organic producers have to comply with the same regulations that must be adhered to in the conventional trade, including those pertaining to exports to the United States and Canada in the NAFTA region. The most important factors relate to the exporting of organic products are as follows: product quality, safety measures, and organic certification.

Organic farming offers—to more than 53,000 Mexican producers—the advantages that conventional producers cannot obtain: better prices for their products in the market; conservation and improvement of their own natural resources such as soil and water; production of healthy food for their families and the market; work in a healthy environment, without danger of illnesses produced by chemo-synthetic products; a better income; and a work alternative for their communities. Moreover, in the case of organized producers, organic agriculture helps them to consolidate their organizational structures in an autogestive way. Organization of small-scale, low-income producers into cooperatives facilitates access to certification, trade, and better prices for their products.

Finally, the importance of organic farming in Mexico is linked to sustainable rural development. This alternative is related to the sustainable production of food, the protection and enhancement of "natural capital", and, above all, the

Endnotes

1. Hubert Carton de Grammont, *Globalización, deterioro ambiental y reorganización social en el campo,* 20.
2. IFOAM, *Organic Agriculture: General Standards.*
3. Jan Holm Ingemann, Food and Agricultural System Development.
4. International Trade Center, in Rudy Kortbech Olesen, "Export potential for organic products," *Ecology and Farming* No. 22 IFOAM, Germany, (1999): 6–7.
5. A post-materialist society gives priority to "soft values," such as quality of life, freedom, self-expression, and environmental protection, all on an individual and collective level. Theory of change in values by Inglehart holds that a higher per capita gross national product will promote a higher proportion of post-materialist values. Also, countries with a rapid increase in living standards will have a higher proportion of post-materialistic values in young people. Ronald Inglehart and Paul R. Abramson, "Economic Security and Value Change."
6. Helga Willer and Monou Yussefi, *Organic Agriculture Worldwide:* Statistics and Perspectives, 22.
7. Nicolas Lampkin, *Organic Farming in the European Union:* Overview, Policies and Perspectives, 4.
8. Helga Willer and Monou Yussefi, *Organic Agriculture Worldwide,* 70.
9. See: Nicolas Lampkin, et al., *The Policy and Regulatory Environment for Organic Farming in Europe,* i-viii.
10. Radical movement in organic agriculture developed by 1924 by Rudolf Steiner. It considers not only the organic technologies but also the interaction of the ecosystem with the telluric and cosmic movements. See Feliciano Ruiz Figueroa, *Tópicos sobre agricultura orgánica,* 7.
11. Theology of Liberalization objectives are to release people from poverty, to improve conditions of social welfare in marginal communities, and to generate a consciousness of exploitative conditions with the outlook of transforming society. See Altamirano Cruz, et. al., "La autogestión indígena una estrategia alternativa de desarrollo: El caso de UCIRI." Theology of Liberalization promotes popular religiousness, indigenous cosmovision, traditional ways of collective work, and the appropriation of the productive process in rural communities. In this context, organic farming is a perfect system of production to develop because it is in accordance with all of these principles.
12. Fair Trade promotes structures, mechanisms, practices, and fair trade attitudes between small-scale, low-income producers' cooperatives in developing countries and processors and trading companies in developed countries. Products are traded through the Max Havelaar and Transfair foundations. These foundations give licenses to the trading companies for using the Fair Trade label. The main characteristics of the fair trade contracts are to guarantee a minimum price, to finance production of the co-operative, and to establish long-term contracts. Equal Exchange, *What is fair trade?* (2001), http://www.equal-exchange.com; *Bob Thomson, Fair Trade—Frequently asked questions* (2001) http://www.web.net/~bthomson/ who/ fair2.html

13. It implies the usage of only a very few agricultural activities mainly weed control and harvest, while the organic type uses additional practices with the objectives of soil conservation, increase of natural fertility, and integral management of the agroecosystem.
14. Laura Gómez Tovar, Manuel Ángel Gómez-Cruz, and Rita Schwentesius Rinder mann, *Desafíos de la Agricultura Orgánica: Certificación y Comercialización,* 30.
15. It allows the product to be sold as organic and obtain the premium price.
16. Based on projections for 2002: M. Á. Gómez-Cruz, et al. (2003).
17. Fieldwork, 2000.
18. Laura Gómez Tovar, Manuel Ángel Gómez-Cruz and Rita Schwentesius Rindermann, *Desafíos de la Agricultura Orgánica,* 119–28.
19. Aurora J. Lobato García, *Segmentación de mercado para productos orgánicos en el área metropolitana (Distrito Federal) y zona conurbada,* 70; and Laura Gómez Tovar, Manuel Ángel Gómez-Cruz, and Rita Schwentesius Rindermann, *Desafíos de la Agricultura Orgánica,* 119–21.
20. UNDP, *Human Development Report.* http://www.undp.org/hdro/report.html
21. Ibid.

Bibliography

Bertinuson, Anne, and Mónica Castillo. "Tendencias, oportunidades y limitaciones en la agricultura orgánica de los EE.UU." *In Producción, Comercialización y Certificación en Agricultura Orgánica en Latinoamérica*. Mexico (and Auna, Cuba): CIESTAAM, 2003.

Carton de Grammont, Hubert. *Globalización, Deterioro Ambiental y Reorganización Social en el Campo*. Edited by Juan Pablos. Mexico: Universidad Nacional Autóma de México, 1995.

Cruz, Altamirano, et al. "La Autogestión Indígena una Estrategia Alternativa de Desarrollo: El Caso de UCIRI." In *Movimientos Campesinos y Reforma Agraria en el Istmo Oaxacaqueño*. Valdivia de Orteda, E. Cuadernos de Centros Regionales, no. 20. Mexico: Universidad Autónoma Chapingo, 1997.

Equal Exchange. *What is Fair Trade?* (2001). http://www.equal-exchange.com.

Gómez Cruz, Manuel Ángel, et al. *La Agricultura Orgánica de México: Datos básicos*. Second Edition. Mexico; Boletín,: SAGARPA-CIESTAAM, 2001.

Gómez-Cruz, Manuel Ángel, Laura Gómez Tovar, and Rita Schwentesius Rindermann. Agricultura Orgánica: *Mercado internacional y propuesta para su desarrollo en México*. Reporte de Investigación No. 62. Chapingo, Mexico: CIESTAAM, 2002.

———. "La agricultura orgánica en México." In *Producción, Comercialización y Certificación en Agricultura Orgánica en Latinoamérica*. México (and Auna, Cuba): CIESTAAM, 2003.

Gómez Tovar Laura. *Proposal for a Structural and Institutional Design for the Development of Organic Farming Technology in Mexico*. Master Thesis, Roskilde University. Denmark: Aalborg University, 2000.

Gómez Tovar, Laura, Manuel Angel Gómez–Cruz, and Rita Schwentesius Rindermann. *Desafíos de la Agricultura Orgánica: Certificación y Comercialización*. Second Edition. Mexico: Mundi-Prensa-Universidad Autónoma Chapingo, 2001.

IFOAM. *Organic Agriculture: General Standards*. (2001). http://www.ifoam.org/whoisifoam/generelhtml.

Ingemann, Jan Holm. *Food and Agricultural System Development*. Draft. Denmark: Aalborg University, 2000.

Inglehart, Ronald, and Paul R. Abramson. "Economic Security and Value Change." *American Journal of Political Science* 88, no. 2 (1998): 336–54.

Kortbech Olesen, Rudy. "Export Potential for Organic Products." *Ecology and Farming* 22 (1999): 6–7.

Lampkin, Nicolas. "Organic Farming in the European Union: Overview, Policies and Perspectives." Paper presented at the conference: Farming in the European Union, Perspectives for the 21st Century. Baden, Austria, 1999.

———, Carolyn Foster, Susanne Padel, and Peter Midmore. *The Policy and Regulatory Environment for Organic Farming in Europe*. Germany: University of Hohenheim, 1999.

Lobato García, Aurora J. *Segmentación de Mercado para Productos Orgánicos en el Area Metropolitana (Distrito Federal) y Zona Conurbada*. Masters thesis, Chapingo, Mexico, 1998.

Ruiz Figueroa, Feliciano. *Tópicos sobre Agricultura Orgánica*. Mexico: CONARAO-Universidad Autonoma Chapingo, 1999.

The Danish Ministry of Food, Agriculture and Fisheries. *Action Plan II: Developments in Organic Farming*. Denmark, 1999.

Thomson, Bob. *Fair Trade—Frequently Asked Questions*. Fair Trade Mark, Canada (2001). http:\\www.web.net\~bthomson/who/fair2.html.

Trujillo Arriaga, Javier. "La Agricultura Tradicional Campesina como Componente del Desarrollo de la Agricultura Sostenible." In *Agricultura Campesina: Orientaciones Agrobiológicas y Agronómicas sobre Bases Sociales Tradicionales vs Tratado de Libre Comercio,* edited by T. Martinez, J. Trujillo, and F. Bejarano. Mexico: Colegio de Postgraduados, 1994.

UNDP. *Human Development Report.* (1999). http://www.undp.org/hdro/ report.html.

Willer, Helga and Monou Yussefi. *Organic Agriculture Worldwide: Statistics and Perspectives.* Germany: Stiftung Ökologie & Landbau (SÖL, Research Institute of Organic Agriculture), 2000.

Yussefi, Minou, and Helga *Willer. The World of Organic Agriculture: Statistics and Future Prospects 2003.* Germany: Stiftung Ökologie & Landbau (SÖL, Research Institute of Organic Agriculture), 2003.

Chapter 8

Bimbo-Coronado and Goat-Keepers in Matehuala

Juan de Dios Trujillo Félix, Elia Patlán Martínez, and Rita Schwentesius Rindermann*

Our study for this chapter was motivated by the search for a greater understanding of large transnational companies that work with small-scale agricultural producers in the Mexican regions where the companies are established. It considers the arrangement for supplying goat's milk between the company (*Productos de Leche Coronado,* a subsidiary of the *Grupo Industrial Bimbo*) and producers from the Matehuala region in the state of San Luis Potosí in Mexico—an arrangement that was facilitated by the Mexican Foundation for Rural Development (*Fundación Mexicana para el Desarrollo Rural* or FMDR). In particular, the study examines the situation of goat-keeping for the members of the producers' group. The participating company is associated with one of the most recognized brand names in the Mexican market: *Cajeta Coronado,* which is a type of jelly made from goat's milk and sugar through a process of evaporation—part of the Mexican tradition of natural desserts. The company markets other types of products from goat's milk,[1] but *Cajeta Coronado* is their most recognized product on the market.

The arrangement or "alliance" referred to by the FMDR seeks to guarantee a market for producers of goat's milk in the region. The 1997 agreement between the goat-milk producers and the company was short-lived, and ended in failure after barely four months. However, the experiment is interesting as a case study because it allows an analysis of the problems between an agro-industrial company and the small-scale producers in a context where an organization mediates between both sides and assumes a helping role beyond that of a technical nature. Additionally, the case allows for an analysis of the situation of this type of small-scale producer, which has specialized in raising goats in the absence of a better alternative. In all, the activities of the small-scale producers in the region studied have contributed to the development of some agro-industrial companies in the same line of products as Coronado, and of a specialized market in goats and in products derived from them.

*This work is derived from a collaborative effort between the Center for Latin American and Caribbean Studies of Michigan State University and the CIESTAAM of the Universidad Autónoma Chapingo.

Natural conditions in the Matehuala region, as well as others in the north central part of Mexico, have made goat-keeping a feasible activity for the local peasants. The area receives less that 600 mm of precipitation, which gives rise to community pastures so poor that the development of other money-making farming activities is very limited. Goat-keeping for milk, meat, leather, and breeding stock has been one of the options for survival that many small-scale producers in this area have found. From the goat's milk, producers make cheese, *cajetas*, and other desserts. A demand for goat meat, especially of kids (young goats), has risen in the kitchens of Mexico as a result of the specializations in meats. Even a popular Mexican dish called *birria* uses the meat from older goats. As far as the *cajeta*, it can be consumed directly as a dessert, spread on bread in the manner of a sandwich or on pancakes, or used as an ingredient in pastries. The Coronado Company, after more than 60 years in existence, was acquired by the Bimbo Industrial Group in 1995. Currently it is integrated with *Ricolino*, one of six organizations that make up the Bimbo Group. The Bimbo Group is considered one of the three largest companies for the production of baked goods worldwide. It was the acquisition of Coronado that motivated the alliance, by virtue of the close relationship between Bimbo's principal stockholder and financier and that of FMDR, an organization in which the same person holds the position of president-for-life.

The FMDR, founded through the initiative of businesspeople, has since its inception attributed basic importance to increasing the productivity of small-scale producers by way of technical assistance, and its activities in the organization and consolidation of agricultural projects have emphasized the transfer of technology. One of its key roles has been the fostering of the relationship as providers of assistance between organized small-scale producers and the large agro-industrial or commercial companies.

The initiator for the supply agreement between Bimbo-Coronado and goat-milk producers was FMDR, which also decided to terminate it in the face of waste, and the impossibility of fulfilling the exchange of quantities originally agreed upon. In this study, the causes for the failure of this arrangement between small-scale producers and the processing agribusiness company will be considered. The study concludes that the failure does not necessarily invalidate this type of an agreement, but that the fundamental problem of raising the income of small-scale producers revolves around their level of organization. The organization not only enables producers to improve their capacity for negotiations with agro-industrial companies, but also expands the range of market options for their development.

The Bimbo Industrial Group and the Coronado Company

Bimbo is a company of Mexican origin founded in 1945 by Lorenzo and Roberto Servitje, Jaime Jorba, Alfonso Velasco, Jaime Sendra, and Jose T. Mata for the production of American-style loaf bread. The company is engaged in the production and distribution of products such as bread, cookies and packaged desserts, party snacks, sweets, *cajeta*, gum, frozen fruits and vegetables, and corn- and wheat-flour tortillas. They also produce equipment for the food industry. Bimbo has become the thirteenth most important company in Mexico and the first in the food industry there.

Bimbo expanded from a regional company in the east central part of Mexico (states of Veracruz, Morelos, Hidalgo, and Puebla) to become a dominant player in the food industry in the Mexican market. After 1989, the expansion of the Bimbo Industrial Group led to a process of internationalization, stimulated in part by the Mexican economic crisis and the downturn of its internal market. In the end, the company not only has a prominent presence in Mexico, but also operates distribution centers and production plants in the United States, Latin America (Brazil, Guatemala, Chile, Venezuela, El Salvador, Argentina, Costa Rica, Colombia, Peru, Honduras, Nicaragua, and Uruguay), and Europe (Germany, Austria, and the Czech Republic). It expanded its presence in the United States with the acquisition of Mrs. Baird's, and in Brazil it has become the first in bread-making since the acquisition of 100% of the stock of Plus Vita, Ltd., which handles prestigious brands in that country such as Pullman, Plus Vita, Ana Maria, Muffs, and Van Mill.

The Bimbo Industrial Group operates with 76 plants and five marketing units, employs more than 60,000 people, sells its product at approximately 550,000 points of sale, and offers more than 750 different products. It handles the brands Bimbo, Marinela, Wonder, Tia Rosa, Barcel, Chip's, Cora, Montecristo, Mrs. Baird's, La Tapatía, Yopi, Park Lane, Ricolino, Milpa Real, Sunbeam, Lara, Candy Max, Freezer, Juicee Gummee, Del Hogar, Coronado, Lonchibón, Suandy, and Paty Lu, and other brands in various countries. In the year 2000, Bimbo reached more than US$3 billion in sales and is currently considered one of the healthiest companies in Mexico, financially speaking.[2]

In April of 1995, the Bimbo Group acquired *Productos de Leche Coronado,* a company dedicated to the manufacture of *cajeta*, eggnog, and other Mexican desserts made from goat's milk. The brand enjoyed a high level of popularity among Mexican consumers. The company was founded in 1938 by José Hernández Guerra, who took the name *Coronado* from one of his country estates as the brand name for his *cajeta*. His product was originally homemade and the formula was derived from a family recipe. The Hernández family initially marketed *cajeta* in the town of Venados, San Luis Potosí, at a railway station where the train had a layover in which passengers were allowed to disembark. From there, recognition of the product extended throughout Mexico without the need for large promotional expenditures. For many years, *cajeta* and *Coronado* were virtually synonymous.

The Hernandez family came to build three plants in various towns in the state of San Luis Potosí—in Venados (its original location), Matehuala, and San Luis Potosí. In the regions where these plants were installed, the keeping of goats developed. The company also expanded operations in other goat-milk supply zones that were situated in other Mexican states. Operations were centralized in San Luis Potosí, the capital of the state, while the Venados plant, located in a town of lesser economic importance, was transferred to one of its employees. After the death of Mr. Hernández,[3] familial disputes among his heirs finally led to the decision to sell the company in December of 1991 to the *Grupo Televisa*, whose line of business had little to do with food.[4] Its executives made the decision to close the Matehuala plant, maintaining only the parent company in San Luis Potosí, which would be provided with "paste" (the resulting ingredient of the first stage in the processing of goat's milk, before it is transformed into cajeta), fabricated in the towns of Jamay (in the state of Jalisco), Torreón (in the state of Coahuila) and Meoqui (in the state of Chihuahua).

Coronado did not stay long in the hands of Televisa, whose principal stockholder was Emilio Azcárraga Milmo. The Televisa Group, however, introduced important changes in that it redefined the company—Productos de Leche Coronado—giving it a market profile as an exporter. To this end, many investments were made to revamp facilities, equipment, boilers, and vehicles, in addition to the contracting of food preparation specialists and FDA personnel. In this way, the Televisa Group attempted to modernize its plants and to improve the quality of its products according to U.S. guidelines. The Mexican economic crisis of 1995, the expansion process that the Televisa Group had in other areas (radio, television, and other media), and problems between principal stockholders, led to a reorganization which necessitated the sale of several of its businesses, including Coronado.

Upon being acquired by the Bimbo Group, Coronado became administrated by *Altex*, one of Bimbo's divisions that comprised diverse companies. Altex did not introduce *significant changes* and gave great independence to the already existing administration. Altex demanded an increase in profits, and changes were made in the operating systems to correlate with those of the Bimbo Group. The separation of Altex from Bimbo in 2000, however, led to the transfer of Coronado to the Ricolino organization, which was also part of the Bimbo Group, and this transfer imposed a new dynamic. Ricolino reassessed the positioning of the Coronado brand, and its potential in the domestic and export markets. It has since intervened more directly to modernize the plants, to facilitate the adoption of Bimbo operating systems, and the application of the quality standards necessary for an export product. Furthermore, they tried to make it so that Coronado products arrived not only to wholesalers and large self-service stores, but also to small dealers, as is the case for Ricolino products.

Coronado has had a dominant position in the Mexican *cajeta* market for many years, though now the market has become more competitive. Other companies marketed similar products in the state of San Luis Potosí, such as *Productos Lácteos San Diego*, and *Productos Medellín* (*Las Sevillanas*), or in other states such as Guanajuato (*Productos Aldama, La Higiénica,* and *La Regia*) or Querétaro (*Productos Don José*). Also, homemade *cajeta* is sold at the local community level in various regions. Furthermore, goat's milk is not only demanded by companies manufacturing *cajeta* and other types of sweets, but by businesses and families who make cheese as well. The market for products derived from goat's milk still has not been faced with any restriction in terms of supply of goat's milk that might limit the expansion of its processing companies.

Sales of Coronado products have been on the rise, but they still do not fulfill expectations in terms of the export market; *Coronado cajeta* is produced largely for domestic consumption. At present, they export around 3% of their production to the United States, but it is probable that this area may increase substantially after their absorption by Ricolino with their greater capacity to invest. Coronado developed without large expenditures on advertising and the Mexican market in the United States—which is familiar with the product and brand—has not been exploited fully.

The Mexican Foundation for Rural Development (FMDR) in San Luis Potosí

The Mexican Foundation for Rural Development (FMDR), a non-governmental organization with more than 30 years experience in promoting small-scale family production, was created by a group of private entrepreneurs through the initiative of Lorenzo Servitje, the primary shareholder of the Bimbo Group. The Foundation gained in importance in the Mexican countryside during the 1990s, due in large part to less government attention to this area, and to the dismantling of a good number of official rural organizations that had existed before. Currently, FMDR is present in 25 states and has 35 Development Offices, a basic component of its organizational structure.

FMDR was founded in 1963 as a private, non-profit institution, motivated by a Christian sense of charity but without being specifically religious in nature. In the beginning, it focused on social welfare and community development, but later placed greater emphasis on economic organization and the realization of productive projects. In its first approach to the area, FMDR directed its efforts toward credit, creating a guaranteed fund to facilitate the farmers' access to credit (Austin 2000). In order to maintain its viability as a support organization, it has established that services not be totally free of charge.

Under the principles of human dignity, solidarity, subrogation, efficiency, and respect for the environment that guide the organization, the FMDR attends to the human development of people in the rural family, and in organized groups' through subsidized support of the foundation and its centers of development. Its general strategy is based on the development of "farm companies," whose plan of action consists of creating cooperative businesses designed to overcome limitations and consolidate supply and demand of goods and services, and the establishment of strategic alliances in order to link itself to other agencies involved in the economic chain (FMDR 1999a). With the concept of the "farm company", an attempt is made to define the small, rural, local unit.

The FMDR is characterized by its having drawn up a plan that emphasizes the need for competitiveness, business sense, adaptation to change, and market orientation. The plan is designed so that producers and their organizations add greater value to their products by using appropriate technology, adequate financing, and professional advising and training. The importance that it assigns to training is one of the most notable aspects of the FMDR.[5] Furthermore, it sees producers not only as proprietors, but also as clients and providers in the agro-industrial chain. These characteristics distinguish it from the majority of organizations that operate in support of farmers in Mexico.

Precisely for these reasons, in recent years (despite the fact that FMDR is a private organization) there has been a coming together of FMDR and programs and institutions sponsored by the public sector that seek to improve efficiency in the allocation of government resources destined for the countryside. Its focus has been more compatible with the reform process of public policy in Mexico. This drawing together, on the other hand, has created a situation where some of its managers have moved into public administration at the state and federal levels, in areas related to land and rural development.[6]

The level of development achieved by the FMDR has defined it as a Foundation Movement (*Movimiento Fundación*), integrated on three levels. The first level consists of farming groups organized around projects of common interest at the local level. The second level is represented by Development Centers resembling regional foundations located in several geographical areas of the country and focused on providing advice and services in such areas as: organization, training, management, access to credit, technical assistance and technology transfer, and marketing and promotion of family development. The final level is the FMDR itself, with its headquarters in Mexico City. This last unit is governed by an advisory council made up of members of the business community, some of whom also serve on the executive committee.

The national operation of the FMDR is quite decentralized. Each of its regional head offices functions with a council made up of prominent people from the local community while it also uses the services of hired professionals and receives input from organized groups of producers. Decisions on policies, strategy, and programs at the local level are largely made by the councils at these regional head offices.

The head offices display different levels of development and adapt themselves to diverse problems; because of this, their activities and members can be very diverse in their characteristics. In the state of San Luis Potosí, where the Coronado headquarters is located, three offices or agencies have been formed: Rural Development of San Luis Potosí (*Desarrollo Rural de San Luis Potosí*, formed in 1976), Rural Development of the North of Potosí (*Desarrollo Rural del Norte Potosino*, established in 1985), and Rural Development of the Central Zone of San Luis Potosí (*Desarrollo Rural de la Zona Media de San Luis Potosí*, formed in 1990). These offices, especially the latter two, have given special attention to rural families dedicated to raising goats, and to their special conditions of poverty and marginalization.

Rural Development of the North of Potosí administers the Matehuala region along with the towns of Catorce, Cedral, Vanegas, Villa de la Paz, Villa De Guadalupe, and Charcas. The current president of the council is the owner of the most important mining company in the region. Rural Development of the Central Zone of San Luis Potosí is present in Rioverde, as well as in the towns of Rayón, Villa Juárez, Cerritos, Ciudad del Maíz, and Ciudad Fernández. As they are introduced, these agencies have been developing a technology package for the raising of goats which was to be transferred to producers, for which they could count on support from researchers at the University of Arizona. In their attention to the goat program, the offices headquartered in Matehuala have a leading role because of the greater importance placed on goat-keeping in the region.

FMDR's agencies in the state of San Luis Potosí have placed much attention on the development of families raising goats, due to the characteristics of the region, the pattern of product specialization already in existence, the potential for creation of jobs, and the type of producer selected to receive support. In the time since the initiation of activities, their personnel have accumulated enough knowledge about goat-keeping to enable them to participate in the regional design of public policies related to the activity.

Furthermore, the need to make FMDR's assistance plans viable has led to situations in which its managers tend to get involved in initiatives that exceed the purpose of simply giving assistance to farming families. Thus, FMDR's local managers often get involved in the development of regional plans and in the drive to coordinate institutional and private efforts for the benefit of the communities at large. This means that FMDR personnel are always ready to help in the areas of technology and community development, which fall more into the realm of public function otherwise reserved for government institutions. Consequently, their relationship with government agencies that serve the communities in which they operate are not exempt from some degree of rivalry.

The FMDR offices not only attend to the production problems but also propose, for example, a plan of action directed toward improving living conditions and nutrition through the establishment of family gardens, the improvement of rainwater collection systems, the installation of latrines, and the provision of equipment for brick-making, among other activities.

Goat-Keeping in the State of San Luis Potosí

Goat-keeping is practiced in almost every state in Mexico, especially in regions where low precipitation rates or poor soil make agriculture difficult. Goats adapt extremely well to drought conditions and poor grazing land. They are also extraordinarily efficient in their eating habits and are capable of producing milk and meat through the consumption of foods which other domesticated species are not able to use. Furthermore, they not only have high rates of fertility and reproduction, but investment and maintenance costs are comparatively low. These characteristics have made it possible for producers lacking technical knowledge and resources to dedicate themselves to this occupation in regions that are also poor in resources.

In Mexico, the most important goat-raising region has been the north of the country (Chihuahua, Durango, Coahuila, Nuevo León, Zacatecas, and San Luis Potosí) which represented 45% of the goat population in the 1980s (Mayén 1989). This geographical area has been declining in importance, however, and in 1999 it made up only 33% (CNG 2001). The activity has gained in importance in zones to the south and in central Mexico, but within the context of an overall falling goat inventory.

According to estimates by the Center for Statistics on Agriculture and Cattle (*Centro de Estadísticas Agropecuarias*) of SAGARPA (CNG 2001), the goat population in Mexico was estimated in 1999 at 9.1 million in total, a number which is lower than in previous years. According to this source, there was a slight decline in the production of goats for meat and for milk, although these volumes show greater fluctuation than the total number. In general, the statistics referring to cattle-raising in Mexico are unreliable—even more so for goat-keeping, due to the fact that the activity is conducted over large tracts of land and by poor families on marginal areas and communities. As a result, absolute figures must not be unquestioningly accepted.

While there is no clear explanation as to why the importance of goat-raising is in decline, our study suggests that this drop is largely due to young people's lack of interest in continuing this family economic activity, as it generates a low income, requires long working hours, and means extensive walking every day. Families have a hard time keeping young people at home, since many people venture to more economically rewarding locales—especially the Unites States. Historically, the labor force of the northern states has been scarce in comparison with states in the central region and in the south of Mexico. As a result, this northern region has a much more severe shortage of goatherds, and goat-keeping has been an occupation practiced largely by adults of advanced age and by children.

According to the source previously mentioned, the three states with the largest goat populations are Puebla, Oaxaca, and San Luis Potosí, with 1.4 million, 1.1 million, and 1.0 million heads respectively. The goat population in San Luis Potosí is equivalent to 10.6% of the total inventory of Mexico, but has shown a decrease that corresponds with the general tendency in the country. In addition, according to information from the FMDR (1998), there are 220,000 producers involved in goat-keeping in San Luis—approximately 11% of the rural population of the state.

The region of San Luis Potosí which specializes most in raising goats is known as the *Altiplano*.[7] It is characterized by a dry steppe-like climate, an inconsistent and scarce rainfall, and lack of developed water-delivery systems. The lack of water and good natural pastureland limits the development of agriculture and cattle grazing. Without better alternatives, the presence of goat-keeping has, to a surprising extent, allowed the development of the goat market (and products derived from them) and an industry that makes Mexican desserts based on goat's milk.

Those who raise goats may earn income from the sale of goat's milk to producers of *cajeta* and other desserts or cheeses, or they may use the milk themselves to produce these same products at home. They may also sell kids (young goats), or waste animals from which meat or skin is obtained, or live animals for breeding (male or female). In states like Oaxaca, Puebla, and Guerrero, "fattened goats" (castrated males that are then fattened) are sold. Kids are marketed 8 - 40 days after birth (on average, 25 days after birth) depending on their development, the breed, and existing prices. Waste goats are old or defective adults, or others that are not productive. Owing to the already long tradition of raising goats in the northern region of the country, as well as in the *Altipla-*

no, an area of Mexican cuisine based on kids or goats has developed. This contrasts with the Midwest of Mexico, where goat meat is used for the typical dish, *birria*—in which case, the meat of adult animals is generally used.

The use of goats may be oriented primarily toward milk production or meat, although one is sold as much as the other. This distinction is important and stems from the type of breed, some of which are better milk producers (Alpine and Saanen), while others are better for their meat (Boer). Those breeds which are better for milk require better nutrition and care. For this reason, their use tends to occur in richer zones and, ideally, in stable conditions. The breeds that are raised in open pasture conditions, in areas similar to that of the highlands (*Altiplano*), tend to be those used for meat and involve lower costs—although the types most suited for these conditions may not be the most efficient for meat production (Nubian and Criollas, or hybrids with a low proportion of Toggenburg, Saanen, and Alpine).

To a large extent, the *Altiplano* has lost its reputation as the center of goat-milk production compared to other zones of production in Mexico,[8] consequently turning the focus there toward meat. Still, two important milk-demanding businesses exist in Matehuala, *Productos Lácteos San Diego* and *Productos Medellín*,[9] which absorb the production from areas that are nearby and accessible. The breeders with flocks located at a lesser distance from the plants tend more toward milk production destined for the dessert industry—due to the fact that they incur fewer transportation expenses and there is less risk of milk souring from long transportation times. It is worth mentioning that the rural communities near Matehuala are quite dispersed and distant from one another. The price is determined by the companies and is adjusted according to the season, being lower in periods of high production and higher in times when it becomes scarce. Milk is produced during the entire year, but goats produce more when there is a greater food supply available due to increased rainfall. The low-production period occurs from August to October, and the high from February to June.

The power of companies to set the prices is restricted by the willingness of producers to sell, since these companies are forced to compete with cheese producers for the milk.[10] If breeders consider the price to be too low, they will prefer to produce cheese or to sell to others. The cheese is sold in nearby communities and villages. A certain quantity of it arrives at the northern border and enters the United States by way of family networks. Milking and cheese-making are activities done by women. Cheese-making, as an alternative for producers, reduces the milk available to the processing companies.

During the 1980s, the activity entered a period of decline due to high inflation in Mexico. The high interest rate existing at that time favored the sale of flocks used for milk production, for the purpose of depositing money earned from sales in the bank. A good number of breeders believed that they could live better with less effort, thanks to income earned from money deposited in the bank. They were mistaken, however, as the loss of buying power of the money led to a decline in their standard of living and they were not able to rebuild their flocks.

The decrease in the number of animals and the deterioration in the quality of the flocks affected milk production. Furthermore, it caused increased emigration and a scarcity of shepherds. To this can be added the greater frequency of droughts, to which hybrid animals of lower productivity adapted more easily. Consequently, the goat population tended to decrease at the same time possibilities for the introduction of better management techniques worsened. This situation wound up causing the closure of the Coronado plant in Matehuala as the region lost its competitive edge to other companies with a greater capacity for milk supply.

In regions of the country where the same tradition of family production does not exist as in the highlands, those breeders either specialized in the sale of milk to companies similar to Coronado, such as Jamay, Jalisco, or Chilchota in Durango, or they allowed kids to consume all of the milk of the goats. In other cases, where goat-raising occurred under more scientific conditions of confinement with breeds more oriented toward milk (as in Guanajuato and Querétaro), production units specializing in higher quality cheese have developed. The existence of a local market for goat-milk cheese in the highlands has allowed breeders to count on this alternative and enabled them to develop double-purpose flocks, in spite of their preference toward the sale of kids. This system tends to reduce the breeders' vulnerability to changes in market conditions and increases their ability to negotiate when dealing with companies that produce *cajeta*.

Politics and public programs of the state government of San Luis Potosí, the action of FMDR offices in this state, and the organization of goat producers have contributed favorably to increased consumer confidence regarding cheeses produced in the highlands region. This in turn has stimulated the development of this market. However, these efforts are still not enough and have not completely eliminated the lack of consumer confidence related to the risk of contracting Malta fever which is caused by the brucellosis virus that is often associated with the consumption of non-pasteurized cheese or milk.

In addition, although the FMDR has encouraged initiatives in this direction, the production of finer, European-style cheeses[11] of the types appreciated by restaurants and higher-income consumers in urban areas, such as Mexico City, Guadalajara, and Monterrey, has not been undertaken. Only a small quantity of goat cheese from the highlands passes into the United States, and the potential of this market has not been exploited, because no company has concentrated its efforts on producing European-style cheese with the control and quality demanded of export products.[12]

Because there are a greater number of buyers, the market for young and waste goats is much wider and more competitive in comparison with that for milk goats; however, it is not exempt from undesirable, non-competitive practices. Thus, there are middlemen who enrich themselves by advancing loans to breeders ahead of the sale of the animals, or sales made through kinship relationships where breeders feel obligated to sell at a lower price. In response to these concerns, the FMDR has encouraged the establishment of contracts and sales agreements at better prices, the organization of producers in order to consolidate the supply, and the introduction of greater training.

The most important markets for young goats are in Mexico City and Monterrey, and for waste goats, in the interior of the Mexican republic. Matehuala has been the main center for the marketing of kids and goats and exercises an influence in the setting of prices. This area attracts the young goat market from various goat-keeping regions in Mexico, which is mostly introduced in Monterrey, Nuevo León, for slaughter and consumption. From Monterrey, the meat is sent to Mexico City and elsewhere. It is worth observing that raising goats in the various regions of Mexico is oriented toward local markets, and this represents a market constraint for the development of goat-keeping.

The extended-range method, which predominates in the highlands region and that requires a low investment, is not very technical and offers a low yield. While it can be adequate for the subsistence of a family and for some savings, it does not guarantee its capitalization and development. According to the FMDR (1998), income from goat raisers is less than 60% of the minimum wage in the San Luis Potosí zone, and 50% of the workers are older than 50 years, with little or no education. Production of milk is 0.2 liters/day per animal, with milking periods of 90 days. A better technology package could extend the period of milk production and increase productivity of the goats by way of feed management and breeding. It would also help in the production of kids of greater size and weight in less time, and contribute to a better scheduling of the shipping of young goats to the market during periods of the highest prices. However, current conditions are not favorable for this.

An environment like the one mentioned represents an obstacle for the initiative designed by the FMDR, since the foundation has been promoting in its areas of influence a model of "family cultivation of goats" of a semi-extensive type,[13] which involves improvements in water-supply systems, the use of feeds and genetic improvements, and the use of better management systems. The FMDR has made proposals for raising existing parameters, such as increasing production from 0.2 liters/day in 90 days of milking to at least 0.6 liters/day in 150 days, and culling kids within 20 days of birth. The goal, based on a plan of greater utilization of the resources upon which goat-raisers rely, is to obtain increases in income for goat-raisers to more than one and one-half times the minimum wage.

Alliance for the Reopening of the Matehuala Plant

An important aspect of the FMDR strategy has been to encourage, through the mediation of their offices, the establishment of alliances of organized producers with agro-industries, with the aim of guaranteeing stable access to the market and making promoted projects work. For this reason, it favored the Bimbo-Coronado agreement for the rehabilitation and opening of the Matehuala plant in 1997. The agreement lasted a few months and was ended with the concurrence of both sides.

The FMDR is not an instrument of the Bimbo Industrial Group. Yet, wherever this group has needed providers for its plants, FMDR offices have responded with assistance, although not always successfully, as in the case documented in this study.

From the point of view of the FMDR, the alliances imply cooperative work and convince producers of the need for organization for the marketing and consolidation of supply, and the introduction of technical improvements to increase productivity. The agro-industries can benefit from the development of their providers, from working with a sole provider with the legal capacity for billing, from an increased volume of raw material of better quality, and from a greater identification of the business with its social environment.

The closing of the Coronado plant in Matehuala, the most important of its kind, had represented a crisis of the activity, given that a demand estimated at 45,000 liters daily disappeared. The closure represented a drastic change since other companies did not have the ability to absorb the existing available milk, and because there were fewer options for sale of the milk in the market. In reaction, breeders felt themselves free to turn their emphasis toward meat, which endangered the quality of their flocks. This adjustment not only caused more emigration and increased the search for alternate sources of income, but also brought a setback in the attempts to bring greater technical improvements to the activity.

The system of milk production is more suited to the participation of women in the administration of income and expenses as they receive money periodically, and not in a single distribution during the season as is the case in the marketing of kids. In contrast, the system of specialization in the production of live animals requires that breeders carefully manage their expenses throughout the cycle and, given the existing cultural pattern, males have the tendency to consume alcohol or participate in diversions such as cock-fighting. Under this system, families are faced with difficult obstacles to improve their level of well-being, in spite of the fact that a greater possibility for capitalization exists.

The Center for Development of the North of Potosí, a unit of FMDR, sought to make a milk-based system viable, although climatic conditions as well as the market were encouraging a slant toward the production of kids. This is the pattern of specialization that has been developing, and currently technical innovations are occurring in this direction, such as the promotion of genetic improvements by way of the Boer breed.

As we have shown, the closure of the Matehuala plant had economic, social, and technological implications. After Bimbo's acquisition of Coronado, the idea of reopening the plant has matured and an agreement has been established with the administration of this company, as motivated by Lorenzo Servitje and the Bimbo Corporation.

The plant's reopening implied support for the poorest producers of the region. Goat-keeping as an activity has the advantage of not requiring a large investment; it also fosters the integration of the family around the woman, and makes viable the adoption of a technology package for a more complete land use (a system of small-scale, family use with a semi-extensive system). This was precisely the package of techniques that the foundation's office considered most adequate and had been implementing. Additionally, in a much larger context, it was important for this organization to create a climate for the advancement of their proposal of medium- and long-term development of goat-keeping in the highlands of Potosí. This program was designed to help through advising, technical assistance, and support of numerous producers and communities, with the goal that in ten years it will cover almost one-third of the goat population in the area.[14]

The contracted agreement was to make the FMDR plan viable in the region, based on the increase of goat-keeping and small-scale production. The belief was that the agreement would overcome the negative effects caused by the plant closure through the willingness of the producers to invest in improving their flocks and to adopt a different management system.

In addition to the rehabilitation of the plant, certain demands were placed on Coronado, including an acceptable market price for milk delivered, while taking into account market conditions, weekly pays, higher pricing according to the percentage of fat, financing of milk-collection centers, and reimbursement for transportation costs. Although the industry was not inclined to agree to the last three points, it invested in the rehabilitation of the plant in exchange for the FMDR's agreement to supply it with 7,500 liters of milk daily, in good condition and before 3:00 in the afternoon. In the good years before closing, the plant required 25,000 liters to make it profitable; afterwards it demanded a lesser quantity.

The industry was not interested in dealing directly with producers; the reopening of the plant was conducted under the assumption that it would be the foundation that would be responsible for collecting the milk and for paying each producer for its deliveries. For the industry, direct dealings with producers represented administration and management costs that it was not willing to assume, and in reality the office of FMDR assumed the role of intermediary. As a result, producers had no contact whatsoever with the processing plant; rather, FMDR appeared to be the purchaser.

Coronado, in the producing regions where it has its offices, transports the milk used to supply its plants through its own personnel and equipment,[15] but it accepts direct delivery from producers and has come to accept deliveries by way of independent deliverers (truck drivers). However, the plan for the existing milk supply in the Matehuala region had been based on collectors who operated with their own vehicles and who maintained close ties with the goat-keepers. The milk was transported in sterilized, stainless steel tanks. The milk that the plants received was required to be clean (without goat excrement) and was subjected to burn tests (to check for colostrums, which elevate acidity) and other laboratory tests to verify acidity, and water and fat content, and to make sure that it was free from brucellosis.

The agreement was not sustainable and the plant was closed again without great conflict between the parties involved. According to the foundation's representatives, it was impossible for them to fulfill the quotas agreed upon due to unforeseen problems, while the company was not inclined to support them with a differential price in compensation for the higher quality of the product in the zone—greater fat content in the milk.[16] Nor was the company willing to assume part of the transportation costs, or to supply producers with a milk-collection and-delivery infrastructure.

The deterioration of milk flocks had already led to a decreased capacity for milk production and the initial estimates for the supply capacity in the region were not correct. The plants that were in operation at that time already had established mechanisms for ensuring supply that also involved supply from remote locations, so that the reopening of Coronado certainly led to increased demand on the capacity of the region, something that was not perceived at the time.

In addition, the technicians of the foundation were not equipped to assume the role of intermediaries; the need to fulfill quotas forced them to bring in milk from more distant places, a fact that elevated transportation costs as well as the risk of deterioration of the product. Given this, they would have had to invest in refrigeration equipment which was unaffordable in the short term, and for which Coronado was not ready to compensate them. Furthermore, they had not considered the seasonal nature of milk production and the climatic conditions which affected their supply.

Technicians discovered that the management of large volumes was very complicated and that this required infrastructure in the form of transport vehicles and refrigeration tanks. Neither was the market price sufficient, given the conditions that other buyers were able to offer. A liter of milk delivered to the plant was paid at a rate of Mex$2.10. Of this price, producers received Mex$1.80–$1.90—by comparison, Productos San Diego paid Mex$2.10 at the farm. Also, the FMDR technicians discovered that placement of the product entailed higher transaction costs, as much for transport as for the need for registering and accounting for the product received from producers. Processing the payments owed the producers (calculation required two days) added to the demand on personnel, causing lost opportunities due to neglect of other tasks. These problems are among those faced when administering contracts with small-scale suppliers.

In addition, another unforeseen problem arose. The loss of milk that had previously been used within the community for the production of cheese generated an imbalance locally between supply and demand, causing prices to rise. This led to a decreased interest on the part of the families to hand in their milk to the foundation offices for delivery to Coronado.

According to information from the FMDR office in Rioverde, this dynamic weakened the cooperative organization that had been forming, which had also made investment in vehicles and refrigeration tanks. Membership in the cooperative declined, while refrigeration equipment went unused. The credits for the acquisition of equipment were covered through other income sources of the members. The behavior of reneging on the supply agreement was promoted, above all, by women who observed that the milk could bring a higher return locally than by being sold through the cooperative. To the extent that they participated in the production of cheese, the women found that they did not have at their disposal the whey that they had used to feed their backyard pigs. In addition, the breeders found that, due to the high cost of transport, it was more profitable to produce cheese than to turn their milk in to the plants (and not only to Coronado). (The area attended to by the FMDR offices of the central zone of San Luis is located at a distance of 200–300 kilometers from the industrial plant.)

The local plant administration, which remained largely independent from Bimbo, was not willing to incur higher costs in the short term in order to make viable the planned alliance proposed by the office of Matehuala—notwithstanding the positive disposition of the corporate directors toward the program. They could not refute the logic of making the reopening profitable, because the factory in San Luis had already established a mechanism for the supply of goat's milk from other production zones which were competing with Matehuala. This refusal notwithstanding, the administration realized that they were in competition with other businesses for the region's milk (a phenomenon that did not occur in other supply areas), where there existed the power of a limited supply such that prices were forced to rise. The other businesses saw themselves compelled to improve their milk-buying conditions.

Coronado wanted to keep the plant viable from the beginning and it was not motivated by articulating a development project for goat-keeping or for the development of providers at that moment, given that the policy of the Bimbo offices was not to provide financing. Furthermore, the FMDR deliveries arrived late and were not of good quality; the milk tended to sour due to the time elapsed between collection and delivery.

In addition, the FMDR did not sufficiently investigate whether the plan could work with personnel that was not moving toward the marketing and handling of the milk, but rather toward the promotion of producers, training, technical assistance, and management of systems. Similarly, it did not possess the appropriate infrastructure to fulfill obligations implied by the agreement.

Conclusions and Alternatives

The case of the Bimbo/Coronado alliance with the FMDR offices in the state of San Luis shows how difficult the establishment of a working business relationship between companies and small-scale producers can be, even when both parties are willing to make it work. Companies operating under the logic of business seek a supply of raw materials at the lowest possible price in order to increase profit levels while producers seek to secure a market at prices that allow them to raise their income. Their interests are not always reconcilable.

The initiative to establish an agreement for the opening of the plant in Matehuala was the responsibility of the FMDR offices in the highlands of San Luis Potosí. The direction of the alliance was that the interests of the company could be compatible with those of the milk producers, which was something not verified in this situation. There was insufficient study and analysis of its viability. In the end, the cancellation of the agreement was the responsibility of the FMDR offices themselves, and the Matehuala plant was closed again. The causes of the failure can be summarized in the following way:

- There was an incorrect estimate of the actual capacity for milk production due to inadequately considering the changes that had occurred in patterns of goat exploitation of the region.

- There was no consideration of the transaction costs that arose due to the management of small-scale milk production, or of the numerous breeders situated at considerable distances from one another.
- The requirements of plant administration were not considered, and the motives of owners could not be compatible with the interest of FMDR's small-scale producers (even if there had been willingness on the part of the Bimbo Group).
- It was not expected that breeders would be reluctant—due to the imbalance between supply and demand in the communities and its negative effects on the cheese production, which constituted a major source of income—to hand over their milk to Coronado.

The first Coronado plant closure in Matehuala was related to the loss of competitiveness of the region as a milk source compared with other goat-keeping zones, as well as their interest in preserving a strong supply-controlled position in the fixing of prices. This closure contributed to a deepening of retrograde tendencies, such as the reduction in the number of heads, the deterioration in the quality of the milk flock, a greater orientation toward meat production, and an increasing scarcity of shepherds. The greater activity of the market for meat in the north of the country has underpinned this process.

In the second closure of the plant there were no greater effects. However, it allowed Coronado to verify that Matehuala had lost its place as a good milk source. Also, the breeders are already very accustomed to combining the sale of kids with the production of cheese, which gives them a power of negotiation in the face of the companies and makes them less inclined to sell at low prices.

The market for products derived from goat's milk has increased, but not consistently between the production of meat and milk. Until now, companies have found sufficient raw material, though this demand has not been totally satisfied with the production of the highlands region, and the raw material has often become scarce. Given this, in order to increase efficiency, Coronado plans to maintain only two plants for its supply, closing one of the three that have been in operation. Thus, a supply problem is not expected.

It is known that the quality of the milk received in the plants could be significantly improved if the companies adopted certain measures to support breeders, such as the sanitary and preventive measures in flock management through specialized personnel, but this is not being done. The companies assume that imposing quality requirements on the milk that is delivered is sufficient to induce better management techniques. While there is no chronic shortage of milk which might be reflected in increased prices, they are not going to take measures to assist the development of providers, as can be inferred from the behavior of Coronado in the supply zones where it is present.

Concern over the activity of goat-keeping is really a matter of public interest and the interest of the families that engage in it, and is more of a social than an economic issue. Goat-keeping has been neglected by governments in most of Mexico. This is not the case in San Luis Potosí where the social importance of the activity, in a situation lacking better alternatives, has sparked greater governmental intervention through aspects such as genetic improvement, vaccination campaigns against brucellosis attacks, and technical assistance. Nevertheless, there have been problems with the budget and efficiency. FMDR offices have intervened in some of the government programs—with a greater level of efficiency than the participating public institutions. San Luis Potosí's experience in the development of the market for goat products, not only of the industry connected to the activity, suggest that—through whatever means—government intervention is very important, especially regarding sanitation and generating consumer confidence. Still, there is much that remains to be done.

The scarcity of shepherds indicates that it is time for a change in the pattern of use of resources by way of better management and techniques, but the majority of goat-keepers do not have the means to make these changes. The solution to the problem is not an increase in inventory, but rather an increase in the milk and meat output through more productive animals and better systems of utilization of the products generated from the goats, in order to increase the income of families who participate in goat-keeping.

FMDR deliberately pursues an alliance between small-scale producers and agro-industry as one of its strategies, with the idea of reinforcing the organization of producers and the income of families by way of assuring a market. The fact that the plan does not always work, as can be seen in this study, does not invalidate the plan as a whole. Organization is the key for small-scale producers to be able to have a greater capacity for improving their production process and facing their buyers (agro-industry included) and improve their position in the market, with or without the alliance. The value of the FMDR's efforts should be recognized. Their activities with goat-keepers in the region under study have had a positive effect on techniques of the production process, the diversification of options (so as not to depend so much on a single buyer and a single product), and small-scale producers' organized incursion into the market.

Endnotes

1. The company produces cajetas of various types, sizes, and appearances, and lollipops made of milk and water, gums made of cajeta and caramel, and candies made from cajeta and water.
2. For information about the Bimbo Industrial Group, visit the following web sites: http://www.grupobimbo.com.mx and http://profiles.wisi.com.
3. José Hernández had five children in his first marriage. After the death of his first wife, he married again and had four more children. Disputes between the two families developed when the children of his second marriage came of age. This information was obtained through a personal interview with Francisco Pérez Porrúa, production manager of Bimbo-Coronado.
4. According to Francisco Pérez Porrúa, the decision to acquire had to do largely with Emilio Azcárraga's nostalgic memories of his father, who loved cajeta.
5. Interest in training led to the creation by the FMDR of the Mexican Institute of Education for Rural Development (*Instituto Mexicano de Educación para el Desarrollo Rural,* or IMEDER) toward the end of 1999.
6. Examples of this at the federal level are those of Antonio Ruiz, who currently acts as the Undersecretary for Rural Development of the Secretary of Agriculture, Livestock, Rural Development, Fishing and Nutrition (SAGARPA), having previously been President of the FMDR; and of *Leticia Deschamps,* current Director of the National Training Institute (*Instituto Nacional de Capacitación, or INCA Rural*).
7. The Altiplano (Highlands) is the part that corresponds to a semi-arid region of Potosí—a dry, steppe-like climate, with very low levels of precipitation which allows only plant species that require very little water (desert scrub, spiny scrub, and pasture scrub).
8. The most important goat-milk-producing region in Mexico is the Lagunera region in the northern states of Coahuila and Durango, which accounts for around 65% of the total production. It is followed, in order of importance, by the central part of Guanajuato, the Chapala marsh between the states of Jalisco and Michoacán, and the northern part of San Luis Postosí (Zavala 2001). The production of goat's milk in Mexico in the year 2000 was 132 million liters (CNG 2001).
9. These businesses tend to supply themselves with goat's milk from Guanajuato as well.
10. The FMDR office in Rioverde, 200 kilometers from Matehuala, has been promoting another option, providing training for the production of homemade cajeta.
11. In Matehuala, there is a pilot project—the responsibility of a specialist—designed to produce a different type of cheese. These cheeses require much more hygienic procedures than those currently practiced by goat-keepers, and require milk-producing goats not fed with the type of vegetation that is available in existing pastures, which leaves a strong odor. This modality excludes producers served by the FMDR. The office located in Rioverde—given the type of breeders which they service, who have a low capacity for investment and raise flocks not specialized in milk—prefers to train them in the production of traditional cheeses that can be sold by families in local markets.

12. It is worth noting that small factories producing finer cheeses exist in other regions. This would be the case of *Productos Finos Caprina,* with the Artisan label in Atotonilco, Jalisco. Likewise, there are companies that market French-style cheese (soft textured, milky) in the state of Guanajuato—under the Normandie label, in León; Lacclette, in Celaya; and Crotte, in Apaseo el Grande (Zavala 2001).
13. A semi-extensive system implies a better combination of management of pasture land and culling and replacement of animals, increasing the intensity of this activity.
14. See FMDR (1997).
15. It seems that there has been a change adopted in this system owing to problems of corruption of the drivers.
16. The milk goats, and those that receive feed supplements, produce a lesser quantity of milk fat, while goats raised in drought or natural pasture conditions generate milk with a better fat content. The fat content is considered important for the production of *cajeta.*

Bibliography

Austin, James. Estudio de Caso. Mexico: Fundación Mexicana para el Desarrollo Rural (FMDR), 2000.

Centro de Estudios Agropecuarios. Crianza de Caprinos. Mexico: Grupo Editorial Iberoamérica, 2001.

Chudnovsky, Daniel, Bernardo Kosacoff, and Andrés López. Las Multinacionales Latinoamericanas: Sus Estrategias en un Mundo Globalizado. Mexico: FCE, 1999.

CIESTAAM. Probisci. Chapingo, Mexico: Mimeo, 1998.

CNG. Información Económica Pecuaria 10. Mexico, 2001.

Harvard Business School. Mexican Foundation for Rural Development. 1999.

———. Grupo Industrial Bimbo S. A. de C.V. 1994.

IMEDER. Educación: Factor Estratégico para Lograr Procesos de Transformación y Desarrollo en el Campo Mexicano. Mexico, 2000.

FMDR. Plan de Desarrollo Integral de Caprinocultores del Altiplano Potosino. Chapingo, Mexico: Mimeo, 1997.

———. Plan de Desarrollo Integral de Familias Rurales del Altiplano Potosino. Chapingo, Mexico: Mimeo, 1998.

———. Informe Anual. México, 1999 (a).

———. Proyecto de Caprino en el Altiplano. Chapingo, Mexico: Mimeo, 1999 (b).

Haro Ortiz, Francisco Javier. Informe de Actividades Año 2000: Desarrollo Rural de la Zona Media de S.L.P., A. C., Rioverde, México, 2000.

Mayén Mena, Javier. Explotación Caprina . Trillas, México, 1989.

Muñoz Rodríguez, Manrrubio, and Horacio Santoyo Cortés. Ganar-ganar: El Arte de los Servicios Profesionales . Chapingo, Mexico: CIESTAAM/UACh, 1998.

SERPAC. Boletín (Agosto/Septiembre). México, 1996.

Zavala Zaragoza, J. "Plan de Negocios para la Creación de una Microempresa de Productos Lácteos (Quesos de Cabra) en el Municipio de Valle de Santiago,

Conclusions

Mexican Agriculture and NAFTA—The Challenges Ahead

Juan M. Rivera

Persistent poverty and oppression can lead to hopelessness and despair. . . . These failed states can become havens for terror.

President George W. Bush
March 2003*

One can trace back the origins of the new economic paradigm in the Mexican economy to the early 1980s. The grave macroeconomic crisis suffered by the country in 1982–83 impelled the government to seek alternative development policies to its inner-looking, import-substitution-based development model of the time. Thus, the De la Madrid regime initiated radical policy changes toward opening the Mexican economy to the rest of the world, lessening or eliminating restrictions to foreign investment, and reducing import controls and trade barriers that had protected but also isolated the inefficient Mexican industrial apparatus. For Mexico, joining the General Agreement on Tariffs and Trade (GATT) in 1986 reaffirmed the new approach to open trade and market orientation. Later on, the emphasis on open trade, free markets, and less governmental control that was the cornerstone of Mexican economic policy during the Salinas presidency culminated in the signing of the NAFTA Treaty in 1993. The endorsement of this trade agreement formalized the change to a neo-liberal market orientation and confirmed, once and for all, the new compass for development that Mexico would follow.

NAFTA strengthened an existing and significant trade link between the United States and Mexico and helped the latter expand its industrial sector and multiply its exports. Thus, between 1990 and 2003, the export of Mexican manufacturing goods (mainly to the United States) increased five-fold, from US$27.8 billion to US$141 billion. The trade boom in Mexico was essentially a manufacturing phenomenon and continues as such today; in 2005, manufacturing exports represented 85.6% of the total non-oil exports, while the trade in primary products paled—at only 4.9 % of that total.[1] In the process, it is estimated that 500,000 new jobs were created in the Mexican manufacturing sector.[2] Over the first ten years of the agreement, the total trade between Mexico and the United States had nearly tripled—a point which elicited praise about NAFTA from some Mexican journalists.[3]

* President George W. Bush, March 2003, as quoted by Rick Lazio, "Some Trade Barriers Won't Fall," *The New York Times*. Opinion section. August 9, 2003

Notwithstanding the growth in the manufacturing sector brought by the wide constellation of new economic policies (of which NAFTA was the key star), there are some sectors of the Mexican economy that did not fare well at all. In the agricultural sector, for example, where about one-fifth of the Mexican people work, 1.3 million jobs have been lost since 1994.[4] Apparently, the wishful prediction by the Mexican government that the "inefficient" displaced farmers would be absorbed by manufacturing plants in the city or by integrated processing farms in the countryside has never materialized. This is evidenced by the relatively unchanged proportions of employment in the manufacturing sector. Although trade increased in raw terms, as a percentage of GDP it has remained relatively constant. After all the restructuring, the Mexican agricultural sector ended up with a significant decrease in importance within the national economy where its share of GDP went from 8.4% in 1980 to 4% in 2003.[5]

There is evidence that the foreign component of the agricultural sector in Mexico expanded as a result of the new free-trade agreement. However, the benefits of this expansion fell mainly to the mass processors of fruits and vegetables who were better financed and better prepared for the market challenges and opportunities that NAFTA presented. In contrast, for the wide majority of the 25 million Mexican farmers traditionally working small plots and accustomed to growing basic staples of corn and beans, the alternatives for survival decreased.

It is true that the NAFTA experiment is only one among many other factors that in the last years have shaped the development of Mexico's economy. It is also true that the agricultural sector in Mexico is quite heterogeneous in the types of producers, products, and regions it encompasses. On the other side of the marginalized majority of agricultural producers represented by ejido farmers (who have not prospered for over 40 years), there is a smaller class of private farmers who have larger lands, grow pricier crops, and/or manage sophisticated plantations. The ejido farmers are still engaged in traditional farming of basic staples and had gotten used to operating under the system of guaranteed prices and government supports of the pre-NAFTA past. The latter class are the integrated, mechanized processors of fruits and vegetables for the domestic and export markets, some of them working in association with international agribusiness firms.

The preceding chapters of this book have presented a mosaic of different situations where the various actors of the Mexican agricultural scene live and interact. Keeping the common thread of focus on the small-scale agricultural producers in Mexico, the studies have discussed the ways and wherewithal (or lack thereof) that Mexican rural producers have used to adapt to the new market and economic conditions created by NAFTA and the neo-liberal economic policies of the Mexican regimes. As evidenced from these studies, the change to the new NAFTA environment has produced winners and losers. For those small-scale agricultural producers who were dependent on agricultural price-support mechanisms and other government subsidies, the new market conditions were hard to negotiate. As has been the experience in other countries, the poor farmers of Mexico have had to diversify their sources of income by seeking part-time work in other occupations, by forcing other family members to find employment in urban centers, or if all else failed, by migrating themselves to other locations in Mexico or in the United States.

During the NAFTA years, the U.S.-trade component of the Mexican agricultural sector has indeed doubled, but it has left Mexico with an average annual trade deficit of US$1.4 billion. The agricultural trade flow that NAFTA facilitated not only displaced many of the small grain producers in Mexico, but also created a persistent trade deficit that could potentially affect the food supply of the country. From 1995 to 2004, the total export of agricultural products from Mexico to the United States went from $3.6 billion to $6.5 billion, while total imports of U.S. agricultural goods by Mexico increased from $3.1 billion to $7.7 billion for the same comparative years. While Mexico exports fresh or frozen fruits and vegetables and beer to the United States, it buys mainly grains, meats, and oilseeds from that country.

A closer view of the reasons behind Mexico's persistent trade imbalance in agricultural products under NAFTA reveals that, in Mexico, there is a double-faulty disarticulation between the local demand-supply forces and the primary-industrial market relation. This is something that cannot be attributed to NAFTA, but rather is associated with local market imperfections and the inability of the Mexican regimes to reengineer agriculture to function better in the new international and competitive economic universe.[6]

The worsening of economic conditions that the small Mexican farmers have experienced has also been linked to the persistent and substantial subsidies that the U.S. government provides to its farmers, which facilitate a flooding of low-priced U.S. grain commodities into the Mexican market. Arguably, the small-scale Mexican producers of grains such as corn and wheat cannot compete against those U.S.-subsidized farm prices. Here, it is true that both the U.S. farm bills of 1996 and 2002 created first, and extended later, a system of guaranteed prices and subsidized market mechanisms that favor U.S. grain producers. The 2002 farm bill has funneled an average of $14.5 billion dollars per year in farm support prices to U.S. farmers, mostly those producing grains such as corn and wheat.[7]

However, this is only a partial point, because on the one hand, in Mexico the production of grains has not only been insufficient in meeting the local demand, but also consists mainly of white corn for human consumption; the grain exported by the United States to Mexico is yellow corn for animal feed and for food processors. On the other hand, a system of decoupled income subsidies to Mexican agricultural producers was instituted by the Mexican government to come into effect during the 15 years of the NAFTA implementation phase. The income supplements given to agricultural producers are not product-specific, but rather are based on size of farming plots and were purposely created to partially compensate for the unfavorable impact on the Mexican grain market caused by NAFTA.

The lavish subsidies and other protective schemes that the rich countries have instituted to favor their domestic agricultural producers have been often associated with the misery and backwardness plaguing the developing world. Agricultural subsidies have been practiced in the United States for a long time, and the Farm Bill of 2002 authorized and extended $200 billion in farm subsidies for ten years,[8] and the trend in federal government support of U.S. agriculture is likely to continue. Thus, at the end of July 2007, the U.S. House of Representatives approved a generous farm bill which, to the tune of over $200 billion dollars for the next five years, would extend subsidies to farmers at a time of record crop prices.[9] In all, the United States is not the main culprit in this unequal world. Every year the European Union (EU) dispenses the equivalent of $58 billion dollars to its farmers—which creates overproduction, lowers farm prices, and translates to lower or no revenues for farmers in poorer countries.[10] On a larger scale, the 30 industrial-nation members of the Organization for Economic Cooperation and Development (OECD) spent $311 billion on domestic agricultural subsidies in 2002, a sum that exceeds the combined GDP for all the countries of Sub-Saharan Africa.[k]

The size and continuity of farm subsidies that the United States has practiced for many years is indeed another factor that has unfavorably impacted the chances for growth and competition by Mexican farmers under NAFTA. Besides the uncontested political reasons behind the transfers of U.S. funds to the American farming communities, the U.S. government support for agriculture rests on questionable assumptions and problems dating back to the turmoil of the Great Depression. Currently, the U.S. farm economy operates under a different system than the one of the mid-1930s. The new U.S. farm economy is characterized by two dominating forces: (a) the consolidation of farms into larger and fewer production units, and (b) the consolidation of ownership and control by food-processing companies that link farm producers with food manufacturers through contract or vertical integration.[12] As a consequence, the system of agricultural subsidies that the U.S. government underwrites ultimately benefits the biggest and richest of the U.S. farmers. There is even a popular countercurrent within the United States to reduce or eliminate farm subsidies[13]—in part because 70% of U.S. subsidies go to the top 10% of its agricultural producers.[14] Recognizing that farm income doubled in the U.S. during the years 2003 and 2004 while subsidies also went up 40% over the same period (and were projected at $15.7 billion for 2004), it becomes clear that the subsidy system in the United States no longer makes sense.[15]

The profound dissimilarities between the agricultural sectors of the United States and Mexico already existing at the time of the NAFTA signing were later accentuated by the increasing farm subsidies and protective policies of the U.S. government. At the same time, the Salinas regime was withdrawing subsidies, guaranteed prices, and any governmental support for the agricultural sector in Mexico. Apparently the Mexican government was more concerned with stabilization policies and industrialization programs. Little attention was given to creating alternative support programs to help the often forgotten rural sector survive and adapt to the new NAFTA markets and neo-liberal economic realities.

NAFTA accelerated Mexico's transition to a more industrialized, open-market economy, but it created a bleak picture for the future of Mexico's rural households. Gone were the threads of the support net that the Mexican government had created in the past. There were no longer guaranteed prices, soft though limited credit, cheaper seeds, subsidized fertilizers, or other similar benefits, which had made the small-scale agricultural producer dependent on government handouts and unable to organize or change strategies to advance.

In order to partially alleviate the more difficult conditions faced by the Mexican small-scale agricultural producers created by NAFTA, in 1994 the Mexican government introduced a direct support program which would assist them during the 15 years of the NAFTA transition to full implementation. The program, known as *Procampo,* resembles a system of decoupling payments to farmers that is similar to the one in the 1996 U.S. farm bill—that is, payments to farmers were to be based on a cultivated land size and not tied to a particular type of product. Procampo has since been the main type of transfer payment for Mexican agricultural producers, and the applicable rates for producers with less than 5 hectares reached $102 for the year 2004. Another support program originally known as "Alliance for the Countryside" (*Alianza para el Campo*), and more recently renamed "Alliance with You" (*Contigo*), is designed to provide farmers with grants that are intended to foster technology transfers, technical assistance, mechanization, and general improvements to production, storage, and marketing activities.

Lastly, a new program of direct market support to agricultural producers has instituted target-income guarantees to Mexican farmers engaged in the production of ten basic crops, mostly grains and oilseeds. This program has some of the elements used in the United States through the countercyclical support payments to basic grains and oilseeds. All in all, the various price-support and aid mechanisms launched by the Mexican government serve as palliatives to ameliorate the income situation of the rural Mexican poor. In all, the level of Producer Support Estimate (PSE)[16] for Mexico has reached an estimated 18% for 2000.[17] Compared to this, the PSE level in the United States for the same year was estimated at 25%.[18]

The ostensible disparity in the level of subsidies, supports, and protectionism granted by the governments of the United States and Mexico has generated increasing protests by diverse groups in the Mexican agricultural sector. Pressing for solutions and further commitment by the Mexican government, the rising voices of despair have petitioned adjustments to NAFTA that include extending the final stages of controlled imports of corn and soybeans beyond the 2008 deadline—and the more drastic step of renegotiating the agricultural chapter in NAFTA. Though the trend in the current world situation and within the WTO framework is to gradually reduce or eliminate the domestic subsidies that are distorting trade, one cannot expect a sudden withdrawal of the existing system of protective subsidies and special accords that are engrained in the fabric of developed economies.

Given the biased preference in the United States toward its more sophisticated, technically advanced, and favorably funded farmers, one can bring an issue for debate from the perspective of the Mexican market. While it is true that U.S. agricultural subsidies depress market prices of basic grains and thus render noncompetitive and unattractive the production of those grains in the Mexican countryside, the lower prices of those subsidized staples serve to reduce the price of foodstuffs prepared with those agricultural goods. Consequently, the flooding of cheap, subsidized grain into the Mexican market helps depress the prices of the foodstuffs produced or imported, where no tariff protection whatsoever applies. In the final analysis, the comparatively lower prices of foodstuffs consumed mainly by the urban population would be possible thanks to the U.S. taxpayers. As a counterpoint, these benefits to the general population would be partially matched against the losses to Mexico's rural population, who are thus precluded from otherwise selling their grain at the higher free-market unsubsidized prices. In true economic analysis, the first benefits would likely surpass the latter costs (losses). However, additional considerations would fog the view, especially those considerations dealing with equality and justice on the basis that the rural poor have endured enough and that it is time for them to recoup part of what they have been denied for so many years.

In view of the myriad of problems and limitations that the agricultural sector in Mexico has been subjected to in the years past, one can reassess the role played by the Mexican government, in order to improve the conditions of the rural poor in Mexico. In retrospect, one can agree that the past regime of President Fox made a concerted effort to approach the agricultural situation of Mexico in a more open and comprehensive fashion with a long-term view. The Law of Sustainable Rural Development[19] enacted by the Mexican Congress in 2002 outlined a comprehensive set of objectives, goals, programs, and instruments to help the development of the rural sector. It called for active cooperation between local and state government units in the implementation of programs to support the local agricultural producers and communities. Additionally, it included the cooperation of the private sector and promoted the associations and links between agricultural producers, industrial processors, and all other participants in food production and distribution. In general, the law offered a plausible framework for agricultural development. The only thing missing was the necessary funding to tackle all those programs to reach their promising results.

On the financial side, notwithstanding the failed attempts at fiscal reform sought by the Fox administration, the agricultural sector has received much more attention in budgeting terms than in the previous administrations. Thus, the approved budget for the Secretary of Agriculture (SAGARPA) for 2004 amounted to $3.7 billion, about the same level in dollar terms as in 2002 but a 20% increase over the amounts received in 2001. Almost two-thirds of the new monies allocated to agriculture were destined to fund the support programs for the rural population, including the Procampo program of fund transfers to small-scale agricultural producers. In addition to the direct budget lines, a new government institution for agricultural finance (*Financiera Rural*) was created to substitute the inefficient and corruption-plagued *Banrural* that was dissolved in 2003. The new agricultural financial unit is a finance facilitator operating through branches of affiliated banks and is intended to increase the role of rural financial intermediaries.

Notwithstanding the efforts of the Fox administration to improve the conditions of the Mexican agricultural producers, segments of the civil society and organizations of displaced farmers considered these efforts insufficient. The voices of discontent were united in street demonstrations by thousands of farmers and concerned citizens, who, in April of 2003, threatened to block the Mexican Congress and the Office of the President. The outcome of this peaceful confrontation resulted in a National Accord for the Countryside (*Acuerdo Nacional para el Campo*) subscribed to by President Fox and a series of peasant organizations. The Accord reemphasized a series of measures and actions that the government should undertake to improve economic conditions in the countryside. There was a reconfirmation of government support for a myriad of policies and programs to reinforce productivity and marketability of the Mexican agricultural sector. In addition, there was a pledge by the Mexican government to allocate additional emergency funds to agriculture from the windfall gains produced by the increases in the price of oil produced and exported by Mexico.

While good intentions and better funding have been evident in the Fox and the new Calderon presidencies in their quest to find solutions to the agricultural problem and seek improvement in the conditions of the Mexican rural poor, one can be sure that the action of the government will be a necessary but insufficient agent for success. The cooperation of other key actors and agents of the socio-political and economic landscape is urgently required. Civil society, non-government organizations, educational institutions, organized farming associations, agribusiness firms, industrial processors, banking institutions, and similar units and organizations must act in coordination toward a common goal.

Some of the preceding chapters of this book portray a historic perspective of the agricultural sector in Mexico, with particular focus on the impact of NAFTA and the Mexican government policies on Mexico's small-scale agricultural producers. Another group of papers address issues related to specific agricultural products, and a few more present results of case studies where different participants joined efforts with small-scale agricultural producers to seek opportunities for growth. From the start, the work for this book was multidisciplinary in nature because the editors firmly believe that the problems of small rural units in Mexico is a multifaceted one that cannot be solved simply with economic cost-benefit analysis or statistical projections based on the past.

Still, looking at the past and recent years of the agricultural sector under NAFTA provides a retrospective of how one could adapt and adjust to a changing environment and how one can cope with the persistent constraints that globalization—combined with imperfect government policies—presents. At the same time, the analysis and experiences of the actual cases discussed in the book should serve as lessons and future guidelines for the areas one needs to focus on when seeking improvements for Mexican small-scale agricultural producers in the future. Whether the NAFTA treaty will be renegotiated—as some of the authors of the chapters have advanced—or not, the various chapters in this book seek to compose a compass to help academicians, government agencies, agribusiness firms, educational institutions, non-governmental organization, and small-scale agricultural producers in Mexico navigate through better waters toward better destinations in years to come.

In lieu of renegotiating the NAFTA accord, one final and strong recommendation to government policy-makers is to extend the scope of NAFTA and formulate agreements on two crucial areas that have been left out of negotiations—problem areas that are in urgent need of solutions. These would be a formal agreement on immigration reform between Mexico and the United States and the creation of a common fund among the three NAFTA partners. The purpose of this fund will be to help finance the growth and development of Mexican agriculture for the years after NAFTA's full implementation, and to help finance both the training and education of the rural poor, and the search for and selection of alternative economic activities for this population.

Endnotes

1. INEGI. *Mexico at a Glance*. External Sector. Trade Balance Mx. 2005. http://www.inegi.gov.
2. John Audley, Demetrios Papademetriou, Sandra Polaski, and Scott Vaughan. *NAFTA's Promise and Reality*, 5–6.
3. Sergio Sarmiento. "Critics Aside, NAFTA Has Been a Boon to Mexico." *The Wall Street Journal* (January 9, 2004), A-11.
4. John Audley, Demetrios Papademetriou, Sandra Polaski, and Scott Vaughan. *NAFTA's Promise and Reality*, 6.
5. Gisele Henriquez and Raj Patel, "NAFTA, Corn, and Mexico's Agricultural Trade Liberation," *Americas Program Special Report*, (Feb. 13, 2004), http://www.americaspolicy.org.
6. Sergio Luna Martinez, "Agribusiness Foreign Trade," Banamex, *Review of the Economic Situation in Mexico*, (Dec. 29, 2004): 48–92, http://www.banamex.com/eng/esem.
7. At the time of this printing, a new farm bill that proposes continuing heavy subsidies to the U.S. agricultural producers had passed both chambers of the U.S. Congress. President Bush threatened to veto it because of the heavy financial burden it would continue to place on the U.S. federal budget (see also endnote 9 below).
8. Laura Carlsen, "The Mexican Experience and Lessons for WTO Negotiations on the Agreement on Agriculture," Americas Program, Interhemispheric Resource Center, (June 11, 2003), http://www.americaspolicy.org.
9. David Henderson, "House Passes Farm Bill, Expanding Food Stamps," *The New York Times* (July 28, 2007).
10. Scott Miller, "Why Not to Cut Farm Aid," *The Wall Street Journal* (December 16, 2004), A-14.
11. Rick Lazio, "Some Trade Barriers Won't Fall," *The New York Times*. (August 9, 2003), A-2
12. Russel L. Lamb, "The New Farm Economy," *Regulation* (Winter 2003–2004): 10–15.
13. Jim Wasserman, "Bush Budget Calls for Subsidy Cuts. Farmers Feel Betrayed by Proposal," Environmental Working Group, http://www.ewg.org, as reported by the *South Bend Tribune* (February 12, 2005), C-9.
14. Timothy Egan, "Big Farms Reap Two Harvests with Subsidies a Bumper Crop," *The New York Times* (December 26, 2004), 2.
15. Ibid.
16. The Producer Support Estimate is a mix of the value of gross transfers to agricultural producers from government programs. It comprises money transfers in the form of price support and budgetary payments to producers.
17. "Effects of NAFTA on Agriculture and the Rural Economy," Economic Research Service, USDA, 6. Briefing Room, Mexico, http://www.ers.usda.gov/Briefing/Mexico.
18. Ibid.
19. Mexican Congress, Ley de Desarrollo Rural Sustentable, (December 7, 2002).

Biographical Notes

Manuel Chávez is the Associate Director of the Center for Latin American and Caribbean Studies, and a Professor at the School of Journalism in the College of Communications Arts and Sciences—both at Michigan State University. Professor Chávez teaches courses on news media, international affairs, and the political economy of Latin America and the Caribbean with special focus on North America. In 1999, he received a Fulbright-Hayes Award to study the economic impacts of globalization in Mexico and Central America. His research focuses on North American security and borders, international news coverage, newsroom practices, and U.S.-Latin American relations.

Cornelia Flora is the Charles F. Curtiss Distinguished Professor of Agriculture and Life Sciences and Sociology at Iowa State University and Director of the North Central Regional Center for Rural Development, 12-state research and extension institute. Previously she held the Endowed Chair in Agricultural Systems at the University of Minnesota, was head of the Sociology Department at Virginia Polytechnic Institute and State University, a University Distinguished Professor at Kansas State University, and a program officer for the Ford Foundation. She has a BA degree from the University of California at Berkeley and MS (1966) and PhD (1970) degrees from Cornell University, where she received the 1994 Outstanding Alumni Award from the College of Agriculture and Life Science. She is a past president of the Rural Sociological Society, the Community Development Society, and the Society for Agriculture, Food, and Human Values. Professor Flora has been the author and editor of a number of recent books, including *Interactions Between Agroecosystems and Rural Communities; Rural Communities: Legacy and Change; Rural Policies for the 1990s*; and *Sustainable Agriculture in Temperate Zones*. Her latest book is *Rural Communities: Legacy and Change, Third Edition*. Her current research addresses alternative strategies for community economic development and community-based, natural-resource management, with particular attention to poverty reduction.

Manuel Angel Gómez Cruz is an Agricultural Engineer from Escuela Nacional de Agricultura (Chapingo) and also holds a Diploma (1989) and PhD (1990) in Agricultural Economics from Humboldt University in Berlin, Germany. He is a member of Mexico's National System of Researchers and his areas of expertise are agricultural policies and agro-industrial systems. He is the author or editor of several books on agricultural development in Mexico and on the impact of NAFTA on Mexican small agricultural producers. Professor Gómez is currently coordinator of the National Program of Research on the Integration of Industry and Agriculture at the Centro de Investigaciones Económicas, Sociales y Tecnológicas de la Agroindustria y la Agricultura Mundial (CIESTAAM) de la Universidad Autónoma de Chapingo in Mexico where he also serves as an academic instructor and researcher on economic and agro-industrial problems in the doctoral program.

Laura Gómez Tovar is a Professor of Agricultural Ecology at the Universidad Autónoma de Chapingo in Mexico and a Researcher at the Center for Economic, Social and Technological Research on Global Agriculture and Agro-industry (CIESTAAM) at the same institution. She holds a degree in Agricultural Ecological Engineering from the Universidad Autónoma de Chapingo in Mexico (1995) and a Master's Degree on Innovative Systems and Ecological and Social Change from Roskilde University and Aalborg University in Denmark (2000).

Mark A. Martínez is Associate Professor and Department Chair in the Department of Political Science at California State University, Bakersfield. He earned his BA degree in Political Science and Economics from California State University, Chico, and his MA and PhD degrees in political science from the University of California, Santa Barbara (1998). He is also a Research Associate at the Universidad Autónoma de Queretaro in Mexico, and served as a Trade Consultant on Mexico for the State of California's Center for International Trade Development in 1999–2000.

Gerardo Otero is a Professor of Sociology at Simon Fraser University in British Columbia, Canada and concurrently an adjunct professor in the Doctoral Program in Development Studies at Universidad Autónoma de Zacatecas in Mexico. He holds a BA degree in Business Administration from the Instituto Tecnológico y de Estudios Superiores de Monterrey, an MA degree in Latin American Studies from the University of Texas at Austin (1977) and a PhD degree in sociology from the University of Wisconsin-Madison (1986). Dr. Otero has held faculty appointments in several universities in Mexico and the United States, and in 1986–87 he was a postdoctoral visiting fellow at the Center for U.S.-Mexican Studies at the University of a California in San Diego. Dr. Otero has published articles in edited collections and scholarly journals including *Canadian Review of Sociology and Anthropology; Canadian Journal of Political Science; Sociological Forum, Rural Sociology; Latin American Research Review; Latin American Perspectives, Latin American Politics and Society;* and *Revista Mexicana de Sociología.* His books include *Farewell to the Peasantry?: Political Class Formation in Rural Mexico* (1999) and his forthcoming edited volume, *Food for the Few: Neoliberal Globalism and the Biotechnology Revolution in Latin America* (2008).

Elia Patlán Martínez is a member of the faculty at the Universidad Autónoma de Chapingo in Mexico and also serves as an Academic Advisor for indigenous students at that university. She has a BA degree in Psychology from the Universidad Autónoma de Mexico (UNAM) in Mexico City, and an MA degree in Mexican History from the same university. She has completed doctoral studies in Agribusiness and Economic Development at the Universidad Autónoma de Chapingo. She has published several papers on the history of agricultural technology and on agribusiness and multinational corporations.

Gaspar Real Cabello is a Professor of Anthropology and Social Sciences at the Universidad Autónoma de Querétaro in México. He holds a PhD degree in Social Anthropology from the Universidad Iberoamericana in Mexico City. His research focuses on industrial anthropology, microeconomic rural units, and agricultural development in Mexico. He has also done extensive research on the impact of NAFTA on the poultry industry in the Bajío region of Mexico.

Juan M. Rivera is a Professor of Accounting in the Mendoza College of Business and a Faculty Fellow of the Kellogg Institute for International Studies at the University of Notre Dame. He has a BA degree in accounting from the Instituto Tecnológico y de Estudios Superiors de Monterrey in Mexico and MA (1967) and PhD (1975) degrees in Accountancy from the University of Illinois at Urbana-Champaign. Professor Rivera is the recipient of two Fulbright Fellowships, one for Panama in 1986 and one for Mexico in 2001. From 2004 to 2007 he directed a Training, Internships, Exchanges and Scholarships (TIES) program on entrepreneurship and small agribusiness units in Mexico which links the University of Notre Dame with the University of Guadalajara in Mexico and is funded by the U.S. Agency for International Development.

Rita Schwentesius Rindermann holds degrees in Agricultural Engineering and a PhD in Agricultural Sciences (1980) from the University of Humboldt in Berlin, Germany. She has published several papers on agricultural economics in national and international journals and is currently on the faculty at the Universidad Autónoma de Chapingo in Mexico. She has conducted prior research at the Timirjasew Academy of Agricultural Sciences in Moscow, and at the University Marthin Luther Halle in Berlin. Professor Schwentesius is a member of Mexico's National System of Researchers and her area of research focus is the trends of agricultural production and the status of world food supplies.

Juan de Dios Trujillo has dual appointments as Professor of Economics and of International Studies and Public Policy at the Universidad Autónoma de Sinaloa in Culiacán, Mexico where he also serves as a Research Fellow in the Instituto de Investigaciones Económicas y Sociales. He has a BA degree in Agronomy from the Universidad de Sinaloa and a PhD in Agro-Industrial Economics from the Universidad Autónoma de Chapingo in Mexico. His recent research has focused on modernization of rain-fed agriculture in the state of Sinaloa, Mexico and on the analysis of competitive advantage for tomato production in Mexico.

Scott Whiteford is Director of the Center for Latin American Studies at the University of Arizona. He holds a Master's degree from Stanford University and a PhD degree from the University of Texas at Austin. Professor Whiteford has written or edited 16 books on resource management, public policy, health, indigenous rights, and food security in Latin America. His recent edited or co-edited books are *Globalization, Water and Health: Resource Management in Times of Scarcity*; *Seguridad, Agua y Desarrollo: El Futuro de la Frontera México-Estados Unidos*; and *Managing a Sacred Gift: Changing Water Management Strategies in Mexico*. His current research focuses on social and environmental impacts of globalization and strategies for a sustainable future.